Grace Stott

Twenty-six Years of Missionary work in China

Grace Stott

Twenty-six Years of Missionary work in China

ISBN/EAN: 9783743342132

Manufactured in Europe, USA, Canada, Australia, Japa

Cover: Foto ©ninafisch / pixelio.de

Manufactured and distributed by brebook publishing software (www.brebook.com)

Grace Stott

Twenty-six Years of Missionary work in China

TWENTY-SIX YEARS OF
MISSIONARY WORK
IN CHINA

BY

GRACE STOTT

OF THE CHINA INLAND MISSION

WITH A PREFACE BY
THE REV. J. HUDSON TAYLOR

WITH EIGHT ILLUSTRATIONS

SECOND EDITION

NEW YORK
AMERICAN TRACT SOCIETY
10 EAST 23RD STREET
1897

"For I am not ashamed of the gospel of Christ: for it is the power of God unto salvation to every one that believeth; to the Jew first, and also to the Greek."—ROM. i. 16.

PREFACE

THE work of God recorded in these pages is no longer an experiment, and it is well that Mrs. Stott has been able, during her furlough, to put in more permanent form some of the incidents which many of us have heard with deepest interest from her own lips in missionary meetings, or on more private occasions.

It has been my privilege to be acquainted with this work from its commencement. With earnest prayer I commended Mr. Stott to God for his difficult journey, for in those times Wunchau was not a free port, and the eight days' overland travel through unknown and mountainous country would have been somewhat formidable for a good walker, while for one on crutches it was much more so. He left Scotland, however, believing that "the lame should take the prey," and he was spared to do so to no small extent.

I had visited Mr. Stott during his early labours there, and seen how much he needed domestic help, and how handicapped he was in the charge of his boys' boarding-school, before I had the pleasure of welcoming Miss Ciggie (whom I had known in Glasgow) on her arrival in China, twenty-six years ago, to become his wife.

Having closely followed the progress of the work through these twenty-five years, and having paid my last visits to Wunchau since Mrs. Stott left, it was with special interest and pleasure that I snatched time to read most of her manuscript. It is emphatically a story of work—earnest, persevering work which God has blessed: an unvarnished account, it brings out clearly the lights and shades of missionary service.

I did not find one dull paragraph. Those who begin to read the book will want to finish it, and it cannot fail to be a blessing to the reader.

It is an unfinished record, and, since Mrs. Stott asked me to write a few lines of preface, a joyful letter from Miss Christabel Williams tells of the conversion of sixteen of the twenty-six girls in the boarding-school: four of the children were previously converted, and several of the remaining six—the little ones of the school—were seeking the Lord.

May many readers be led to pray for the work and workers in Wunchau!

J. HUDSON TAYLOR.

CHINA INLAND MISSION,
NEWINGTON GREEN, LONDON, N.
January, 1897.

CONTENTS

CHAPTER I.
PAGE
"Follow Me, and I will make you fishers of men."—MATT. iv. 19   1

CHAPTER II.
"In due season we shall reap, if we faint not."—GAL. vi. 9   .   10

CHAPTER III.
"They that make them are like unto them ; so is every one that trusteth in them."—PSA. cxv. 8.   20

CHAPTER IV.
"They imagined a mischievous device, which they are not able to perform."—PSA. xxi. 11   35

CHAPTER V.
"Our Lord is above all gods."—PSA. cxxxv. 5   .   .   .   52

CHAPTER VI.

"And He said unto them, Lacked ye anything? And they said, Nothing."—LUKE xxii. 35 68

CHAPTER VII.

"If any man will come after Me, let him deny himself, and take up his cross daily, and follow Me."—LUKE ix. 23 . 83

CHAPTER VIII.

"Why do the heathen rage, and the people imagine a vain thing?"—PSA. ii. 1 98

CHAPTER IX.

"And ye shall be witnesses unto Me."—ACTS i. 8 . 114

CHAPTER X.

"How beautiful are the feet of them that preach the gospel of peace, and bring glad tidings of good things!"—ROM. x. 15 129

CHAPTER XI.

"When thou passest through the waters I will be with thee; and through the rivers, they shall not overflow thee."—ISA. xliii. 2 145

CHAPTER XII.

"The memory of the just is blessed."—PROV. x. 7 . . 160

CONTENTS

CHAPTER XIII.

"He will be very gracious unto thee at the voice of thy cry; when He shall hear it, He will answer thee."—ISA. xxx. 19 . . . 176

CHAPTER XIV.

"And both Jesus was called, and His disciples, to the marriage."—JOHN ii. 2 197

CHAPTER XV.

"And the common people heard Him gladly."—MARK xii. 37 . 213

CHAPTER XVI.

"In the morning sow thy seed, and in the evening withhold not thine hand: for thou knowest not whether shall prosper, either this or that, or whether they both shall be alike good."—ECCLES. xi. 6 226

CHAPTER XVII.

"Ye shall be sorrowful, but your sorrow shall be turned into joy."—JOHN xvi. 20 241

CHAPTER XVIII.

"All Thy works shall praise Thee, O Lord; and Thy saints shall bless Thee."—PSA. cxlv. 10. 258

CHAPTER XIX

"The kingdom of God is come nigh unto you."—LUKE x. 9 . 266

CHAPTER XX.

"In the fear of the Lord is strong confidence."—PROV. xiv. 26 . 288

CHAPTER XXI.

"Thy expectation shall not be cut off."—Prov. xxiv. 14 . . 300

CHAPTER XXII.

"Thou therefore endure hardness, as a good soldier of Jesus Christ."—2 Tim. ii. 3 314

CHAPTER XXIII.

"Both he that soweth and he that reapeth may rejoice together."—John iv. 36 330

CHAPTER XXIV.

"Be not afraid of them that kill the body, and after that have no more that they can do."—Luke xii. 4 . . . 345

CHAPTER XXV.

"I was dumb, I opened not my mouth, because Thou didst it." —Psa. xxxix. 9. "As for God, His way is perfect."—2 Sam. xxii. 31 355

CHAPTER I

"Follow Me, and I will make you fishers of men."—MATT. iv. 19

MY first interest in China began in the spring of 1865 when Mr. Hudson Taylor, accompanied by Mr. (now Dr.) Barchet and his companion, visited Glasgow. The two latter were *en route* for China, sailing in a few days, and Mr. Taylor had come to wish them good-bye and God-speed. They addressed a small meeting, and as I listened to Mr. Taylor's tale of the darkness of China and the terrible need of workers there, there came a question that would be answered, "Why may not you go to tell of a Saviour's love?"

I had been converted four years, and had begun in a feeble way to serve the Lord—who had bought me—at first by tract distribution, then Sunday-school teaching. The Lord had often also graciously used me to lead many an anxious soul into the light, but up to this time I had never thought of mission work, never supposed I had any call beyond my native city of Glasgow.

For days this question kept ringing in my heart. I had no home ties, it was true; but was I fit? Then, too, at that time I had never heard of a young girl going to a heathen land—was it practicable? This latter question I decided to ask Mr. Taylor. He saw no reason why I should not go, even though but twenty years of age, if called of God, and if called, surely the fitness would be given by Him.

After much prayer and consideration, Mr. Taylor invited me to go to London, that by mutual prayer and knowledge of one another, God's way might be made clear. I arrived just the day before Mr. and Mrs. Stevenson's marriage. They and Mr. Stott, whom I then met for the first time, sailed three weeks afterwards for China.

Mr. Stott had been brought up to farm work, but when he was about nineteen years of age he slipped on the road and knocked his knee against a stone. This simple accident resulted in white swelling, which, two years later, necessitated the amputation of the left leg. For nine months he lay a helpless invalid, and it was during this time that the Lord graciously saved his soul. So far he had been careless and indifferent to the love of God in Christ Jesus, but now, in his helpless condition, and what seemed his ruined future, how precious that love became! After his recovery he began to teach in a school, and had been thus employed several years when he first heard of China's needs through a friend, who himself was going out.

In accepting Mr. Stott for mission work, Mr. Taylor manifested that faith which has so eminently characterised him, for surely no Society would have sent a lame man to such a country to pioneer work, and Mr. Stott often referred with gratitude to Mr. Taylor's acceptance of him. When asked why he, with only one leg, should think of going to China, his remark was, "I do not see those with two legs going, so I must." As I saw them slowly sail out of the docks a great hope welled up in my heart that I should soon follow, though at that time I little thought that my life and work would be blended with his.

I continued in London a few months, when it was definitely settled that I should accompany Mr. and Mrs. Taylor and party, who were to sail the following May. Almost as soon as that decision was arrived at my health began to give way, though up to that time I scarce remember one day of sickness. After trying several places, with the vain hope my illness might prove a temporary weakness, and that I might still be able to go forward, the doctors gave it as their definite decision that I ought not to go to China at present. Mr. Taylor reluctantly communicated this decision to me, but added, "I hope you will be able to follow us in a year." This news was a great blow to me; I had thought I was willing, for God's will only, that I would be content to go or stay, just as He called; but when the word came "stay" I was bitterly disappointed. This led to much heart searching: for the first time I saw how easy it was to deceive oneself, and night after night I cried to God to save me from self-deception.

One night, when on my knees, with tearful confession of self-will, it seemed as if I heard a voice saying, "If you still want to serve me go back to Glasgow, and take my messages to the Salt Market and the district round about." My heart almost stood still: the Salt Market was one of the vilest and most wicked places in Glasgow, inhabited almost exclusively by thieves and women of ill-repute. It was hardly fit for a man to go into such a place— could it be God was sending a young girl there, uncalled by man, unprotected, and without means of support—could that be God's will for me? I knelt in silence; I dare not speak. I had had one lesson in self-will, and dared not say "No," while I feared to say "Yes." At last the answer came, "Yes Lord; if Thou wilt go with me every step of the way." I then told the Lord that as I could not go alone I should refuse to go any day I did not feel His presence and power with me. From that hour strength seemed slowly to return. Meantime arrangements were being made for the sailing of the

Lammermuir party. I offered to remain a few weeks and help with the outfits.

About a fortnight before the ship sailed, one of the party withdrew through the illness of her mother. Passages had been paid, and unless another took her place the money would be lost. Mr. Taylor turned to me: I had been getting stronger—was it not possible that God, having made me willing to stay, was now opening the way for me to go? To Mr. Taylor it almost appeared so. I prayed, but could get no light; it seemed as if the Lord, having given me His orders, would hear nothing more on the subject, so I had to say, "I can't go," even though it almost broke my heart to say the word.

The *Lammermuir* sailed on May 26, 1866, and as I watched her towed slowly out from the docks I felt China must be left behind for the present. Mr. Taylor's home was broken up the day they left, but friends had kindly invited me to spend a few days with them previous to returning to Glasgow, and it was here I had my first lesson in faith. The friend who had been as a mother to me after my grandmother's death had died during my stay in London. I had, therefore, no home to return to. I had paid all my incidental personal expenses, and never having referred to money matters, friends must have supposed I had plenty, but in fact I only had just enough to take me by rail to Glasgow. Wishing to have a few shillings in my pocket, by which to obtain lodgings, I wanted to go by steamer, that being the cheaper way. Friends tried to dissuade me, not knowing my reason; the expenses were figured up and after removal of luggage, &c., &c., I found I would save but 4s. 6d., and they urged it was not worth taking so long a journey for that sum. I had been asked to visit a young lady on that day, and was about to write a note to say that, leaving by steamer, I could not keep my engagement, when the thought came to me, could I not give up that 4s. 6d. for the Lord's sake? Perhaps He had some service for me to do, or I might interest her in China, so I decided to go by the night train and keep my engagement. We had a time of sweet fellowship together, and, when leaving, she pressed a small packet into my hand, saying, "Take this as from Him." When I opened it there was exactly 4s. 6d. inside. Oh, how strengthened and helped I was by that simple act It seemed as if God had said, "Do not doubt; I will care for you."

I had never heard of living by faith, and if asked could hardly have told the meaning of the words; but I did know if an earthly master sent his servant to do some special work for him, he would at least see that he had enough to eat, and I dared not think my heavenly Father would treat His child worse than that, so I was "without carefulness" in this matter. I had learned to use my needle well, and thought I might help to support myself in that way. Having some warm Christian friends, I had no doubt that if I told them I wanted needlework they would be sure to let me have some, and for the rest the Lord would provide. My business was to do His will.

On my return to Glasgow I was still far from strong, but gave from ten till two daily in visiting the poor degraded outcasts of Salt Market district. No needlework offered, my Father seeing I was too weak to do anything more than the daily visiting. I soon learned why God had sent me in this way, for almost the first questions fiercely asked were: "What Church has sent you here?" "No Church." "Who has sent you?" "No one." "Are you not paid for coming?" "No." "Then why do you come?" "Because I love you; I have been saved myself, and I want you to be saved too." And when they found that I was not only willing to read with and pray for them, but to nurse poor sick ones, kindle a fire, make beef tea, or sweep a hearth if need be, beside nursing their babies, both hearts and homes were opened to me at once. At first the elders of the Church to which I belonged were uneasy at so young a girl going into dens of such wretchedness, and one elderly man warned me of the dangers to which I was exposing myself, and feared that evil might befall me; but I felt that was God's business.

He had sent me, and He was responsible, and never during the three and a half years I laboured amongst them did I receive the least insult or hear unbecoming language if they knew I was present.

After three months, during which time God had provided for all my wants in a remarkable manner, sending money from whence I did not know, so that I had lacked nothing, I was one day asked to speak with a few of the elders. They said they thought perhaps God had called me, and they would like a share in the work—would I accept a small sum from them weekly? I told them I could not be put under any rule whatever ; I had to feel my way to depend on God for wisdom by the hour, and must work just when and how I could ; that if their money would mean being under their control, I must decline ; but if they would like to help, no matter in how small a sum, leaving me quite free, I would rejoice in their fellowship. From that hour, until I left for China, three and a half years afterwards, they stood by me, helping me on, but never interfering. In this way the Lord supplied all my wants.

It was not long before I began to see that I was the one God wanted to train through these means. I had all my life had a hatred and dread of sin and sinners. A bad person filled me with disgust, and it was not till I was sent down there among the utterly lost that I began to separate between sin and the sinner, and while hating the one to love the other. They had human hearts, and readily responded to the touch of love, and I felt circumstances and God's grace alone had made me to differ. During that time, so far as I knew, only two had been converted, but God had put His child into His own school, and He was teaching her lessons that would have to be lived out when He gave her her life's work. Never, never shall I cease to give God thanks for those years of contact with sin and for the faith lessons learned there, yet during all the time I never once lost the consciousness that my life's work lay in China, and I had but to wait His time.

CHAPTER II

" In due season we shall reap, if we faint not."—GAL. vi. 9.

IN the meantime, Mr. Stott had, after eighteen months spent in the neighbourhood of Ning-po, acquiring that dialect, gone to Wenchow, arriving there in November, 1867. He met with but scant courtesy. For three months he and Mr. Jackson, who had accompanied him from Tai-chow, lived in an inn. All feared them, and no one would rent a house to the hated foreigner. Again and again negotiations were almost complete, when the money would be returned and the weary search begin again.

At last a man of some influence, who had brought himself to despair by opium-smoking and gambling, offered a house, and was bold enough to brave all the consequences. Mr. Stott moved there as quietly as possible, but next day the news had spread, and a large angry crowd assembled, determined to turn him out. They battered in the gate, bent on mischief. Mr. Stott came out and stood before them, and said, "You see I am a lame man; if I wanted to run away from you I could not ; if you kill me you will, perhaps, get into trouble ; if you let me alone you will find I shall do no harm ; anyhow, I have come and mean to stay." They were taken aback by his quiet, strong words, and contenting themselves by throwing a few stones they dispersed and left him in peace

As soon as possible he tried to begin a boys' school, and thought to induce regular attendance by providing them with a mid-day meal. A fair number attended, and they seemed to have made a good start, when one day, going into the schoolroom, he found the teacher, but no boys. He asked the meaning of it all, and was told that a report had spread abroad that he was inveigling children in on purpose to take out their hearts and liver to compound into medicine, and their parents were afraid to expose their children to such terrible dangers. No respectable person would take the position of servant, and so weary months had to be passed alone, in the midst of many dangers and discomforts, before confidence was fairly won.

Over two years he laboured alone, and for more than a year of that time never saw an English face, or ever heard a word of the English language, for from the time he arrived in Wenchow, in November, 1867, until he left, in February, 1870, to meet me, he had never left the city for a single night.

By that time he had established his boys' boarding school and had twelve boys entirely under his care; but only two men in the city had been baptized, and they proved disappointments in after years.

How much of his time was spent during these two years is given in a letter to a friend, written in 1869. He says, "My household consists of twelve boys, schoolmaster, my own teacher, two servant men, and an old washerwoman: if I rule them as I ought, it is well, but that is an open question. I shall give you a short account of how I spend my time. Getting up in the morning at six o'clock, meditation, prayer, and breakfast over, I have a short lecture or exposition in the school, and prayers; then the needs of the family have to be examined and provided for, such as buying rice, vegetables, fish and firewood, needles, buttons, shoes, &c., the size, number, quality of each having to be decided upon. Marketing done, I go to my study, and prepare discourses for Sundays and evenings, or attend to any important visitor, ever seeking an opportunity of telling him of the true God, of sin, and salvation. After dinner I resume study, receive visitors, or ride out in the country, taking with me a few tracts, and find an opportunity to speak a word for Christ Jesus, for I dare not yet venture to preach in the streets. By the time I get home the boys are out of school, and then I have to keep them busy and out of mischief till supper-time, which takes place after dark. This over we have some recreation, recital of some tale from memory, or exhibition of pictures, with some music until 'prayer time,' when a few friends join us, when all who can, read the Scriptures verse about, then a short address, and close with prayer. After comes the children's question time, then I try to stretch their intellect as soon as it offers to peep out, and to foster it where it does not exist. My health is perfect; the climate agrees with me very well; sometimes I am in good spirits, and sometimes I have the dumps, and think hard things of everything and everybody, myself included. You cannot understand my position till you have been two years and more tied to your post, eight days' journey from the nearest settlement; yet, if any one would give me my choice to-day of any position, I could only say 'Wenchow.' I would not change it, if I could, to rule a nation."

After three and a half years' labour in the slums of Glasgow, my health being restored, I felt the time had come for me to go forth to China, and having in the meantime become engaged to Mr. Stott, I was sent out by the C.I.M. to share his labours, to be as far as possible a helpmeet to him.

I sailed alone from London in the sailing ship *Kai-sow*, on December 4, 1869, and prepared for the usual four months' journey. A few days after, I laughingly said to the captain, "I want to get into Shang-hai on the 12th of March." He thought a moment and answered, "Not likely; if we do, it will be one of the fastest voyages on record. But," he asked, "why on the 12th of March?" I answered, "I had a fancy to get in on my birthday."

The captain was a kind and good man, and his influence was so felt over the ship that during that long voyage I never heard a word a lady might not hear from those sailors. He also encouraged me with meetings with the men, and as we had a pretty fair voyage, I was able to have one twice a week with them, nearly all the time. Two or three professed to receive blessing, but I do not know if they stood the test of after years. The captain and his dear wife became life-long friends. In the Chinese seas we had a terrific storm, and as I had often longed to witness a real storm at sea, the captain jokingly said that he was sure I had prayed for this; the only consolation he had was, that we could not now reach Shang-hai on the 12th of March. Nevertheless we anchored at Woo-sung on the eve of the 11th, and on the 12th, my twenty-fifth birthday, we arrived in Shang-hai. Mr. Stott met me there, and took me on to Ning-po, where I was kindly welcomed by Dr. Lord. According to Consular regulations then, I had to wait a month before we could be married, and on the 26th of April, 1870, we were made one in life, as we already were in heart. The day after our wedding, the cook Mr.

Stott had brought with him from Wenchow was baptized on profession of his faith.

It was my husband's desire to return at once to Wenchow to his work, but nearly three weeks passed before he could find a junk to take us down. The coast was infested at that time with pirates, and junks were afraid to sail unless in fleets, under the protection of a war junk. At last we sailed, and as we had a fair wind, expected to reach Wenchow in three or four days; but alas! for our hopes, when we reached Chu-san, only one tide from Ning-po river, the war junk refused to proceed until other junks had joined the fleet; so there we had to stay for nine days, while the fairest of winds was blowing.

I was anxious to see my new home, and being fresh out from England, and unaccustomed to the slow ways of the Chinese, my active temperament was sorely tried, as day after day we were put off with the promise we should leave by the next tide. I bore the disappointment as well as I could, until the eighth day, when, woman-like, I had a good cry, which relieved my pent-up feelings. We were fifteen days between Ning-po and Wenchow, a distance of only 150 miles. Wenchow itself is "beautiful for situation," having fertile mountains all round, and as we sailed slowly for days in and out amongst the islands, and then up the beautiful river, with grand mountains on either side, I almost fancied myself in dear old Scotland. Indeed the similarity has been remarked by many, except that instead of the clear blue lakes of the latter, we had the thick muddy water of the river. At that time Wenchow was not an open port, and indeed it was not until seven years after this date that trading steamers were permitted to sail up her waters.

On reaching there we got a very hearty welcome from Mr. Jackson, who had come from Tai-chow to take charge of Mr. Stott's work during his absence, but left soon after for his own station. Never shall I forget the amount of excitement my presence caused; daily crowds of women came to see the first foreign lady who had been in their midst, and when I ventured out, it seemed as if the whole city was gathered to see me. At first I only went out in a sedan-chair, but the bearers were compelled to stand still while they looked at the strange object. Nor did they get easily over their curiosity. For a long time I was a strange thing to them, as if hardly human.

My first year in China was full of trial, being the ever memorable year of the "Tien-tsin Massacre." It was long after the event before we got details of that horrible crime. The natives seemed to know all about it before we did, and very soon the city was placarded with the vilest reports about us. They said that at Tien-tsin all the foreigners had been killed or driven out of the place, because they kidnapped and murdered children, taking out their eyes, heart, and liver to compound into medicine. The same evil deeds were being done in this city. "Was it not known that we pretended to keep a school?" "Was it not true that so many children were missing?" "Had not some seen barrels in which were salted down babies?" "What was hard at Tien-tsin, was easy here, for there were but two ; drive out the pests and let the city be at rest." Such were some of the expressions of the placards. For about three months I hardly dared venture out of the house, and my husband was often met with stones and vile curses. For a few days there was a stream of people looking in every conceivable place for the said barrels ; one of the school-boys was asked where the missing children were, and when he said it was all nonsense and lies, they said he had eaten the foreign medicine and would not tell. For a time my husband felt very anxious ; if he had been alone he could have braved it, but the responsibility of another life seemed to weigh upon him.

One day he asked what I thought of a plan to leave for a few days in a junk, hoping when we returned all would be quiet. I saw it was on my account he made this suggestion, and when I answered that I feared if we left we might never get back again, and that I would rather stay and trust the Lord, he felt quite relieved. Through the Lord's mercy we weathered that and many another storm; indeed, we got so used to threatening placards and having the day of our death posted up, which passed by as quietly as other days, that we began to feel less anxious about their threats. But in the midst of this time of suffering we were not without encouragement. Mr. Stott wrote in September, 1870, to a dear friend :—

"Since I wrote you last, we have met with a few cheering circumstances. One came at a time when I was feeling cast down a little about the work. Owing to the massacre at Tien-tsin, we were in trouble and could not get out, and very few were coming in. One day a man came from the neighbouring prefecture, and said he wanted to see me. He told me he had been in company with a man who was a member here, and had heard him speak stories of Jesus Christ and of the God who created the heavens and the earth, and sent His Son to die for sinners; that they read the Bible every night together, and prayed to God to pardon and redeem them, and that he believed the 'doctrine' of Jesus and trusted on His merits for salvation, and that three or four others also believed. These I have never seen, but the man, who was a pedlar, and was in the city a few days refilling his pack, attended our evening worship every night, but has now gone again to pursue his business; also two of the boys are taking an interest in the truth ; their minds are expanding and they most readily understand the Scriptures. Thus often the Lord encourages us even in our darkest moments, though not always does the fruit, which seems so promising at the time, mature."

CHAPTER III

'They that make them are like unto them; so is every one that trusteth in them."—PSA. cxv. 8.

ANOTHER letter, dated March, 1871, describing idol worship and processions, gives some idea how excited the people get at such a time :—

"It is difficult to give information of idol worship, although I witnessed it daily, and idol processions are legion.

"Idols in Wenchow are usually made of a cross piece of wood to represent the body and arms, other pieces being fixed for legs; then on the wood is twisted straw ropes to bring it as much as possible to the form required; on the straw is added clay, laid on in coats or layers, each having to dry before the next coat is added, the whole process taking some months if the idol is a large one; the outer layer of clay is put on with much skill and care, as this must give expression to the countenance, &c. When dry, the painter smooths the cracks with putty, and paints in the orthodox fashion of its class. When all is finished there is generally a dedication feast, according to the rank of the idol; then it is established. The idol is first worshipped at the feast of its dedication, and according to the merits it is said to possess. The worshipper brings two small candles and lights them on the altar with a few sticks of incense. After placing them on the altar, he kneels on the kneeboard (I have seen very many kneel, go through a course of bowing, and then turn round for their pipe, light it composedly at the burning candle, sit, and enjoy a smoke on the kneeboard); a few more prostrations, and the affair is over. Processions are generally got up in honour of some festival. There are shops where all the fixings are kept, and they usually contract for so many articles, according to the money they are able to raise, and only those streets get the procession through which can afford to contribute well. All the beauties in the neighbourhood wear their gala dresses, and come and sit in their doors, or at the street crossing, to see and be seen. The procession is usually preceded by a band of boys gaudily dressed, bearing banners of gay and fantastic shapes, then a band of musicians, making the most unmusical, hideous sounds. A kind of pipe is conspicuous, but the universal gong is the most prominent, and pours forth a torrent of sound almost deafening. Then comes the idol seated in an enormous sedan-chair carried by many bearers, the people kneeling and worshipping as it passes. I have seen the bearers streaming with perspiration under a vertical sun, and when it was set down wiping their tanned faces and falling on their knees before the disgusting object that was wasting their strength."

We lived at first in a small three-roomed Chinese house, having only the three upper rooms for ourselves—a bedroom, my husband's study, and the centre our living-room. The rooms below were the bedrooms of the schoolboys. We had then a fairly decent man for a cook, but utterly untaught; my husband had existed on any kind of food they could provide, and suffered much from indigestion as the result. An amusing incident could be related of his experiences during this time; once being tired of rice three times a day, he asked his cook if he could not make him some cakes for breakfast. He beamed encouragingly, and next morning there were hot cakes; but, oh! so solid and hard and with a lump of fat pork in the centre. Not relishing this, and yet not willing to discourage budding genius, he waited till all had gone to bed that night, and abstracted from the tiny larder all the pork that could be found. Next morning the hot cakes came as before. What could be in the centre this time? There was no pork in the house; the very suspiciously white mass was found to be nothing more hurtful than a piece of turnip. After that cakes were given up.

Instead of sitting down quietly and learning the language, as I would have liked, I had to put my house in order, which was not to be done in a day; the cook had to be taught how to cook, and the coolie had to be taught how to wash and iron clothes, clean, scrub, &c. Thanks to the early training of a careful grandmother, these things were not much of a trouble to me, except in the matter of bread-making; time after time I tried to produce bread without yeast, following the recipes of cookery books, with the result that the bread might have done for hearthstones, but not for food. My husband encouraged me by saying it had a good taste, though it was a little hard; but for his patience I would probably have given up long before success crowned my efforts.

Some of my experiences in those early days were both trying and amusing. I remember one day, after having spent the morning teaching the coolie how to wash clothes, I had put a boilerful on to boil, and telling him not to touch them till I came back, I retired for an hour's rest. On returning I lifted the lid of the boiler, when to my horror I saw dark blue water and my clothes dyed dark; the coolie thought it a good opportunity of putting in his blue calico shirt, which was more lively than comfortable Of course my work had to be done all over again

I found not only the school-children's clothing but my husband's claimed my attention. He had been put to some queer straits in his efforts to keep his stockings mended. Of course no native knew how to mend such things, and he had nearly as little idea himself. One day, while looking in his box for something to fill up a large hole, he spied a dress-coat which he had brought from England with him. It was useless as it was, so he thought it would do for mending; cutting off one of the tails and spreading it on the floor, he put his foot on the top, made a chalk mark all round, leaving a good flap to turn over. It was a good evening's work, and when I ruthlessly cut off the feet of the said stockings he boasted they had lasted two years. The coat afterwards was given to his teacher, and, though minus a tail, kept him warm for several years under his Chinese garment. Flannels, too, were in a sad condition; of course they did not know how to wash such things. When I asked how they came to be this peculiar colour (a greenish yellow), he explained that the first time they were washed the coolie had put them into a tub, and poured the thick muddy water of the river over them, thus leaving them for a day or two; when washed and returned to Mr. Stott the hardness suggested a shaking, when the clouds of dust almost blinded him.

With so many other duties it was not to be expected that I could learn the language very fast. I was distressed after nearly two years to find, though able to speak enough for household matters, I was unable to teach the gospel to the women who almost daily visited me. My husband had engaged a Christian woman at Ning-po to help me in caring for the schoolboys; she loved to go with her hymnbook and New Testament visiting among the women. I was too ignorant at the time to know how little her Ning-po dialect was understood by our Wenchow women; perhaps it was well I did not know, for it comforted me greatly to do her work, while I sent her out daily to teach the poorer women around of the Saviour's love.

My health, too, suffered much from the climate; the second year I had a very severe illness, which nearly cost me my life. One day, while in a very low condition, my husband was called away to save a man who had eaten opium; he was loth to leave me, too weak to make my wants known to others, but I urged him to go, for I was sorely tried by the thought that I was hindering instead of helping him, as I so longed to do. He had been gone, perhaps, about an hour. It was a hot day in July, and I suppose partly from the heat and partly from my weakness I fainted; when I recovered consciousness my bed was surrounded on all sides by schoolboys, teachers, and servants who had come to wail thinking I was dead. One had run off for Mr. Stott, and meeting him on the way back, cried: "Oh, master, come back; mistress is dead!" Hoping it might be only a faint, he hurried home and found me restored to consciousness. I remember so well, when able to sit up a little, how I longed for two things, either of which I thought would make me well—the sight of one of my countrywomen, or a little beef-tea, neither of which were within my reach.

In those days we were not well off in the matter of food; we had but little communication with the outside world except by letter. Once in two years we took a holiday, when we brought in necessary stores to last us the next two years, for in the city of Wenchow we could neither get beef or mutton, milk, potatoes, or butter.

But these were by no means our greatest hardships; the indifference of the people affected us more than our surroundings. After the second year I had the servants trained, so that I could give most of my time to missionary work. I began first by visiting in their homes, and everywhere I was well received, being a curiosity to be looked and wondered at. They thought it strange I should speak their language, but they had little heart for my message. Alas! they did not know they needed a Saviour.

About this time my husband and Mr. Jackson, who had joined us about the end of my first year, rented a large shop in the busy part of the city for a chapel; they fitted up one part of it as a bookshop, and a native preacher sat daily selling books and preaching to all who might come in, and in the afternoon the large chapel was thrown open, when either my husband or Mr. Jackson preached. At first crowds came to hear, but after a time they dropped off, and the ones and the twos who really wanted to be taught came to listen. An extract from Mr. Stott's letter describes the kind of crowd he often had to deal with :—

"When the gates are opened, in rushes every one near—street strollers and loungers, rowdies, travelling tradesmen of all kinds, hawkers crying out their wares, conjurors, fortune-tellers, musicians, thieves and beggars; the shaven pate of a Bhuddist priest, the cowl of the Touist priest may also be seen, and the noise is almost beyond description. I assure you it is no easy task to arrest or keep the attention of such a crowd, and it is a great strain upon the lungs and intellect, as I have proved yesterday by experience. In the forenoon I kept nearly every eye fixed, every mouth open, and every tongue quiet for more than three-quarters of an hour, while I told them of the origin of sin, its effects, and salvation through our Redeemer. Many listened attentively all the time; the greater portion flit about, go and come, and never sit down. My daily prayer is that our chapel may be the birthplace of many souls. Yesterday far more than a thousand people heard; it takes long for them to understand, but by God's blessing we are giving 'line upon line' as they are able to receive it."

About the same time he refers to the conversion of the two eldest boys in the school; they, with two other boys, were baptized soon after. A letter written by these boys to the same friend, who had shown them much kindness, is here inserted, and may be interesting as a specimen of Chinese composition :—

"Honoured and respected Sir,—We, the undermentioned boys, in the tenth moon and twenty-seventh day received a letter from you, which our teacher, Mr. Stott, translated for us. You have for a long time shown us much kindness, and your kind exhortations to us are very good.

"We Wenchow boys, although the road is very long, seem so near as almost to eat with you at the same table; we cannot thank you enough for the interest you take in us.

"In the first place, we want to thank you for the beautiful pictures you sent us, although in themselves not of infinite value, yet they manifest a loving heart. Also you continually pray for us ignorant boys, that in school we may increase knowledge and continue in good bodily condition; also that in reading the

Wenchow School-boys, School Teacher, Mrs. Stott, and Miss Bardsley. The front row were converted and three of the six are now unpaid preachers.

Bible we may understand and know about God. We also do a little at the books of the native sages, and are able to understand somewhat, because you pray for us, but your very humble servants know but little of propriety; we also forget your grace, and have no grace to give you in return; our faces are like brass, and our necks stiff as iron—forgive us.

"By the grace of God in the former part of this year a chapel was opened in the Five Horse Street, and very many have heard the gospel. At first they were very noisy and understood but little, now there is a great difference for the better; they are willing to sit quietly and listen. To preach is also far less difficult. Also, before we removed, our sleeping rooms were much hampered; but we are better here —the rooms are large and can accommodate five or six easily: no matter how many come, there is room.

"At worship we every morning and evening read the Scriptures and pray to God. At present in the mornings we are reading the Book of Jeremiah the prophet of God, how the Lord sent him to the King of Judah with a message; but the king would not listen to him, but hardened his heart, and disgraced the prophet by putting him into a dungeon; but the Lord vindicated His servant, and manifested His power by punishing that king and his people. At evening worship we are reading the fifth book of the New Testament, the Acts of the Apostles; we are at the ninth chapter, where Saul persecuted the disciples of Jesus. He was fierce as a lion, and intended to eat up the disciples, by means of a letter from the authorities at Jerusalem; but on the way to Damascus he met the Lord, who changed his heart, and from that day till the day of his death he served the Lord. The mystery of God we are unable to understand, but we are sincere in our worship. We pray that the grace of God may be abundantly to you, and yours, to all generations.

"P.S.—When you see errors in our writing or our composition, pass lightly over, and don't laugh at us, for we are already ashamed of ourselves.

"Written at the school-house of Wenchow, tenth moon, twenty-seventh day.

"SENG SI NYU,
"TSIU DIE CHENG,
"For all the rest."

Mr. Stott writes:—"There are many things to give trouble and anxiety; it is not all smooth sailing, nor yet all success. If we were to sum up our defeats, I am sure it would be easy for me to show ten failures for one success." In writing of the difficulties of sustained teaching, he adds: "When the novelty of reading or speaking God's Word wears off, it needs a strong hold within the veil to sustain us; only close living and walking with God can do this, and my experience leads me to the conclusion that it can only be got or maintained by living, active faith and prayer—real prayer, the soul grappling like Jacob, getting strength, not weakness, from the struggle."

In November, 1871, we had an interesting case of conversion—that of a Bhuddist priest. After he had believed the truth he left his monastery, returned to his native village, and began farm work. He was most earnest in telling all whom he met of the God who had saved him, and we had hoped for fresh openings through his efforts; but only a few months after his baptism, while on his way to join us in a communion service, his boat was overturned in a storm, and our brother, with twenty-eight others, found a watery grave. It is to this man Mr. Stott refers in the following :—

"Last night three elderly men from the country remained to inquire further about the 'doctrine,' and seemed in earnest. Our friend, the Bhuddist priest, has come, and begs not to be sent away again without baptism. He says that in and round his village twenty-eight people believe the gospel, and have turned from idolatry. That statement must be modified, and perhaps really means that about that number acquiesce in what he says about worshipping idols, and of the only living and true God ; but allowing it to be modified, there is still a good margin in his favour. If he has faithfully told twenty-eight persons all he knows, that is something. He says he is known for ten miles round as the turncoat priest."

Two years later there was another interesting case of a man who had been a priest all his life, and was over seventy when he first heard the gospel; he attended more or less regularly for two or three years, and then asked to be baptized; but was told he could not be a follower of Christ while wearing the priestly garb, and living on the gains of idolatry. This was a sore disappointment; he was an old man, unable to work, and had no other means of livelihood.

This was a case we longed to help, but feared the result upon the young church. He continued in the temple, but got others to perform his priestly duties; he was troubled at not being baptized, so one day, putting on clean garments, he went to a mountain stream near by, prayed on the bank, then plunged in and baptized himself. A few days afterwards he met with one of the Christians, and asked whether he thought that baptism would do; but the Christian was unable to give him any information, never having heard of such a case before.

It was not long ere we heard of the fruit of this man's labour. Mr. Stott, writing to a friend a few months afterwards, says:

"During the last ten days three new inquirers have come; one, an old man near seventy, has been a vegetarian for nearly forty years, and has been to all the temples in the district worshipping. Lately, he went to a temple some distance from his home to burn candles, &c.; while worshipping, the priest saw him, and after making sure there was no one to hear, said, 'Elder brother, I have been a priest for sixty years, and worshipped these things until two years ago; but they never did me any good, and never will. You, like myself, are an old man, and must soon die. Come inside and I will tell you who, and how, to worship.' He then took him into his room and preached Jesus to him. The question naturally arose, 'Where did you hear such things?' 'From the foreigners in the city.' 'From the foreigners!' he exclaimed; 'why, there is no crime under heaven but the foreigners have committed, and they are going to be beheaded one of these days, if indeed it be not already done.' The priest assured him that was untrue, and told him he had been to Wenchow only three days before, and had listened to the true words of God. The priest informed him that some tens of good men had entered the religion, and were going to eternal happiness in heaven; he, too, would have joined them, but he was too old to earn his rice, and had nothing to depend on but the temple, and the missionary had said he could not be a disciple of Jesus and eat the rice of idols. All this and much more the poor old priest told him; also of pardon and peace through Jesus, God's Son. He died in the temple, but, we believe, a true disciple."

About this time a man from Dong-ling dropped in to hear the foreigner. He was interested, and had a long talk with the native preacher. He had a good many questions to ask, and returned home to think. He came again and again, and, after a while, truly received the truth. He had been told that opium growing was nearly as bad as opium smoking. He had some growing in his fields, and his conscience became troubled. One night he was trying to argue with himself: he was poor; it paid better than anything else; it was too late in the season to grow wheat; he would let it alone this year, but give it up the following. He could not sleep, however; the question troubled him more than he liked. At last he rose by dawn, took his scythe, and cut down every root of opium. He was baptized soon after, and, when we visited him two years later, we found his wife and mother true Christians; he also conducted morning and evening prayers, when eleven of his neighbours joined him.

Surely this was an instance of what a sincere heart and simple eye to God can do. He had but little ability, but what he had he used for God.

CHAPTER IV

"They imagined a mischievous device, which they are not able to perform."—PSA. xxi. 11.

IN April, 1873, Mr. Stott paid his first visit into the Dong-ling district, and thus writes:—
"Last week I made a journey into the country, to a place distant about twenty miles from here. Two days before I went to a village about six miles off, and when I returned I found my pony's back sadly hurt by the saddle. There was nothing for it but to rest him for two days and re-stuff my saddle, which was a difficult job for me. At the time appointed, accompanied by one of the members, and a man to carry my bed, I got off pretty early. It was a lovely spring morning, and the road we had to travel was beautiful in the extreme. I heard the frogs croaking for the first time this season; the oil plant was in full bloom, filling the air with fragrance; farmers were sowing the early rice, and the bamboo groves were full of the melody of singing birds; the snakes also were out sunning themselves, and wriggling their

ugly forms on the sides of the path. After riding about five miles or so, we struck the foot of the hills, and after dinner we came to the district we had in view, and I rode from hamlet to hamlet, preaching and selling books. The whole district soon turned out to see and hear, for there had never been a foreigner in that place before. We could see men in the fields a mile off throw down their hoes and run as if for life, and all to see your humble servant. As we advanced the crowds gathered more thick and noisy. One cannot judge of the noise of a Chinese crowd till they have heard one; nobody listens, but everybody shouts at the top of his voice, and such shrill, piercing sounds, no Saxon throat could produce anything like them.

"I continued preaching until nearly sundown, then went to the house where we were to pass the night; but the scene there would need a livelier pen than mine to give even an outline of it. At last, almost in despair, I took my crutch and gave a knock on the wooden partition, and ordered every tongue to be still and listen to me. To my surprise I succeeded in getting them quieted pretty well, and then preached salvation through Jesus Christ till my throat was sore. Then the man who carried my bed took up the subject and showed them that idols made of wood and clay could not do any one good, and exhorted them all to worship the only living and true God, who had sent

Jesus Christ, His dear Son, to open the way of heaven for them, and who is now there interceding for those who trust Him. Most of the people left to get their evening rice, but soon returned in greater force than ever; and, though tired and weary, I had to begin again and preach to a late hour. Then I asked all to leave and return in the morning, but just as I was going to bed a deputation from the elders of the village came, saying that all the wisest of the old men were in a house near by and wanted a quiet interview, to hear and see for themselves, for the youngsters had brought strange news. This was a rare good chance of speaking for our blessed Saviour, and lifting up my heart to Him for guidance, He gave it, and enabled me to speak of His Holy Name.

"I continued for nearly an hour to address fourteen men, who listened most attentively all the time. One asked 'how to worship this true God.' I told him, and knelt on the wet mud floor and prayed for them all, thanked God for His goodness in giving them life and food, and asked Him to send the Holy Spirit to teach them and open their hearts. When I got up they all were surprised; some looking at me with amazement, not knowing what to make of it. One asked, 'But will God hear you?' I answered, 'Your own books tell you that heaven has eyes, which is true ; would it not be strange if heaven had eyes and no ears?' They all replied, ' True, true.'

"At a very late hour they left, and I could not help thanking God for such a golden opportunity of setting His Name before so many people."

These preaching tours were continued as often as possible. Sometimes I would accompany him to the nearer places, but more often I had to remain to look after home affairs.

Referring to another of these tours, Mr. Stott writes:—

"Some three weeks ago I had an interesting preaching tour. We visited a good many towns and villages, and had often over a thousand listeners; sometimes we preached from the theatre stand, or in the village temple, or again, when no good situation was obtainable, from my horse's back. I had two Christian natives with me, who also preached in turn. One, however, lost his voice after the second day, but the other continued to speak. He could be heard a quarter of a mile off. I have seldom listened to a voice equal to his; perhaps the late lamented Duncan Matheson's was as good, but Duncan's was a deep bass, and the native I refer to was a shrill tenor, and anything but pleasing. However, he preached Jesus Christ plainly and fully. These stayed about ten days after I left, and preached in a few other places.

"I did not feel comfortable in staying away too long, with Mrs. Stott all alone, and so many people to look after; but she can get along much better now, can speak pretty well, and is making good progress in the Chinese character. She goes out to visit twice a week, and has a daily class of the smaller boys, and an advanced Bible-class on Sunday afternoons. Besides, she takes the entire charge of the food and clothing of the school; that, with the addition of our own affairs and her Chinese studies, keeps her busy, so that she seldom has an hour to spare; but I am thankful to say she is in good health.

"I wish I had time to refer in greater detail to the many places visited at this time. One, in particular, struck me as being the most lovely I have ever seen; but the people seemed sadly degraded. The village was situated in a glen of almost horse-shoe shape; at the back and sides the hills rose high and abrupt, assuming almost the aspect of mountains, while on in front was a long plain, widening as it went. A beautiful stream ran past the village, which we crossed; the gardens seemed full of fruit, oranges, pomeloes, and pomegranates, all ripening on the trees. The head family of the village took us in for the night and treated us well. After supper the people came crowding in, and I preached to them to a late hour, while the natives who were with me had a still larger audience in the reception hall. They treated me thus kindly because I had formerly cured one of the ladies when ill with fever.

"Next morning I was up, had breakfast, and in the saddle again at sunrise, and made our way to another village, when the whole population turned out to the temple yard. I climbed on to the theatre stand and preached in turn with the native assistant. By and by the head priest raised some objection to our preaching in front of the gods. I said if the people objected I would go somewhere else; but most cried, 'No, no, stop where you are.' One of the crowd called out, 'If the priest is not quiet, we will carry him to the top of the hill and make him fast to a tree.' That remark caused a good deal of merriment at the expense of the poor priest, who remained quiet for the rest of the time. As I wanted to push on I did not accept the kind hospitality of the village schoolmaster, who wished to detain me to dinner."

After this quite a number in Dong-ling became interested, and my husband was invited to go and preach to them. He did so, with the result that a little church was formed in the house of one of the members.

One day Mr. Stott had gone to Dong-ling in the hope of finding a house he could rent as a chapel. On the day I expected him home a man came from there bringing me a large fish as a present, and saying Mr. Stott had found a place for a chapel, and had sent him for money to settle the matter. The present of the fish was a little suspicious. I asked whether he had not a letter for me, and he said he had, but on stepping out of the boat it had dropped into the canal and was lost. A few more questions revealed the rogue, and as I spoke of sending for Yamen runners, he ran off, leaving the fish behind him. A little later my husband returned, and as we discussed the fish at tea we laughed over the clumsy attempt at fraud.

I think it was in 1873 or 1874 we were surprised one morning by a strange man coming in with a small bundle of bedding on his back. Almost his first words were, " I have come to stay and be taught the doctrine." We did not receive people in that easy fashion, but when my husband sat down to talk with him he heard a strange story. The man had been a soldier during the Taiping rebellion. He left father, mother, and a young wife to serve his country, and was absent two or three years. During his absence his wife had died, though his father and mother were still alive. He had become disgusted with what he had seen of the world, and had determined to give himself up to a religious life. What money he had he spent in purchasing coffins for his father and mother, and making their graves. Having fulfilled this filial duty he retired to the hills to lead a holy life. He built himself a very small hut, with bed and bedding too short to lie down in, compelling himself to rest in a sitting posture. He soon got a name for sanctity, and the people of the neighbouring villages brought him presents of food in return for his prayers. One day a man was passing the house of a Christian, and on being asked by him where he was going, replied, "To the hermit with a present." "Oh," said the Christian; "wait a moment, I, too, have a present for him." He brought out a Gospel, and asking the young man to give it to the holy man on the hill, went on with his work, probably thinking no more of the matter. Some days after this the hermit saw the young man again, and asked where that book came from. He answered, "I suppose from the foreigner in Wenchow, but I know little about it. My neighbour talks about a true God, and one Jesus Christ; but I don't understand." The poor hermit became restless to know something more about this strange doctrine, and for the first time in three years he came down the hill and walked to Wenchow to inquire after the true God. After hearing his story, my husband invited him to stay with us for a week, and seeing his diligent study of the Bible and eagerness to learn, asked him to stay on a few weeks longer.

One morning, while I was having a Bible-class with the schoolboys and others who had joined, the subject being John iii., I saw this man weeping. My husband took him aside and asked him what was the matter. He only answered, "My sins, my sins!"

It was the first time we had seen a Chinaman weep because of sin, and it thrilled us through and through. He never returned to the hill again, but in his home he found too much opposition to contend with, and, strange to say, though we sent time after time, and prayed much for him, he never entered into the truth. After a year or so he led us to understand he did not care for us to send to him any more, as his parents did not want him to become a Christian.

But the young man who had carried the book to him, and of whom we had never thought, began to wonder what was in that book, to cause the man to come down from the hill and break his vow of sanctity. He inquired further into the truth, and, after a time, was converted, and through him his father, mother, and aunt became Christians, and are still in the church.

We had often trials and disappointments through the duplicity and love of gain, which is so common in the Chinese character; a man would profess a most earnest desire for the truth, and seem to hold it very precious, while all the time his hope was that he would get employment of some kind. A case in point was a school teacher, who seemed to be converted, and almost daily would, of his own accord, stop the boys in their studies to read the Bible and pray with them. He had been an opium smoker, but professed to have given it up when he became a

Christian; but later on he went back to his opium and gave up all profession of faith in Christ. He had two boys in school, who, after the usual term of education, were apprenticed to trades; for a long while we lost sight of them, but a few years ago the eldest of them was truly converted, and is now one of our volunteer unpaid preachers.

There was another who deceived us for years; he had been a fortune-teller, but when he professed to receive the gospel he gave up everything of the kind, and seemed to be very earnest in telling his friends and neighbours the good news. This brought some persecution upon him, which he bore bravely. At last they trumped up a case against him; he was taken to the Yamen and accused of crimes he had never committed. The mandarin told him plainly that if he would renounce this foreign religion he might be set free; but he answered, "You may cut my head off, but I will never renounce the Christian religion." He was kept in prison for nearly three months, and we were powerless to help him.

We were much touched by his steadfastness, and began to think that after all we must be wrong in our want of confidence in him, for somehow we never could quite trust him. He farmed his own land, but spent much of his time in volunteer preaching, so that through his efforts the work began to grow much in the Dong-ling district. The question of employing him often came up in our minds, for we were sorely in need of teachers in those early days, but this feeling we had, of not being quite sure of our man, kept my husband from doing so. He grew tired of waiting, and, after a little agitation, boldly went over to the Roman Catholics, saying that he had waited for seven years in the hope of employment, and that if we would not pay him he would have nothing to do with us. The Roman Catholics employed him, and the true character came out in his determined efforts to upset our work; he had brought many of these men into the church, and meant to take them out if he could, but happily he had been the means of bringing in better men than himself, and only a very few halting ones followed him; but he was a thorn in our flesh for many years.

About the year 1874 we passed through a series of difficulties through evil reports; if there was evil in the city the foreigner must be at the bottom of it. A secret society, called the "ring" society, had sprung up; Mr. Stott was said to be the head and moving spirit; all who chose to join would receive a gold ring and four dollars, but they would be pledged to do all in their power to upset the present government. Mr. Stott was pestered for gold rings and dollars, and one day, making sure that an applicant knew what he was doing, and was ready for any villainy, he felt the time had come to put a stop to it. Sending his card to the Yamen, he asked them to take charge of the man and to inquire into the case. Two Yamen runners were at once sent, and before they had taken him outside the gate they had possessed themselves of his best garments and hat. After a few days my husband requested the man might be set at liberty, and we were no more troubled with the " ring " society.

An uneasy feeling was all over the city at this time. A band had been organised amongst the hills for a raid upon the city. They were known to be strong, and of course the foreigner was said to be at the head. It had been working for months. The authorities took alarm, and sent to Tai-chow for troops. Cannons were placed upon the city walls, the gates closed each night at sunset, and a mandarin placed upon guard until daybreak. We knew our name was connected with this uprising, but we had passed through so many storms of the kind that my husband and Mr. Jackson left me, as usual, to visit the out-stations, and expected to be away nearly a fortnight. They had only been gone a few days, when the school teacher came to me in great alarm, and said the city was posted with violent placards. Mr. Stott, they said, had gone to train and organise the band, while I was taking in large quantities of rice in order to feed them when they came. The teacher said there was great danger of an attack upon us, and urged me to write to the mandarin and request protection. I thought and prayed over the matter, and finally decided to wait patiently the return of my husband. In answer to prayer they came home four or five days earlier than expected. Mr. Stott at once wrote the authorities denying these statements, stating we were quiet and peaceable people, bent only on preaching peace to all men, and that we had nothing to do with any kind of society, and asking for a proclamation to this effect. This the mandarin granted, but his proclamations were no sooner up than they were torn down, or bespattered with mud. The people seemed bent on mischief, and we were warned by friendly neighbours we had better leave. But how could we leave the few sheep we had gathered in from the wilderness? They did not know the heart of the Shepherd.

At last things got so threatening that our servants were warned to leave us; an attack, they said, had been decided upon for the following Tuesday, and if they did not go they would probably share our fate. So on the Saturday our two servants, and the woman who looked after the boys, said they must leave us that day. My husband called me downstairs to tell me the sorrowful news. It was evident the servants were frightened, and I thought we should be better without timid people about us. Our coolie had recently professed conversion, and it was a bitter disappointment that he should leave us in our hour of need. We had expected the hatred of the heathen, but not the desertion of the Christian. Without expressing any regret we offered him his wages with the others, but he refused to take them, saying he would be back in a week. "Yes, after we are killed, or the danger over," were the words that arose in my heart. But I was soon to be ashamed of such unkind thoughts, for in about an hour he returned and begged to be allowed to stay. The others returned a week later, when they saw we were still alive.

This coolie had rather a hasty temper, which sometimes brought him into trouble. One evening, while we were at prayer, we could hardly hear our own voices for the noise of quarrelling downstairs. Mr. Stott went to see what was the matter, and found the coolie and one of the elder boys had quarrelled. He spoke seriously to them, remarking that it was very sad, after all the teaching, that we should be disturbed while in prayer by their quarrels. The coolie hastily produced the horsewhip; putting it in front of Mr. Stott, and himself in position for whipping, he remarked, "I am the one most to blame, whip me." He was told he must go to God to seek and find forgiveness; and this, I have no doubt, he did, but he seemed disappointed that he was not whipped also.

Of course I had all the housework to do in the

meantime. We were not, however, without real anxiety, for there was no doubt that an attack upon the city was intended, and we knew if the robbers came we should suffer both at their hands and at the hands of the enraged people, who looked upon us as the cause of all their suffering. So we made a few private plans. A long rope was secured and kept in a convenient place; this was to let us over the city wall, where we could fly towards the sea. But we hardly knew what to do with a few of our school boys who had no homes. A friendly neighbour promised that he would give us the first alarm, so that we might have time to escape. One midnight a terrific knocking at the gate aroused us from our first sleep. In a moment we were on the verandah listening breathlessly to know what it could be. The man who had promised to tell us of the first danger rushed in crying, " Mr. Stott, get away as soon as you can; the insurgents have broken in the west gate, trampled upon the mandarin, and are now making their way through the city." My husband went down to gather our people together, to see who would go with us to share our uncertain fate, but first he despatched a messenger to find out if the news were really true. Downstairs they were having prayer, commending us all to God, while I was upstairs preparing for flight. It was warm weather, so I only had to roll a flannel coat for my husband

and a thin gown for myself, which made a very small parcel, tying twenty dollars round my waist, and putting the rest into a bag tied to the neck of a bottle in which were secured the title-deeds of the house, intending to sink them into the well. These few preparations being completed I went downstairs, rope in one hand and small bundle in the other. Even to this sad picture there was a ludicrous side, for we were gravely asked by one of the elder boys "what were we going to do with the furniture?" The messenger returned saying the news was true, and we had better get off as soon as possible; but I knew from the short time I had been upstairs it was impossible for him to have been to the west gate and back: I suggested to Mr. Stott to ask him, and he acknowledged that he had not, but all the city was talking about it. He was again despatched, with orders to run all the way, and, if true, to run back with all haste, and we might still have time to escape. Oh, what a long, long time it seemed; every moment was precious, and might mean life to us. At last he returned, only to say it was a false alarm; a band of thieves had spread the report, and when the poor people, panic-stricken, ran from their houses, they went in and helped themselves. We thanked God, went to bed, and slept soundly till morning.

During those early years it seemed impossible to live without offence before the people. For instance, my husband built a chimney, and though not very high, immediately it was conjectured to be a signalling apparatus to communicate with steamers; a neighbour's child took ill and died, and the unfortunate chimney was found to be the cause. A deputation waited upon us to request that the chimney should be pulled down; this was done, but soon afterwards some one else in the neighbourhood took ill, and the cause this time was found to be my husband's stable —that, too, must come down. My husband explained that he could not afford the expense, but as it was for their own benefit they were at liberty to pull down the obnoxious thing and rebuild any shape they approved at their own expense. This settled the question, and the poor horse's stable was left untouched. Another time, while Mr. Stott was preaching in the chapel to a large and seemingly attentive audience, he happened to look at his watch, when a man asked, "What is that he is looking at?" The reply was, " A kind of hocus-pocus instrument whereby he can tell how many are to be hocussed by his preaching, and when they are hocussed to the desired number and extent he will stop." Mr. Stott knew nothing of this till some time afterwards when, going into the country, he found the whole place full of the absurd story.

CHAPTER V

"Our Lord is above all gods."—PSA. cxxxv. 5.

IT was about this time my husband sent a preacher to open up work in the city of Bing-yie. As usual, crowds came to listen at first, but soon dropped off, and he, feeling rather lonely, asked that some one might be sent to help him. We had no one to send, so my husband sent a Christian schoolboy, named Z-nüe, thirteen years of age, for a few months to keep him company. One day the lad entered into a heathen temple; he could not see worshippers, but at every shrine there were lighted candles and incense, showing some one had been there. Turning round, he saw an old man just finishing his obeisance to the last of the numerous gods, and as he sat down to rest the lad addressed him. "Venerable grandfather," said he, "why do you worship these idols? They are made of clay, and can neither see, hear, or help you. Indeed they cannot help themselves, for see, some of their fingers are broken off, and others have had the hair of their moustachios stolen by rats. Rats do not steal the hair of your moustache: why? Because you are a living man. How foolish, then, to worship these things which even the rats may rob with impunity. Not only so; do not the rats make their nests inside these very idols?" The old man sighed, and said, "What am I to do?" The lad then told him of the God in heaven, and of Jesus Christ His Son, and the way of salvation that had been provided for "whosoever will."

The old man listened with great astonishment, he had never heard such wisdom. As he was deeply interested, he was invited to the chapel to hear more from the preacher. He not only came himself, but brought his old wife; and after a time they both became truly converted, and for years led godly, consistent lives. The aged couple are now in glory.

This young lad, who was converted when he was about twelve, afterwards became an earnest and successful preacher in this very city of Bing-yie. I remember Mr. Stott, in speaking, before sending him out on his first mission, told him he was to preach Christ, and to leave idolatry and their idols and idol customs alone; for as soon as truth entered into their heart the other would soon go out. After talking for some time he asked the boy if he understood what he meant. He said," Yes; you mean like this: the people are now living in an old tumbled-down hut, and you don't want me to pull this down about their ears. I am, as it were, to build a beautiful house, furnished with all good things, and then invite them to leave their old broken-down hut and enter into their new possession." That young man laboured earnestly, preaching often in the open air ; by and by consumption manifested itself, and in spite of all our efforts, so precious, and as it seemed to us so necessary, a life in the early stage of our work, ended. He died, twenty-five years of age. That was a great loss to the young church, for he had been well taught and trained by Mr. Stott.

In 1872, our cook, who was baptized the day after our marriage, married a heathen girl. We were grieved, yet what could we do? To insist that the Christians should marry "only in the Lord" was practically to forbid marriage, seeing there were no Christian women within seven days' journey of them. The influence of the heathen wife was soon apparent, first in coldness of heart, then in utter indifference to spiritual things, and before two years were over we had to dismiss him from the church. This led us to see something must be done to supply the great need of Christian wives for our Christian young men, if we would have a strong and healthy church. So after much prayer and thought on the subject we decided to commence a girls' boarding-school. There were many difficulties in the way; we had no suitable accommodation for girls; then we determined we would have no bound feet, and that we knew would probably prevent our getting the kind of girls we wanted. Some other schools had felt it necessary to continue this evil practice, because of this very difficulty; and one school that I knew of had found it very hard to contend against this almost universal custom. But we felt the importance of being pioneers, and were anxious to begin on a solid basis, that others could build upon. It was better we should fight these questions at first, rather than start on easier lines and have the battle to face later on. We therefore gave out that we were prepared to take in a few girls under ten years of age, that we should feed, clothe and educate them free of expense to their parents, but we should require that their feet be unbound, and that we should have the right to betroth them to those whom we thought fit persons, and that the parents should have no power to betroth them without our consent.

At this time we only had one old woman in the church, and she was the first to bring me her granddaughter. I explained clearly that her feet would be unbound. To this and the other rules she cheerfully consented. The child was a dear little thing, nine years of age, and being the only one, I had her with me a good deal and of course became very fond of her. When the parents saw this, they thought the time had come to make a fuss about her feet. They seemed to think I should be sure to give way rather than lose the pretty little thing that was so winning; so one day a message was brought to me that the child's mother had been crying night and day, for some time; that she was then tearing her hair, bemoaning the fate of her child who should grow up with feet like a man; she would never get a husband, for who would care for a girl with large feet? She therefore requested me to send her home, as she would rather beg from door to door than see her daughter so disgraced. I told the messenger they had brought her of their own free will; they understood our terms, and had agreed to them; that if they wanted her back they must come and fetch her: but first they must pay me the expenses of food and clothing, the amount which I had expended upon her. Of course they were unable to do this, and as I was firm they unwillingly gave in, and so our first battle against foot-binding was fought and won.

Still there was a great difficulty in getting girls, owing to this question, and for several years we had to be content with four, two of whom we certainly would not have received later on when our position was established and the benefits of the school manifested.

The girls' school has now been in existence twenty-

Wenchow School-girls and Teachers. Left, Miss Whitford ; right, Miss Chalmers.

two years, and has proved a great blessing to the church. The girls have had a thoroughly practical training, and most of them become Christian workers after they leave school. During the last ten years, twenty-two girls have been married, three only of whom have left school unconverted. There are seven or eight of our married girls who take regular classes among women and children. For nearly ten years we saw but little spiritual fruit, two or three professed to believe on Jesus, but there was no corresponding power or change in their lives. Our Bible-readings seemed the most wearisome part of the day to them, and they appeared to have no spiritual perception. For the first few years, while the children were young, I did not feel the burden, perhaps, as heavily as I ought to have done; but as years passed on I became almost desperate. Many a time I have gone from the school to my room with literal tears, sobbing, " Will these girls never be saved?" But in 1884 the Lord was pleased to visit us with a very gracious revival.

There was no indication of the coming blessing, save that the elder girls were more attentive than usual with the Bible lessons. One morning in June we were sitting as usual at our work, the elder girls a little apart with their needlework, while I was surrounded by a group of little ones whom I was teaching to sew and knit. The quiet was suddenly disturbed by the eldest girl saying : " Teacher, do you think if I came to Christ now, He would save me?" I looked at the girl, there was an expression of earnestness on her face I never had seen before. She continued, "You have often urged me to come to Christ, but I have never been willing; will He take me now?" I could hardly speak for the joy that welled up in my heart. I answered, "Oh, yes," and began to tell her of my own conversion when I was two years younger than she. While I spoke, she burst into tears, and with a cry and sob ran from the room. I could contain myself no longer, but with tears of joy I ran into my husband's study, and cried: "Blessing is coming at last; Ah-mai is seeking the Lord." We knelt together to pour out our thanksgiving, after which I returned to the girls. I found Ah-mai in her room. We knelt together by her bed while I asked God to have mercy upon her soul, to save her then and there; and thinking it best to leave her alone for a time, I returned to the schoolroom. Two other girls were sobbing, and when I asked what was the matter they answered, "We are such sinners." I called them upstairs, that I might quietly point them to the Saviour, but their distress was so great they could hardly listen.

One sobbed, "You don't know how bad I have been," and going to her cupboard she took out pieces of calico and little odds and ends I had given them to mend their clothes with, also one hundred cash (about fourpence); she put these into my hand and said: "Take them away; they are not mine, I stole them.". She explained that she had purloined little bits of material, &c., and with them had made little stomachers, and the hundred cash was the money she had received for them. The whole thing was of very little value, yet I did not wish her to think lightly of sin. I reminded her that Christ had saved a thief once.

The other girl said: "I have been worse than that. Do you remember, years ago, losing your silver brooch? Search was made, and it was found under Ah-yung's pillow; everybody thought she had taken it, but I stole it, and fearing to be found out, I put it there." I did feel indignant, and asked how she could stand by and see me punish an innocent child. I was so grieved I scarce knew what to say, but felt the first thing was to put this right with the one who had suffered. Assembling the whole school, and calling the little one to me, I asked if she remembered my having punished her a few years before for stealing a brooch? The child did not remember anything about it. I tried to refresh her memory, but it was no use, she had completely forgotten the circumstance. I told her how grieved I was I had accused her, but had done so ignorantly; it was nevertheless a wrong, and in presence of the school I asked her to forgive me.

Quite a number of little eyes twinkled that morning ; it was the first time their teacher had to confess to them her wrong-doing, and they rather enjoyed it. I then told the guilty girl that I had made all the reparation I could, and it was for her to find out in what way *she* could repair her fault. I was pleased afterwards to hear that she had given the little girl the whole of her month's money in compensation, but that the child generously returned half.

In a few days those three were clearly and distinctly converted, and in three weeks afterwards three more. One girl had already left the school to be married, and was still unsaved. As soon as the others were converted themselves they began in earnest to pray for this one ; I was delighted when they asked me to join them in prayer. The following Sunday one of the newly converted girls took the opportunity to speak to her, and told her how we were praying she might be saved. She answered carelessly, " It is no use, my heart is cold and hard ; I do not seem even to care to be saved." The following Saturday they asked if, in company with another Christian, they might visit her ; and on their return they almost rushed into my study, calling out breathlessly, " Sy-mo, our eldest sister is saved." My husband just coming in, and hearing only the last word, called, " Wait, I want to hear too." They then told us that the Sunday before, after the services, she had gone home in such heaviness of heart, and asked the Lord why she, the eldest of the number, should be so hard of heart? She said, while she prayed, light broke upon her, and she believed her sins were washed away. She was baptized some months afterwards, but I am sorry to say she has not turned out a satisfactory Christian. Her husband, though a believer, is somewhat trying in temper, and want of harmony at home has led to coldness on the part of both.

Since then there have been periodical revivals, at which time three, four, or five have been converted; and only three have left the school unsaved—for these we still pray.

During the second gracious revival amongst the girls, which took place in about two or three years after the first, when four more were converted, our coolie's wife was also saved. He had come to us almost destitute, but with diligent work and carefulness he saved enough to get a wife, and as he had no home for her, he asked if she might live in his room for a few months, to which I consented. She was a young girl, only fifteen, quiet and diligent, and the six months turned into many years, for they are still here with their five children, the three eldest in our schools. For about three years this young woman seemed very indifferent to the gospel; she attended the services because she lived inside, and all were expected to do so; but at this time she became deeply concerned about sin, and one day, while in the act of washing clothes, it seemed as though a horror of darkness came over her. She left her work, went to Mrs. Liü, and begged her to pray that God would forgive her sins. For two or three days she continued in an anxious state of soul, and then, yielding herself to Christ, she rejoiced in the knowledge of salvation.

In 1873 Mr. Jackson was married in Ning-po, and in due time brought his young wife to Wenchow. We had by that time got possession of the three lower rooms as well as the three upper, and for some months they lived with us. Mrs. Jackson's ill-health, however, called them away to Tai-chow, and later on to Ning-po, and when they returned, nearly a year after, they were able to rent a house in another part of the city. It was a great comfort to have another lady here, and we had no small fellowship one with another. They had to leave again and again for ill-health, but when it became necessary for us to take a furlough they willingly took the responsibility of the boys' and girls' school, and the little church which had been formed. Mrs. Jackson died in September, 1878, leaving a little girl only nine days old.

The boys' school had given a good deal of encouragement, not so much in the numbers converted as the character of the converts; and at this time

Die-chang and two others were preachers. Mr. Stott, writing a little earlier, says, " Si-nüe is now nineteen years of age, and is at present acting teacher, as I have lent the school-teacher to Mr. Jackson to assist him in his difficulties in Chu-chow. Si-nüe is a smart lad, a good scholar, and understands the Scriptures well, but I hardly expect him to equal Tsiu-die-chang (who is now in charge of the station at Bing-yie as a preacher); he speaks at times with almost burning earnestness, enough to persuade any one of the truth. Si-nüe is bashful and proud, and needs very careful treatment, but there is a good deal of capital material in him. I have heard him several times in hot discussions with literary men ; he can patter off the native classics glibly, and turn many passages against their silly notions with biting power. A younger boy, Z-nue, is nearly sixteen years of age, has been a member of the church about three years, and has all through behaved in a Christ-like manner. He is highly esteemed by the members for his consistent life ; he is very quiet, but ever ready, and seldom fails to establish himself in the good graces of the people he speaks to. I expect him to be a successful evangelist; often when school is over, instead of going to amuse himself with the others, he has gone out with a bundle of books and tracts to the crowded thoroughfares to sell. Would that they were more deeply taught by the Spirit of God, and lived nearer to the fountain of all heat and light and love."

A letter from Si-niie written to a friend mentioned before may prove interesting. Translated by Mr. Stott.

"In the year of grace 1874, first moon: Because I have formerly heard that for a long time you have been writing letters to Wenchow to inquire about the welfare of the boys; but we have hardly courage to receive your messages, for we are unworthy of them, but your kindness and love abound, it is beyond our understanding. Not only this, but many beautiful pictures you have sent for us. All who have seen them admire them; your kindness [lit. grace] is deep as the sea and heavy as the hills. The boys would like to go to your place and thank you personally before your face, but the way is long, seas and hills and impassable barriers intervene, therefore we are unable to come. Also we are so unworthy, that it would be presumption in us to appear before you.

"To speak of the pictures, some of them are hung in the schoolroom, some in the dining-hall, and some new ones are in the hands of a paper-hanger being done. Also there is hanging up a map of the world.

"At present there are in the school sixteen boys, and we read various books, including the native classics; but the Scriptures are the text-book for morning and evening worship. We are born with stupid minds, and our bodies are very lazy, therefore we do not know much; in our daily habits we are not diligent, we ought to hang down our heads and feel ashamed.

"To speak of the church, there have not been many added for a long time, but there are a few inquiring. At present, although there is little fruit, if the Holy Spirit were only in the heart of every one who believes, the time might soon come when we should see a great increase, thirty, sixty, or a hundredfold.

"I have used this small piece of paper to thank you, and pay our respects to yourself, your brothers, and all your father's house. Many things I have not made plain to you, for my composition is despicable; I only ask you not to despise it. At present let this suffice, I will write you longer at another time. May the glory of the Triune God be upon you, world without end.

" P.S.—This is the new year, so I will add a word more. We have heard that you have a Sunday school; how many scholars have you? We know that if you teach them anything it will be the Word of God, which is incomparably the best. I ask if you would, instead of me, salute all your scholars and convey to them a message. 'You have been born in a country where there are no idols; you have not been defiled by them like us, their defilement has gone into us like dye into the fabric.' Although you are free of that sin, do not forget that you are the seed of Adam, in *that* you are the same as us; if you do not trust in the precious blood of Jesus Christ, our middle man, all is vain and useless. The Holy Book says, 'Believe on the Lord Jesus Christ and thou shalt be saved,' but 'he that believeth not shall be condemned.' Do lay these words to heart. Would that all of you would earnestly pray God to interest the minds of many of your countrymen to come to China and point out the way to heaven. Revered master, no more, but all the boys in the school join in salutations to you.

" Written by
" SI-NÜE."

Up to that time much seed had been sown, but little fruit gathered in ; we had evangelised in nearly all the villages around the city. Frequently we would start in the morning, taking lunch with us, preaching in various villages ; my husband gathering the men, and I the women, under some spreading tree. Many heard, but, alas, few believed that Jesus was the only Saviour. But is it not always so? We need constantly to remember the promise that " He that goeth forth weeping, bearing precious seed, shall *doubtless* come again with rejoicing, bringing his sheaves with him." It is for us to observe the conditions "precious seed," the Word of God; "weeping hearts" longing for souls, that will not be satisfied without fruit. As the result of our first ten years' labour a little church of only eighteen or twenty was formed; how meagre apparently the return for so much labour: we had often in those days to assure ourselves of His faithfulness, who has said, "In due season ye shall reap *if* ye faint not." But besides this mere handful of Christians there were many hopeful inquirers, and during our absence of eighteen months thirty-seven were baptized on profession of their faith.

CHAPTER VI

"And He said unto them, Lacked ye anything? And they said, Nothing."—LUKE xxii. 35.

ON the 1st of April, 1877, Wenchow became an open port. It was a new thing for us to see a steamer in the river, and we had a feeling almost of intrusion when we went on the hill and met other foreigners there. The state of my health in that year rendered it necessary to take a furlough to England, and we left by the first trading steamer that came to Wenchow. Mr. Stott had been over eleven years in China, and his health being good, he at first thought of sending me home while he remained at his post. Mr. Taylor, however, kindly suggested he should take me, and that suggestion was carried out.

At that time the little girls were beginning to grow up, and we felt keenly the need of a separate house for them. The state of the mission funds did not encourage us to look to them for the rather large sum that would be needed to build a girls' school-house. We took our need to the Lord, told Him if *that work* had to be carried on a home must be provided for them. We decided to make no appeal of any kind, not even to mention our need publicly, but that we should tell our private friends of our desire, and leave the rest to God.

We told Mr. Taylor of our plan, and said we thought £250 would be needed; he said he thought not less than £300 would suffice. We had asked the Lord for £250, but we told Him about the £300, and if it was needed to send us that sum. When we returned to China in the autumn of the following year we had received unsolicited £304, besides having spent £10 upon school materials; it was another of the "exceeding abundantly" which the Lord has ever loved to give us. We had decided together that we should limit our own expenses to the sums received from the mission for our own support, and whatever gifts were given to us should be put to the school fund.

During this time we had some very singular experiences. When in Ireland my husband was asked to address a few Christians who lived in a quiet out-of-the-way village; the people were poor, they had nothing to give but their prayers; but Mr. Stott felt prayer was a mightier power than money, so he went seeking to interest these godly people. The meeting was held in a farmhouse; not more than twenty were present, but they were deeply interested in all they heard. When the meeting was over, one and another pressed up to shake hands with the missionary, and one woman, with tears in her eyes, pressed a coin in his hand, he putting it into a pocket where there was no other money. When he retired to his room he looked to see what the coin might be, and was deeply touched to find it one "halfpenny." He felt it was like the "widow's mite," and at once knelt down to ask God to bless her gift. He then entered in his book, "A poor woman unknown, a halfpenny." Next day when he returned to me he said, "I was deeply humbled, and had to confess to God that if I had had only a halfpenny to give I should have been too much ashamed to have put it into the hand; she had much more faith and love than I." Then he added, "Do you know God seems to have shown me that He is going to send £50." I answered, "Oh, I have not faith for that, but according to *your* faith be it unto you." We then knelt down together and asked God again to bless that woman who had so nobly given all she could, and was not ashamed of the smallness of the sum.

The next day we went to spend a few days with a friend in another part of the country. The day after, while the lady and I were out for a drive, our host came to the room where my husband was writing, and said, "God has told me to give you this money for your work." He put down a bundle of notes and left the room. On counting them Mr. Stott found there were just £50! It was entered as the next donation to the halfpenny, and up to this time we had never received more than £5 in a single gift.

We then went on to Dublin, where we were hospitably entertained by a dear Christian couple, and while sitting by the fire recounting the Lord's wonderful dealings with us, my husband mentioned the incident of the halfpenny and £50. He then added, much to my confusion, " And I have the same strong conviction, that God is sending me £5." When we retired to rest I asked why he had said such a thing. "It was as good as asking, and no doubt next day when we are leaving £5 will be given." He answered, "Oh, I never thought of that, but of course I can explain and refuse." Next day, as I expected, a cheque for £5 was handed; my husband refused to touch it, expressed his regret for having mentioned his conviction in the way he did: it was all right to tell of what God had done, but what He was going to do seemed too like a hint, and if he wished to spare his feelings he must not ask him to accept this. Our host replied, " That £5 was given to me two days ago by another; it is not my money at all. My wife and I laughed when we went upstairs; it is no use trying to cheat you, for God evidently tells you beforehand."

These are a few of the remarkable ways in which God supplied all our need very abundantly. Our visit home was productive of much interest and prayer; I had specially asked that friends would plead that some suitable woman might be converted who would be a real help in work amongst others, for up to that time we had only one Christian woman, and she was over seventy. I felt the drawback of being alone, and longed for such a helper. Little did we think that, while they prayed, God was working out His own plans in that direction.

We arrived back in Wenchow on the last day of 1878; two days afterwards I was asked to visit two women who were interested in the truth and wanted to see me. Oh! what good news! two women interested in the grand story of the Cross. Of course I went without delay, and was delighted to find them not only interested, but truly converted. They told me that one of our members, a firewood seller, had every time he brought their wood, sat down to tell them of God and His Christ. At first they were indifferent, but by and by they began to long for his coming, that they might hear more and more. Afterwards they were visited by schoolboys, and others who could teach them. One of these women mentioned how in former years she had closed her door when she saw me coming up the street, lest I should try to get into her house as I did others; but

Mrs. Liu, our former Bible-woman; her son, now labouring in Taichow; his wife, a former school-girl; and their three children, the eldest of whom is converted.

added, "Now I am longing for you to teach me the Bible."

This lady, Mrs. Liu, was of a refined literary family, and when young was married to a man of wealth; but alas, he, his father, and two brothers were opium smokers, and as they had no business of any kind, the property grew less and less each year, until the death of her husband. After paying his debts she had but a remnant of property left, not enough to keep herself and son—at that time a lad of seven or eight. After her husband's death she gave herself up very largely to the worship of idols, but in that she found no comfort for her weary spirit.

The other woman was a working man's wife, Mrs. Oae, very bright and earnest. Her husband was bitterly opposed to her being a Christian, and would not allow her to attend any services, nor would he consent to any Christian visiting her in her home; but as these two women lived in opposite sides of the same house, he could not prevent our going to Mrs. Liu's, nor his wife from listening.

I at once began a Bible-class each Wednesday afternoon in Mrs. Liu's house. Neither had ever attended a Christian service—one prevented by her husband, the other too much ashamed to be seen outside. Now I look back with great joy to the time spent teaching those women. Their hearts were indeed opened, and eagerly they drank in the precious words of life; week by week they repeated almost word by word the lesson of the week before, and it was wonderful to see their rapid growth in grace.

One Wednesday I went as usual, but found Mrs. Liu was not at home. Mrs. Oae told me that her mother-in-law had died two days before, and that she had been called to the funeral ceremonies: she left a message that we were to pray for her, as she did not know what to do under such circumstances. So that afternoon, instead of our Bible lesson, we spent the time in prayer, that God would keep His child in the midst of difficulty and sore temptation.

The next two or three days I was very anxious and much in prayer for her. I feared the effect of all the deadening influences of idolatry; wondered if she would have courage to confess Christ before her proud literary relations.

Three days afterwards she came to see me, and the first glance of her told all was well, for her face fairly beamed. Her first words were, "It is wonderful, wonderful! God stood by me all the time." She then told me that when being carried in her chair she was greatly perplexed what to do, and could only cry, "God, help me to glorify Thee." When she arrived and saw all her relatives going through the idolatrous ceremonies, her heart smote her, and she felt she must confess Christ. She called them together and told them how that, since they had last met, a wonderful change had come over her : she had heard of a true and living God, who could wash away her sins and make her more happy than any earthly treasure could ; that the knowledge of an everlasting home in heaven was more than earthly gain, and that though she and her son were the nearest relatives, and had a right to most of the property of the deceased, yet she could not offend God by performing the necessary ancestral rights. Her son was young, but she hoped he, too, would become a Christian by and by, and that he must not undertake those rites either. She therefore gave up all claim to the property, and would leave it with themselves to give what they thought right, on the understanding that she and her son would be for ever free from ancestral worship. She also added that they began to ask what kind of a religion it was that could make her do such a thing, and so, she said, "for three days I have been doing little else but telling them of Jesus, and just before coming away God let me know I had glorified Him, for I heard one of my relatives say, 'That must be a good religion, for if you searched the city through you could not find another who would give up property like that.'"

I am ashamed to say that they only gave her the sixteenth part of what she ought to have had, but with that she got a written statement that at her decease none of them were to interfere with her funeral, or perform idolatrous rites. For many years she has been a faithful and valuable helper in the work here. Her son was trained for several years under Dr. Douthwaite, and there converted. He is now doing medical work in the city of Tai-chow.

Mrs. Oae, who had been prevented by her husband from making any public confession of her faith, began to feel an earnest desire to be baptized : I counselled waiting upon the Lord in the matter, hoping that her husband might give consent. One day on going to the class she told me, with a beaming face, that her husband was going away next day to do some work in the country, and would be away till the following Monday or Tuesday. She said, "For three days I have been praying that God would open up my way to be baptized, and this is His answer." I reminded her that it was very cold weather (we baptized by immersion, and the baptistry was an open one in our courtyard), and asked if she was not afraid. She answered, "Oh, no ; God has given me this opportunity, and if I do not take it He may never give me another."

I was a little doubtful about her taking this step without the knowledge and consent of her husband ; but she seemed so certain that God had given her a chance not to be thrown away, that I could but be silent.

On Saturday evening she came out for the first time in her life to a Christian service, and gave such a testimony to the power and preciousness of the blood of Jesus Christ as quite astonished the little group of Christians. She was unanimously accepted by them for baptism the following morning, after which she joined in our communion service. How strange it must all have seemed to her; she had never seen memorials of Christ's broken body before, but her Spirit-taught soul greatly rejoiced at being able to join with others in thus publicly remembering her Lord.

After the afternoon service she returned home, and had only just laid aside her outdoor garments, when to her astonishment in walked her husband. He saw from her appearance she had been out, and questioned her, when she boldly acknowledged she had been to the chapel. He grumbled something about being disgraced in the eyes of his fellow-workmen by his wife going after a foreign religion, but on the whole took it very quietly, much to her relief.

This dear woman led a bright, earnest, consistent life for some years. She was one from whom I had hoped much, but one Sunday morning in 1888, while we were in England, she died quite suddenly just as she was preparing to go out to the service.

About this time (1879) another bright woman was converted. She impressed me so much by her intelligence and ability to receive the truth, that for about two years I went regularly to her house one afternoon each week to teach her. Work in China in the earlier years had to be done among the ones and twos. For two years I carried on two classes a week, one composed of two women, the other only of one, but it was well-repaid labour, for the lives of these three were bright and shining witnesses for Christ. This woman, Ah-Chang-na, was very poor, yet had a joy in giving to the Lord that surprised us all; for when we began our native women's missionary band, she was one of the most regular contributors. Day by day, from her housekeeping money, she would put aside one cash for God, and often in the middle of the month she would bring the money to me to keep for her, lest in her extreme poverty she might be tempted to use it. She had a young family, and could do little beyond her household duties; but if she earned a little money with her own hands, she always gave one-half of it to God as a thank-offering.

I remember, one New Year's time, at our native missionary meeting, telling the women God would be no man's debtor, and that whenever we from a true heart desired to spread the knowledge of His name and gave what we could ill afford, He would be sure to reward. I looked to this woman for confirmation, and said, "Ah-Chang-na, you are one of the poorest of us, yet you have given to God this year more than ever before, and more than any of the others; will you tell us how God has dealt with you—has it been harder for you to pass this year than formerly?" I asked this in faith, yet tremblingly, not knowing what the answer would be. With a beaming face she declared, before all, that at the end of the year, after paying off her little debts, she had one dollar left upon which to enter a new year, and, she said, "never in my whole life have I had one dollar to begin the New Year with before." We did praise God for that blessed testimony, and often has it been quoted since. This dear woman, too, passed away in 1888, while we were at home in England.

It seemed to us so sad, that two out of our three brightest and best Christians should be called away so near each other, and at a time when they seemed more than ever needed. Before they were called home, however, they saw a goodly band of women gathered out of darkness into God's wondrous light. I must say, Ah-Chang-na was a Christian who never gave me an hour's anxiety, so consistent and bright was her life throughout. She had much power in prayer, and literally prayed her husband and mother into the kingdom. We had a meeting amongst the women every Thursday afternoon, especially to pray for unsaved relatives, and this dear woman often broke down while pleading for others. It will be interesting to note that during the first few years of its existence no fewer than four husbands, and seven children, of our praying women were brought to the Lord.

It was out of this prayer-meeting grew our Missionary Band. I was a little perplexed to know how to get them out of the narrow groove of themselves and circumstances, into interest in and sympathy for others. I knew it would be a benefit to their own souls to do something for those around. We began in a very simple way, contributing what we could once a month, to enable one of their own number to go out as a Bible-woman. Mrs. Liu was chosen, and, as long as health permitted, faithfully represented them. This Missionary Band was a great blessing to the women themselves; the missionary information I was able to give them, month by month, stirred up their hearts and interest and stimulated prayer, besides producing a self-denying spirit in the matter of giving. This Missionary Band has now (1895) been in existence for ten years. Of course it has grown with our Christian women, and for some years they have almost entirely supported their own Bible-women. Our schoolgirls, though having no money of their own, were most desirous of helping in this effort; a barber had to be called twice a month to shave the heads of the little girls according to the Chinese custom, and one day the elder girls asked if I would allow them to do the head shaving. I asked why; they replied, "We do want to help with the Bible-women, and we thought if we could do the work instead of the barber, the money might go to the missionary fund." I was only too glad to accede to their wish, and the effort has been continued ever since by those, who in turn, become the elder girls of the school.

In the summer of 1879, we began building the girls school for which God had so graciously supplied the funds. At first we intended only to build a house large enough for a school, but felt led to build instead a double house, where the school could be at one end and our rooms at the other, so that I might be in a better position to superintend them ; and also that the native house we had lived in for ten years might be available for a married couple whom we hoped would soon join us. With our enlarged plans we knew we should need more money, but as this seemed the right thing, and God had proved Himself so faithful in the past, we felt sure He would supply unasked all that was needed.

The house was to be built by piecework, and we determined to go on only as far as we had money in hand. We paid men and materials week by week ; twice we thought we should have to tell the head workmen to withdraw their men for a time, and twice fresh supplies came before that was necessary. The whole was finished without a single day's stoppage for want of funds, and of course without one penny of debt. We had to wait a little time before we could put up the necessary outhouses; but they, too, were provided in answer to believing prayer.

These buildings, native houses, chapel, &c., were all destroyed in the riot of 1884.

CHAPTER VII

"If any man will come after Me, let him deny himself, and take up his cross daily, and follow Me."—LUKE ix. 23.

AS soon as building operations were finished, regular itinerations were again commenced, mostly by Mr. Stott alone, as the girls' and women's work occupied my time more and more. He had to make occasional visits to Chü-chow, which was then an out-station from Wenchow, as well as to Bing-yie and Dong-ling, where the work was growing steadily. Referring to a few of these journeys, Mr. Stott writes:

"Jan., 1880. My dear Mr. A.,—When yours came to hand I felt conscience-stricken; there was no time to reply, as I was just starting for Chü-chow. I had to go up the river ninety miles in a small miserable boat; the weather was very cold, a bleak north wind, sleet and hail driving in our teeth. The boat cover was in such bad condition that I had to compel the boatman to get a new one; and by urging and coaxing I reached my destination in a little less than three days.

"On both sides of the river there are many villages

and small towns which have not yet been visited by any Christian. I trust I may be able to give them the offer of salvation ere long. Every one travelling in China and seeing the countless towns and villages, with their thousands of inhabitants, could not remain unmoved; they are born, live, and die, generation after generation, seeking nothing higher than to have enough to eat and wear, and leave a small portion for their children.

"On arriving there, it was no better than the boat for comfort—the hail came through the roof and left no place dry; the room where my bed was had only two sides to it, and I can assure you the ventilation was perfect! However, the day following, I got some boards and a carpenter and closed it in a bit, but then all the light I had was through the tiles. The silver lining in my cloud was a small stove, which I had brought with me, and I assure you the warmth from was grateful to a degree. I remained there four days, and tried to strengthen the hearts of those who are looking forward to the house of many mansions in the skies.

"More recently I have been to Bing-yie, south of Wenchow, and spent a very happy time, having met thirty persons all interested and more or less instructed in the truth. There are ten or twelve more in the same country, but as they live a long way off I did not see them. Ten of the best out of the thirty were invited to come to the city and spend a little time with us in Bible study. There are a good many inquirers in the district where I go to-morrow, and perhaps three or four may be accepted. Last Lord's day, a woman came about sixteen miles, and got one of the Christians to introduce her to us. She wanted to be 'baptized and made a disciple of Jesus.' After talking to her some time, we found that she and her husband had been taught by one of the native Christians, who sometimes visit their village on business. Their idols were thrown away some months ago, and the husband had been to the chapel a good many times, but never made himself known.

"We expect Mr. and Mrs. Douthwaite, of our Mission, soon. They have been six or seven years in China and he has practised medicine, I believe very successfully. We hope that blessing may follow his medical work here ; but he is far from strong, and it is doubtful whether the damp climate of this district will suit his health. Mrs. Stott and I do a little in the practice of homeopathy. Mrs. Stott got a nice chest from Mr. R., whom we met in your brother's house at Pinner. Mr. R. also gave me a small bottle of a special preparation called 'Neuraline,' said to be an instant cure for sciatica. I tried it once when an attack was coming on, and in half an hour the pain was gone. I left the bottle in the bedroom, and when the old woman went to make the bed she was attracted by its fragrant, pleasing smell; afterwards, on meeting the old withered beauty, I could not make out what she had been anointing herself with, as she really distilled fragrance at every step, and, as the cook remarked, 'You could hear the fragrance of her all over the yard.' But when I discovered my loss, I felt as an Irishman at Limerick once expressed himself, 'An' shure it was a little riled that I was, sur.'

"I hope you are not thinking too highly of the C.I.M. It is not perfect, nor ever will be as long as I am connected with it; but it is as near perfection as any mission I know of. I am glad you are no enemy to system and order in connection with service for our Master; if there was no organisation or system I do not think the C.I.M. could do as good or as much work as it does, and instead of less, I think we need more of it. Did it ever strike you that some of these good men who are so afraid of system in the Lord's work are yet very systematic in their habits? Take, for instance, their systematic reading and study of God's Word, meeting with kindred spirits for prayer, &c., at stated hours and places, which many of them would not forego for any worldly gain. To give an illustration of this kind of inconsistency, I met in —— a good man and pillar of the church of ——, and we talked about missions in general and the C.I.M. in particular. He liked the mission very well, but was afraid it was running too much into system; he complained that a council was now formed in London, Hudson Taylor was Bishop in China, and every member was under his thumb: that he used his power rather unsparingly, and perhaps it was a mistake that he should have so much power over the brethren. My part, of course, was to defend as best I could; then the conversation turned upon our own work in particular. I told him much of what had been done, and more that was still undone, and the conclusion he came to was, that one man could not do well the work on hand. To ease his mind I informed him that Hudson Taylor had promised me help as soon as circumstances would allow; a young man, or perhaps two, would join me soon. So far, so good; did I know either of the young men? I could not say that I did. Then he said, 'It was most important that a proper understanding should exist, to begin with; the work was already established, and if some young man or men were to join who would not work willingly on the lines already laid down, but upset here and overturn there, they would do more harm than good, and damage the work of the Lord by unskilled hands.' I told him it was understood by all parties that the new-comers must work on the lines already laid down, and were not at liberty to tear up old or lay down new ones. He felt relieved and happy then, and said, 'That was just as it should be,' but the dear man did not see that he had cut away the foundation from his own remarks about Hudson Taylor having control over the members. I think it is a scriptural thing for the younger to be in submission to the elder. Yea, more than that, if it is not put into practice, confusion will be the result, as is often but too plainly seen.

"Two Sundays ago we had eight persons baptized here, who gave us much comfort and hope, which I pray may not be disappointed. Others, by God's grace seem to be pressing forward. For some time past, I think the Spirit of God has been helping me in making the way of salvation through Christ clear; for oh, it is hard for them to understand the precious truths, their minds are so dark. Yesterday was the Lord's day, and I think His Spirit was with us in power. At evening prayer the word spoken seemed to touch every heart, and at the close I asked two of the brethren to lead us in prayer. One of the Christians prayed first; then an inquirer began for the first time. Inquirers are not expected to pray, but I did not like to stop him; he is an elderly, grey-haired man, venerable in appearance and highly esteemed by all who know him. At first I feared his attempt would cause an explosion among the young folk, but to their credit be it said they behaved better than your scholars would have done. I think his simple earnestness overawed every one, and at the end there was such a hearty 'Amen' from all present as if they really meant to thank God for opening another mouth to worship Him. This old gentleman and two of his neighbours had been constant attendants for about a year. There is no doubt that they like the gospel, but whether they are all subjects of the saving grace of God it would be hard to say; but I think the one who prayed last night is.

"It is very good of the Lord to give us even a little success. We are so unworthy of it, but He saves in spite of our unworthiness. Thirty-four in all have been gathered in since our return a year ago. It is much to thank God for, but what are they among the many thousands who hear as though they heard not? Many listen for a long time before they ever dream that any object of worship can or ought to exist besides what they already possess."

A little later he writes:—"Since writing you last we have accepted and baptized ten persons; most have been coming to the services one, two, or three years. Last Lord's day the chapel was full, and in the afternoon Mrs. Stott had thirty women in her class; she calls this a class for teaching them the Scriptures, but I fancy there is some preaching goes on as well. I have not been there to see, but I think most of her meetings contain more or less of the preaching element; but as long as souls are saved and God's blessing rests on them, I think it would be a mistake for her to stop, even if the Archbishop of Canterbury were to condemn her. The Lord has given His seal, and that is what we look, long, pray, and give thanks for. This year, 1881, more have been gathered into the church than any one year since the work began; but during this time a few have been put under discipline: one man long in fellowship, and who had a good deal of influence and had been the means of bringing a goodly number under the sound of the Word, has departed from the faith and godliness, and since his suspension has been behaving in a very unbecoming manner. These things are our trials, but the work is the Lord's, not ours, and He will bring into His kingdom all that are His. Satan seems to have greater power than ever in hurting the saints of God, by causing many to turn from the faith and accept unsound doctrine. It all points to the fact that the Lord is at hand. I sometimes so long for His appearing, because our whole hope for the Church and the world is centred in His coming to take the government of the world into His own hands; the sadness and suffering all around is great indeed, the misery day by day is appalling.

"As an instance, only last month a poor man, in a country village, whose daughter was ill and supposed to be dying, had, according to custom, lighted two candles, put them in paper lanterns and hung one at the head and the other at the foot of the bed. He then fastened both door and window and went on to the top of the house to call back his daughter's spirit. He stood and called long, and during the time one of the candles fell down and set the bed on fire before the people of the house knew it, and then they could not get in; by the time they reached the fire it had taken such a hold that six houses were destroyed before it could be conquered. The man's daughter was burnt to death, as well as a woman in another house; and a young man was so severely injured in trying to save his family and property that he died the next day. More than half the fires that take place in China result from idolatry or from opium smoking.

"I have lately come in from the Dong-ling station. I had a good time on the whole, but a shake of ague prevented me from extending my journey. Concerning four persons baptized, one or two things were a little remarkable. One lad was about fourteen years of age; I have only once baptized one so young (Z-nüe), and he is now twenty-two years of age, and went into the water with them and performed the rite. I only hope this lad may turn out as well. Two others were husband and wife; the fourth, a very nice young woman, daughter of two of our Christians, is married into a family who are opposed to the truth, and has a great deal to bear for Christ's sake, and seems to bear it cheerfully. She was engaged to be married into this family before she or her parents heard the gospel."

(In after years this young woman led her husband to the truth, and gained the goodwill of her other relatives, so that her mother-in-law, though never a Christian, was changed from a persecutor into a friend. I remember when visiting there, the mother-in-law spoke gratefully of her daughter's goodness.) "I thank God and take courage, but must confess that every time there is a baptism I am filled almost as much with fear as with joy—fear lest I should have committed any mistake, or that Satan may lead them away into sin, thus causing shame and dishonour to God and His Word.

"Here in the city we baptized three persons last week, and hope to receive more soon. Some of them have been giving us much comfort; they are mostly from Mrs. Stott's Bible-class. The Lord has been and still is blessing her efforts among the women, many of whom seem to accept the truth more readily than their husbands, and also walk more consistently than the rougher sex. Indeed some of our best Christians are women, and Mrs. Stott has often told me that at their prayer-meetings they seem to unburden the very secret of their souls to the Lord, and confess their sins, temptations, and failures with an openness and earnestness unknown at home; they often pray for twenty or twenty-five minutes at a time. They begin with their hearts full almost to bursting, and are not happy till they have told all their story (not the half);

and having told it, their faces beam with delight, and they go on their way strengthened with faith, hope, and love. Prayer is very real to them, and the answers as real. At the same time there is a good deal of persecution; at one place some have been badly beaten, and at another they are afraid almost daily that their houses will be pulled down and themselves maltreated.

"I think I told you that one poor woman who was ill-used last year never recovered from the effects of the cruelty she was subjected to, and has lately died. At another place an old man had his house set on fire twice; he was at last driven away, and is now ill, not expected to live. Another is a very sad case; a brother's wife died, and the neighbours would not allow him to bury her without going through all the heathen rites for the dead, nor would they allow him to bring the coffin into the village, nor carry the corpse out. Several of the members went to visit him, but they were beaten, one of them very badly. At last our brother escaped, and ran here as if for his life. We had a good deal of trouble in arranging the matter, and ere then the corpse was much decayed. Then the neighbours insisted upon the other Christians performing the rites, and on their refusing they were beaten, and their hands bound and tied to the bed over the decaying corpse, while the heathen neighbours went through the rites; they then brought in the coffin, and tied two of the Christians to it by their tails.

"I hope the trouble is over now, and that we have strengthened our position. It seems impossible to advance one step without stirring up the devil, and having to maintain our ground inch by inch. I pray this may be a real blow at the supremacy of his power in that place. There are a few inquirers there, and when Mr. Jackson went up to see about the burying of the brother's wife, all the Christians and inquirers came to see him, except one young man who was tied up to a post by his father lest he should catch the 'Jesus disease.' He had been too late in tying him up, for he caught the disease more than a year ago, and now the father finds it difficult to cure him.

"There are others I could tell you of, suffering the loss of their little all for Christ's sake. Since I wrote you last the Lord has been blessing us; one Lord's day we had ten persons baptized and last Sunday three. There is a spirit of inquiry abroad in many places, but we are much hampered for want of native assistants. The people are willing to hear, but we have hardly any one to tell them the way of salvation. We have been specially crying to God about this matter. We have few in the church fitted for teaching others, and it takes a long time to train so as to fit them for this work. Our hope and confidence is in God; He has provided many things for us, He is able to provide this also.

"I came in from the country yesterday; had a rainy, disagreeable time, and some unpleasant things to do. Satan seems to break loose every now and again, and do all the mischief he can to the Christians. One man who steadily refused to contribute to the support of the heathen temple had half his standing corn cut, and what was left was trampled, so that he suffered a serious loss; others have had their farming implements broken to pieces, been denied the use of the public road, and annoyed in many ways, for they are adepts in the art of petty persecution. It is surely a testing time for us all, and makes me long for the time when our Lord Himself shall come and save His own out of the hand of the wicked.

"July 1, 1884. This is quarter-day, when accounts have to be made up and despatched. A great deal of pastoral work has claimed my attention of late. My dear wife is feeling fagged out with extra work, and I give her an hour's *help* daily. We are hard worked certainly, but thanks be to God, His presence is with us, sustaining and helping. Last Saturday evening I was up until 11 p.m. examining sixteen candidates for baptism; eleven were accepted, and baptized on Sunday morning, and afterwards sat down at the Lord's table. Some of those deferred will soon be received, I think, as they were put off only until some family matters could be arranged. This year we have already received thirty-two, and I hope God will give us a great many more before the end. I long to get into that state of soul-communion with God in which the good man is supposed to be, when 'all he doeth shall prosper.'

"The rumours of war so near us have given me a good deal of extra work. Many of the Christians in distant places are having rough times ; the heathen are persecuting them fiercely, but as yet no blows have been struck. The Romanists are getting it worse than we, and a rupture has taken place, but I have not heard the details. The Chinese are not so enlightened as to make much if any distinction between one foreigner and another; here they distinguish our nationalities by our religion : Protestants are British and are very bad—they produce the opium ; Romanists are French, they are even more abominable and ought to be exterminated. Such is the expressed feeling of many. Our most southern station is near the border of Foh-kien, and with hostilities going on so near there is much to try them. There is also a great deal of excitement in the city, and some days we can hardly walk out without being reminded of the dislike with which many regard us ; they will sometimes get behind us and make a harsh whirring noise like sharpening a knife, and if they can draw our attention will take their fan and make a significant slash at their necks, and then disappear as soon as they can. But if matters do not get worse we will be thankful; the Lord reigneth, and our confidence is in Him. I do not go out more than I can help, and so far have been treated with respect. The mandarins seem in earnest in trying to keep the peace, and have issued a good proclamation. I am told they have soldiers parading the streets and secret spies loitering about, and any detected stirring up the people are taken to the Yamen and soundly thrashed. What we all fear is bands of marauders, who are always on the alert to embrace the first opportunity of plunder that presents itself.

"But our souls are in God's mighty hand, and our bodies too; and He will take care of us till our work is done. We are more anxious about our friends in the far interior, and daily pray that they may be kept in peace; we trust their distance from the seat of hostilities may be some protection to them.

"I propose to send Mrs. Stott to Shanghai for a month, when the cool weather comes. She has had heavy work during the summer, and is purposing taking in a number of women during the winter for Bible instruction that they may be the more intelligent witnesses for our Lord and Saviour. There is a great difference between a well-taught Christian and an ill-taught one—I mean in their being able to bear witness for Jesus. If we can only give all the native converts a good hold of the Scriptures, we might in a great measure dispense with native preachers."

CHAPTER VIII

"Why do the heathen rage, and the people imagine a vain thing?"
—Psa. ii. 1.

THERE was at this time a war between France and China, and during the summer of that year the French had bombarded Foo-chow, sunk several gunboats, and destroyed the arsenal there. Foo-chow was the next port south of us, and when the news came of these disasters the people were greatly alarmed. The excitement was increased by the officials issuing orders that each household was to provide a basket of stones, which were to be placed in junks and sunk at the mouth of the river, to block it in case the French should come here. All July and August the excitement prevailed, and had a riot happened then we should not have been so much surprised; but things quieted down and our fears were allayed.

It was during this summer that the conversion of the six girls of which I have spoken took place; new life had brought new desires for further teaching.

At the end of September my husband insisted I should go to Shanghai for a fortnight's rest, before beginning some fresh work contemplated for the autumn. My last words were, "I can go away contented and happy, for the people are so quiet and contented again": little did I anticipate the blow that was to fall so soon.

On Saturday evening, October the 4th, just one week after I had left, while Mr. Soothill, of the Methodist Free Church, was conducting their usual prayer meeting, a few rowdies collected at his chapel door and noisily demanded admittance; when the door was opened they ran away. This was repeated two or three times, and on the door being again opened several rushed in throwing stones, and evidently bent on mischief. Some one raised the cry, "Burn the foreigners out," and almost before the words were uttered they lighted torches, and, with paraffin oil, set the place in flames. The chapel was close by the house, and Mr. Soothill, fearing a general conflagration, went to the Yamen to beseech help. The magistrate, thinking Mr. Soothill might meet with bodily injury, refused to let him out again; but he, accompanied by some soldiers, went in the hope of quelling what had now become a serious riot. He was told, however, he had better go back; the people were bent upon mischief, and he might get injured in the fray. His chair was, indeed, considerably battered, and, mandarin like, he thought discretion the better part of valour; and the soldiers sent to intimidate the rioters joined with them in their evil work. When Mr. Soothill's house, chapel, and all he possessed were in ruins, they made for the Roman Catholic premises. The poor priest had a hard time of it; frightened almost out of his senses, he lay hid for three days in the firewood house of a friendly neighbour, and was at last disguised as a Chinese coolie and taken to the Yamen. The destruction there was thorough also; the mob now seemed like tigers who had tasted blood, and they determined to make a clean sweep of everything belonging to the hated foreigner. From the Roman Catholic place they went to Mr. Jackson's, of our own mission, and when they reached our chapel, only three minutes' walk from our house, Mr. Stott felt it was time to seek a place of safety.

Dr. McGowan, of the Chinese Customs, had, at great personal risk, come to Mr. Stott's help. They collected our sixteen school girls (the younger of whom had to be taken from their beds), servants, and all others within our gates, in order to seek shelter in the magistrate's Yamen. As they went out at the back gate the first contingent of the rioters burst in at the front, and in a few moments were in possession of the place. Happily the Yamen was near, or it might have fared badly with them, for they were freely pelted with stones, one of which struck Mr. Stott's pith helmet a heavy blow, which made his hat roll on the ground, and caused him to run the gauntlet bare-headed. A moment after Dr. McGowan staggered under the blow of another, and the frightened school children, who were clinging to his coat-tails, were scattered here and there.

When they reached the Yamen several of the girls were missing, and our cook, an active, earnest man, went out in search of them, but it was the next day before the family was complete; two or three of them spent the night in a temple courtyard, scarcely daring to breathe, lest their hiding-place should be discovered. I have said complete, but there was one dear little thing three years of age, pet of the household, who was carried off, and we never saw her again.

In a few hours the destruction was general, not only the effects of the missionaries, but also of the foreigners in the Chinese Customs employ; everything foreign was destroyed: they showed a nice discrimination, for the latter, who lived in old temples, had all their goods, furniture, &c., carried out, even partition boards and flooring which they had put down, burnt in the front yard, while the buildings were left intact.

After completing their work of destruction in the city they tried to reach the English Consulate, which is situated on a small island in the middle of the river; but the magistrate had anticipated their intention, and had ordered all boats to the other side. They tried to make a raft, but failed, and the next day the homeless refugees were escorted by a strong band to the island.

On the Monday the rioters went to our country chapel in Dong-ling, twenty English miles away, and burnt it also to the ground. We all shared the same fate, proving that the feeling was anti-foreign, not anti-missionary. The officials acted with creditable promptness in paying the indemnity demanded by the consul, and in six weeks from the date of the riot Mr. Stott was able to return and begin rebuilding, leaving our school children in the kind care of Dr. and Mrs. Lord, of Ning-po, who most unselfishly received them into their school, although it was at the time quite full, and kept them under the care of their own matron, Mrs. Liu, for five months, during which time we were rebuilding.

It was an anxious time; the war had upset our steamer communication, and Ning-po was blockaded. For three months we were without letters, and heard vague rumours of the bombardment of Ning-po and flight of the foreigners there, which happily proved untrue; while they, poor things, suffered also through false reports concerning us. But in all this the Lord kept our hearts resting upon Himself. The news of

Mr. Stott's arrival soon spread, and it was a great joy for pastor and people to be united once more.

In February, 1885, Mr. Stott writes: " My dear Mr. A., I have just finished the duties of the day, and will now indulge in the pleasure of a chat with you ; you are one of my oldest friends, and that gives me license. I am here alone as yet, for my dear wife could not leave Shanghai owing to the death of Miss Minchin—and, indeed, I was not in a state to receive her sooner. After getting official liberty to return I came by first steamer, and at once began to search for a temporary home. After many failures the Lord gave me success. I have bought a small house adjoining my former property, and I am now living in it in tolerable comfort. I had to pull down the ruined walls of our dear old home, and I must confess it cost me many a pang to stand by and see it done ; and our dear little garden, which was such a pleasure to my wife, all disfigured, not a plant, shrub, or even a weed left. We had a large number of flowers in pots, which were mostly thrown down the well. At every corner were signs of the most wanton destruction. Surely their mischievous ingenuity came from near the bottom of the bottomless pit. And now quiet has been restored, the mandarins are doing very little to bring the rioters to justice. Many of the native Christians have been looted of their all, and the mandarins will not even look at their petitions for redress.

Very few out of China have any idea of the weakness and corruption of the Mandarinate and their hatred of all Europeans. Those brought to justice are comforted and consoled by the mandarins telling them that they must apprehend and punish them through pressure, for the "foreign devils" are very cruel, and destitute of any mercy.

I am now rebuilding, and the girls' school will be finished next month, also the chapel at Dong-ling; our own house is some distance on, but the city chapel still lies in abeyance. Hitherto the Lord has helped me, and I do need His help, for I am poor and needy.

The British Consul has entered into the case with much spirit, and has done for every one as well as he could. Two instalments of the indemnity have been paid, and another is almost due.

I am glad to say I have found nearly all the Christians have stood firm, only one having gone back. He seems to have lacked stamina to endure the long strain they were all exposed to after I left for Ning-po; and as I was over a month absent, it was a testing time for them all, for the worst was over before I could return. Others have got a new start, and are bolder in the faith than formerly, and some new converts have been drawn out; so on the whole I do not think we have lost much, and may be all the better for this searching. It has been a time to bring out all that was in us, both natives and foreigners; but those who put their trust in God shall never be ashamed. Ever since the night of the riot the Lord has been showering blessings on us, and since the buildings began we have not been stopped an hour by rain. It has come now, but the roofs are on, and no harm or hindrance will result, which is a boon."

We had, about that time, two hundred Christians and inquirers, and out of that number only two turned back through fear. The poor, scattered flock had met in little groups in each other's houses, the stronger visiting and cheering on the weaker and more timid. Mr. Stott arrived on Friday and at once set a few men to clear away the débris and erect a few upright poles and cross-beams, over which were thrown bamboo mats; and by Saturday afternoon the extempore chapel was ready to receive the flock who came to welcome their pastor back. And what a day of thanksgiving it was, both rejoicing together. God was very gracious to us in this time of sore trial; the blow had been especially heavy, because unexpected. We had gone through so much in the earlier years, had lived down opposition and hatred, had gathered a goodly number of warm-hearted Christians—it seemed as if our difficulties were over and we had reached the reaping time; but with one stroke all our hopes appeared laid in the grave—yet, only appeared. When I received the letter from my husband which told me everything we possessed was destroyed, and that he and the helpless band of eighteen natives were in Ning-po and had taken possession of a large empty house, homeless and almost clotheless, the blow seemed cruel; yet, at the same time, God brought His own Word to my comfort. It was as though the question was asked afresh, "Why do the heathen rage and the people imagine a vain thing?" that one word *vain* had a power I never felt before. Thank God all should be vain, we should yet go back, gather our scattered people, build up our ruined home and chapels, and win many more souls for our Lord and Master. The vision filled me with hope and comfort, and when, three hours afterwards, I left to join my husband, it was with a heart profoundly thankful, for had not the precious lives been spared, and was there not good hope for the future? I thought God had comforted me, so that I might be able to speak words of cheer and comfort to the dear ones who had passed through the storm; but when we met next morning they had no need of my comfort—God had gone before and cheered them with His own assurance that all would yet be well: and wonderfully did God fulfil His promise, for on the first Sunday at the opening of our new chapel, five persons were baptized and received into the church; and for years after, few months passed without some being added to our number.

We had been told that no indemnity would be paid until we had first sent in an inventory of all our losses. Anxious to get back as soon as possible, we set ourselves to prepare an inventory to forward to the Consul by the first steamer which should return from Wenchow. In all former cases, months of negotiation had preceded settlement, and though we feared delay, we determined it should not be on our side. What was our astonishment, when the Consul wrote by the first steamer to say that the magistrates had accepted the rough estimate of losses, which had been handed in a few days after the riot, and that the first instalment of money should be paid in a few days.

Thus, my husband was able to return as soon as he could purchase clothes, &c., and was received by the people as kindly as if a riot had never taken place. For five months he personally superintended the building operations. Many men were employed, so that the school and chapel might be finished with as little delay as possible.

Services were held each night for the workmen; but, with that exception and our Sunday services, our missionary work was at a standstill. One day, upon my remarking to Mr. Stott that he was building substantial walls, he replied, "I want to build this specially strong, for I believe Christ is coming very soon and the Jews are to be the evangelisers of the world, and when they come to Wenchow it is my desire they shall find a place ready for them."

About a year after this, we had a letter from the Rev. David Hill, of Hankow, saying that he had just baptized a man who dated his first interest in the Gospel to the time of the riot. He had come to Wenchow on business, and when he saw the missionary robbed of all he possessed, pelted with stones, making his way very quietly to the Yamen without one word of cursing or bitterness, such as he expected; and when, a few weeks later, that missionary returned quietly to rebuild, with as much grace as if all the city were his friends, he said to himself, the religion which could bring forth fruit like that was worth inquiring into. On returning to his home, he attended Mr. Hill's chapel, and was in due time baptized by him: thus the Lord gave us fruit in the very midst of the fire.

But we were not allowed to go without personal suffering. We were living in a low, damp Chinese house, and the wet season coming on, we were compelled to move into the new home before it was dry. Miss Littlejohn, a young missionary, who had joined us but a few months, was taken seriously ill and died in the autumn of the same year at Che-foo. I take an extract from a letter written to a friend at this time:—

"*September* 14, 1885.

"DEAR B.,—Very many thanks for your cheering letter received two weeks ago. Just when it came we were getting weary and discouraged, and your sympathy cheered us not a little. It is not often we feel down-hearted, but I fear we are somewhat in that condition at present. We are still left single-handed (Miss Littlejohn being away invalided), and we begin to feel the strain heavier than we can bear. We do not mind hard work, but it is discouraging to feel that, work as we will, one half is left undone. I have now twenty-five girls entirely under my care, who need and ought to have all my time. The dear ones who were converted last year are growing in grace, and their thirst for the Word of God *must* be satisfied. On the other hand, the Christian women and inquirers need much teaching, and in trying *to do* both, neither is done thoroughly. The same is true of my husband. The church in this city has grown to need all his time and care, yet he is grieved that the out-stations are not visited oftener. May our Father lead us in a right way. I am sure you will pray for us. Miss Littlejohn, who joined us last December, may be ill for a long time; she was very delicate and, indeed, seemed worn out when she came. In the beginning of summer she took ill. After a few weeks she went on to Shanghai, and was there two months without getting any better; she has now gone to Che-foo, where I trust she may gain strength. She is a dear, earnest Christian, and we love her much, but we fear she is too delicate for this trying climate.

"Let me now turn from the *dis*couraging to the *en*couraging. I never like to look long at the dark side, it does not pay; we need all the hope and joy we can bring into this work, especially in such a dry and thirsty land. Praise the Lord, we find Him a well-spring in the desert; He gives strength according to our day, filling our hands full of sheaves and causing our hearts to rejoice, so that we should not, if we could, change places with any one.

"Month by month, some are coming out on the Lord's side. At Bing-yei, where Mrs. Liu has gone for a month, quite a number have put away their idols and are inquiring after the truth—four young men at one hamlet, three women at another, and so on. Mrs. Liu has gone to teach them. At the same place, one of our old Christians passed away lately; he was an old man and failing for some time. One day he felt unable to get up, and said to his wife that Jesus was coming for him soon; in the afternoon he asked for some food, and when he had taken a little, he said, 'Jesus is coming for me now, I will just sleep a little till He comes; don't wake me.' He fell asleep and never opened his eyes on earth again. (This was the old man found worshipping in the temple by the schoolboy Z-nüe.)

"At another station, Dong-ling, where there are about forty Christians, eight families have put away their idols and are asking after the truth; no doubt some of them are chosen of the Lord.

"As soon as the weather gets a little cooler, my husband hopes to take on some young men students again, and I a few women, for training during the winter months. I can take in ten or twelve women to teach, without adding very much to my labour. They can share morning and evening Bible classes with the girls, and a class every afternoon for them would be all the extra work it would give me. We have also begun a boys' day school; this was much needed for the sons of the Christians, and there are ten pupils.

"This has been a very sickly summer; a kind of cholera and dysentery has carried off many victims—two of our women died within a few days of each other, and several others are still very ill; all around us can be heard the death-wail. We have given medicines and saved a few lives. One of our girls is very ill with dysentery. We trust it may please the Lord to restore her. My husband began a boys' school seventeen years ago, and though we have had schools ever since, we have never had one death either among boys or girls. This, for the first few years, was in answer to prayer. We had to win our way amongst the people, and we felt that a death in the school might, in those early days, be the means of driving us from the city.

But, in this, as in everything else, the Lord has given us more than we asked.

"I will now close with the good news that four more were baptized yesterday. Since May, twenty-seven candidates have been examined, and out of that number fourteen have been accepted and baptized. They have all been inquirers one, two, or three years. The mind works slowly in China, and it is often long after they hear the truth that they lay hold of it. We like rather to wait and be sure, as it is saved souls we want, not numbers."

My husband and myself both suffered, and it was then seeds of the disease in Mr. Stott, which two years later compelled us to go to England, were sown, and afterwards developed into the painful complications which in the spring of 1889 ended in his translation to glory. Thus we were called to be sufferers together with Christ in no ordinary way, yet no word of regret ever passed his lips. He was full of praise that God had enabled him to serve more than twenty years in China.

In the beginning of the year 1886, my husband felt much led to ask God to give him at least one soul each Sunday; week by week he kept this request before the Lord, pleading there might be no barren week during the year; and at its close we were much interested to find that just fifty-two persons had been added to our church. I remember my husband looking into my face with a sad expression as he said, "Why did I not ask more? Oh, how we limit God, when He might do great things for us if only we would open our mouths wide unto Him!"

CHAPTER IX

"And ye shall be witnesses unto Me."—ACTS i. 8.

IT will be interesting to give a few instances of the kind of men and women whom God has chosen as instruments for the furtherance of His own work.

In 1880 Mr., now Dr., Douthwaite had for a time a hospital in this city for the cure of opium-smokers, and amongst the degraded applicants was a silversmith named Li Ao-ming. This man was in the last stage of degradation and poverty. He had to borrow the dollars necessary to ensure his admittance into the refuge, and the only shirt he possessed was borrowed too. He had a bold, defiant, repulsive look, had been an opium-smoker for many years, and was such a desperately wicked character that his own mother did not like to own him. After he had been in the refuge a few days he began to take an interest in the services held by the assistant, and slowly his mind opened up to receive the truth; few knew what was going on in the man's mind until one day, when going upstairs to his room, another opium patient deliberately spilt the dirty water he was carrying down over Ao-ming's clothes! Instead of flying into a passion and cursing the man, as he would have done a week or two before, he stepped down until the man descended; then looking him steadily in the face, said, "If you had done this to me a week ago, I would have cursed you, your parents, and your ancestors for generations; but I have heard of the love of Jesus, dying for such guilty men as we are, and I will not curse you again." When the time came for him to leave, having got rid of that terrible opium habit, which is as a chain which closely binds its poor victims, he begged to be allowed to remain a fortnight longer, so that he might learn more of the precious truth. As soon as he left the refuge, he went home to tell his mother and two brothers of the wonderful gospel which he had heard and believed, and which had changed his heart and made him hate the things he loved before. His mother and brothers were much interested and began to attend the services. They lived in a part of the city where no work had been begun, and at my request the mother opened her house for a meeting once a week. This was continued for over a year, so that the neighbours had the opportunity of hearing of a Saviour's love. The mother became a true Christian, and more than a year afterwards fell asleep rejoicing in her Saviour. His two brothers were baptized with him, but one of them has shown by his life that he was never saved, and was expelled from the church four years afterwards. The other brother still remains with us, but has never been much more than a dead-and-alive Christian.

Ao-ming very soon took up his trade again as a silversmith. Sometimes he would be two days in a village, sometimes a week, according to the amount of work he had to do, but every night after the day's work was over, and every Sunday wherever he happened to be, he spent in telling the glad good news. He was a wonder to himself, and as is often the case with such people, he was mostly taken up with telling what God had done for him. His earnest, fearless manner arrested attention, and it was not long before we had many inquirers asking for more teaching, saying the silversmith had first told them of a Saviour's love. His zeal sometimes went beyond his knowledge, and we had often to undo some of his work, but he was much used of God nevertheless.

After some years my husband, being in need of an evangelist, decided to try the silversmith. He worked both hard and earnestly, but he had an overbearing manner which spoilt much of his work, and after a time he was allowed to go back to his trade as being the best thing for a man of his disposition. It was all the same whether he was a paid evangelist or a working silversmith, preach he would, and preach he did, and he was the means of the salvation of many souls. He has never been an easy man to guide; bold, hasty, and self-conceited, he has had to be kept in with a firm hand, but when his faults are firmly though kindly pointed out, he often confesses with bitter tears. About five years ago he opened a shop in the village of Bahzie, about thirteen miles from here, and after settling his shop affairs, the next thing he did was to look out for a room in which he could preach on Sundays, the rent of which he paid himself; and on the first Sunday morning he closed his shop, hanging a board outside which announced that no business could be transacted that day, and it was well known that the time was spent in preaching. After a time a number of inquirers gathered round him, and it became necessary to have a chapel. This matter he took up entirely himself, giving what he could and seeking help from the city Christians until he had received about seventy dollars. With this money he tiened (mortgaged) a small house, which he had repaired and put in order for a chapel, and since he has become the pastor of this little self-supporting church. But though doing a good work the people sometimes get tired of him, for after all there is a great mixture of Christ and Ao-ming in all he says; still God has blessed and is blessing his labours, and we rejoice, though, if we had our way, he would be a different man. Once a month we send a fresh preacher to help the few Christians. Ao-ming is now a prosperous tradesman, liberal and open-handed, very hospitable, and in spite of many faults we praise God for him. On the anniversary of my twenty-five years' work in Wenchow, he felt very proud to present me with a silk banner entirely on his own account, as a token of his love and esteem.

Boa-sang-tsang, former firewood seller: I cannot recall anything about this man's conversion. He was baptized in 1877, about the time we left for England on our first furlough. By the time we returned at the end of 1878 he had already won several persons to Christ. He was very poor, carrying his firewood from door to door, but in whichever house he entered where he had opportunity he preached Christ to the inmates. It was thus Mrs. Liu and others were won to Christ. Fearless and utterly careless of rebuke, it could be said literally that as he went he preached. After a few years of such soul-winning, he was sent out as an evangelist; faithfully and earnestly he worked, never weary, though often unwise. Later on my husband had, for a time, to suspend him from preaching, because he had taken needless offence at a trifle, and seemed to be doing more harm than good amongst the Christians. He was spoken to very gently, but firmly, and helped back to his old trade again for a short time ; but his repentance was truly beautiful, and when in 1887 we left on our second furlough, it was very touching to see Mr. Boa, though suspended as a preacher, following my husband's chair weeping like a child, proving that " faithful are the wounds of a friend." The year after he was made a colporteur, and ever since has been doing noble work in that line. He has been the means of opening up many new districts, one of which, O-dzing, had very soon afterwards to go through the baptism of fire.

O-dzing is a small village situated amongst the hills, about fourteen miles from Wenchow. The first believers were mother and two sons of a well-to-do family. Mr. Boa remained two or three weeks instructing them in the truth, and quite a number in the village began to show interest. The head-man of the district, feeling annoyed at the desertion from the ranks of those who supported the idols, determined, if possible, to intimidate the believers. After Mr. Boa left, a younger and more inexperienced preacher was sent, and while he was there persecution began. The preacher was beaten, and the Christian and her son tied up by the thumbs until she should recant. An attack was then made upon their house, the inmates had to escape out of doors or windows any way they could, while everything within was either smashed or stolen. The granaries were opened and the grain carried away. The family fled to Wenchow, and the matter had to be put into the Consul's hands, and it was over a year before a settlement could be arrived at. Both sides suffered heavily. The Christians, who had lost over two hundred dollars, were only compensated to the extent of fifty-two dollars; while it cost their enemies three hundred dollars to get the case out of the Yamen. This has left a bitter feeling which has never been entirely uprooted, and the gospel has been much hindered in that place through it.

It is remarkable that in every case where a lawsuit has been necessary, hindrance to the gospel has been the result. We have always found it better for both Christians and heathen to settle disputes in a friendly way out of court. This becomes increasingly easy as the heathen gain confidence in the just judgment of the missionary; when they find that he does not take the part of the Christian because he is a Christian, they are willing to submit the case to him and abide by his decision. This is the last case of persecution which I have had to deal with through the Consul and I trust it will long remain the last. We have had many troubles since, but I have never failed in a friendly settlement.

Another interesting case was that of a husband and wife who had formerly been beggars. They had one little girl, whom they betrothed to a little orphan boy, who had a small house and an acre or two of ground. Yaih-zing-pah and his wife worked this little bit of ground diligently, which, however, only supported them part of the year; for the rest they had to beg. Wandering into the chapel one day, he heard the gospel preached, believed the truth, and was baptized in 1883. As soon as the little boy's relations knew, they insisted he must either give up this new doctrine or their relative. Everything was done to induce them to change their decision, but in vain. Yaih-zing-pah told them he could not give up Christ, who had done so much for him, saving his soul and giving heavenly riches which were beyond all this world could bestow. There was nothing for it but to turn out again into the cold world as homeless beggars. Mr. Stott advised him to get work if possible, and for this purpose gave him a little money to erect a hut on an uncultivated hill, which he was allowed to work for a merely nominal rent. Surely never were twenty dollars more usefully invested. Ten dollars were spent on building a house and ten dollars upon farming implements; the good couple setting to work with a will. They asked if their house might be used for services on Sunday, so that those living near might hear the gospel. One day, a young man came to their door begging. He was the victim of the dreadful opium habit, of a respectable family, and could read well; but cast out from his home, he had no resource but begging from those nearly as poor as himself. Our friends told this young man of the God they worshipped, who was able to help him to break off the opium. They invited him to stay with them, promising to give him his food if he would work. In the meantime they taught, helped, and prayed with him until the desire for opium was overcome, and he felt himself a free man once more. This poor fellow, the fruit of their labours, has been an earnest, consistent Christian for the last ten years, and is now an unpaid local preacher. He continued working with them as a son, and three years ago was married to a deaf-and-dumb girl (he was too poor to pay for any other), and a year after she was received into the church. She is in all things consistent, but we can never know how she received the truths of the gospel.

Yaih-zing-pah and his wife were also the means indirectly of opening up Tung-tsö work; a beggar family called, who were friends in their old begging days, and were as usual invited to stay a few days and hear of Christ. After their begging tour of a few months they returned to their home in Tung-tsö, and began to tell their neighbours of the new doctrine they had heard, but did not believe. This created interest, so that when Mr. Boa some time afterwards on a book-selling tour visited the place, he found quite a number of people desiring to be taught. Upon his report we sent a preacher, and thus the work was begun in a district which heretofore the truth had never entered, and we have now a little church with out-stations. These beggars never believed the truth for themselves, though they were the means of stirring up interest in others. Amongst the believers in that place were four young lads, very bright and earnest. These we brought into Wenchow for two years' Bible training ; two are now unpaid local preachers in their own district, while earning their living as farmers, and two are learning useful trades in the city, and teach in Sunday school.

A few months ago Yaih-sing-pah's wife was crossing the river in a boat with twenty others, when on her way to the chapel ; a strong wind capsized the boat, and our dear sister and sixteen others were drowned. We mourn her untimely end ; they had lost their daughter, who was a bright little Christian, some years ago, and now the old man is left alone in his sorrow.

Another worker is Mr. Dzing, who was brought to us when quite a little lad ; his mother was dead, and his father a wretched opium-smoker, who had sold his younger brother for a few dollars to a man who took him off in a Fuhkien junk, where he knew not. He was about to sell this little fellow, when a relative rescued and brought him to our school. He was a nervous boy, and for months Mr. Stott was pained to see him timidly shrink from him ; but love and kindness won its way, and he became quite confiding. His father left the district and troubled no more about his child, who was thus left absolutely on our hands. He was a quiet, studious lad, and it was seldom we had to find fault with his conduct ; he was good and obedient, and outwardly all we could desire, but several years passed before the truth took possession of his heart. When he was old enough he wanted to learn foreign printing, and our mission press being in Chin-kiang, we sent him there in the hope he would learn that trade. The reports we had of his conduct were satisfactory, but there was no one to teach printing, and as far as learning the trade was concerned it was a failure. He had the advantage, however, of going to several places, visiting Japan amongst the others, so that he returned to us quite a travelled Chinaman. About 1878 he was converted and began to take part in preaching, and after a while he was employed as an evangelist and did good work, until in an hour of temptation he fell into sin, and had not only to be dismissed from preaching, but suspended from the church. His repentance proving sincere, he was restored ; and three years after again became a preacher, and has ever since been a faithful, earnest, and most helpful worker. He is now pastor of the Bing-yie church ; it was formerly an out-station from Wenchow, but is now itself a centre, having out-stations of its own.

One of our disappointments in connection with the young man was his marrying a heathen girl in preference to a Christian, because the latter have large or natural feet; the disgrace of a wife with these seemed more than he could bear, when there were but few such, and each one had to bear reproach. Now it is different. Not only have our girls increased in numbers, but many of our Christian women have unbound their feet, and are no longer the laughing stock of their neighbours. Mr. Dzing did not suffer from this false step so severely as some have had to do; his wife was a quiet, nice girl, and after some years was converted, but she has never been much help to him, either in the home or in spiritual life, through the lack of early training.

Another of our old boys is Mr. Tsiu; he was the first lad brought to Mr. Stott when he began his school in 1868. A more hopeless-looking, blank-faced boy you could hardly meet, and had it not been for the necessity of making a beginning with any kind of material that was brought to one's hand, he might never have been received. His father was dead; his mother a hard-hearted woman from the Fuhkien border, who had drowned two of her girls kept a low-class inn, and was utterly without principle; his elder brother was a wretched opium-smoker. This boy had been born paralysed down one side, and it was because he could neither work nor walk properly, and was therefore only a burden, that he was brought to the foreigner.

Mr. Stott's faith in the power of God was great, and he trusted that even this unpromising lad might yet be a useful witness for Christ, and he was not disappointed. He learned quickly and became a good scholar; he had been in the school about four years, and understood well the plan of salvation, though he had not accepted it. Our old Ning-po woman induced him to read the Scriptures to her every night, and on one occasion she said to him, " How is it you can read so beautifully and yet don't believe?" He replied, "I am not good enough." "Oh," she answered, "you are like the man who went into the feast without the wedding garment; you don't want Christ's robe, but are trying to make your own do." A few nights after he dreamed a strange dream : he thought he heard the trumpet announce the Lord's coming ; that in terror he got up, dressed, and went out to meet Him. When he got into the courtyard he thought he saw Mr. Stott going out of the gate ; he called upon him to wait, but Mr. Stott answered, " No, the Lord has come : I must go out to meet Him; you are not saved, you must be left behind." In terror he awoke, and was glad to find it only a dream ; but the next day, on telling his strange story to one of the Christians, the question was brought home, " What if it had been true?" He saw his danger, and at once yielded his heart to the Lord, and we have never had cause to doubt the reality of his conversion, though some weak points have often given us sorrow. He became an eloquent effective preacher, and was for several years my husband's right hand.

When he was about twenty-eight years of age, his mother, without consulting him, engaged him to a girl from a disreputable family. We feared that such a union could only lead to trouble, and strongly urged him to cancel the engagement. This he several times tried to do, but his mother always went into floods of tears, and the girl said the disgrace would be more than she could bear, and that she would certainly drown herself. The sight of his mother's tears and the girl's distress would overcome him, and they were not slow to see their advantage. We tried every way to get him out of the difficulty, even offered to refund the money that had been paid for her, for we could foresee that a girl brought up as she had been, and with the evil tendencies which she undoubtedly had, could be nothing but a curse to him. For a few years he waited in the hope that some way would be found out of the difficulty, but at last he married her, much to our distress. It turned out as we feared : a blot and a curse seemed to follow him ; his Christian life, bright and unsullied, began to be heartless ; he hardly dared to lift his head among other honourable men, for his wife, careless and extravagant, brought him to endless difficulties. Again and again he was helped, only to have the old story repeated, his wife could not keep out of debt. Several children were born, but were ill cared for. He began to lose the respect and confidence of the church members, and at last we had to remove him from being pastor, through no actual sin of his own, though certainly through his weakness, for a stronger minded man would have managed better.

He is now a teacher of the language to two of the young ladies. It is seldom one can set aside God's revealed will without suffering, and he has suffered sorely. Many a time he has said to me, " If her soul were only saved, I could wish her dead." Still in many ways he is useful, both in taking gospel meetings and Bible classes.

CHAPTER X

"How beautiful are the feet of them that preach the gospel of peace, and bring glad tidings of good things!"—ROM. x. 15.

Z-NÜE was another of our schoolboys who was much owned of God; he was brought to us when about eleven years of age. I well remember seeing a little bright-faced lad led in, clad in a rather nice though worn silk garment. I was surprised to see a boy of such well-to-do appearance, for surely, thought I, the father who could clothe his son in silk, could afford to give him rice; for up to this point no one had come to the school for the sake of the education and training, in every case they were too poor to give them food. Now here is an exception, thought I, the first of a superior set of boys. But alas! the next morning the father came with a profuse apology—the silk garment had been borrowed, and must be returned to its owner; and when it was taken off, oh! what rags, and dirty rags too. I had at once to have new clothes made for the little fellow, and the old ones burnt. From the first he took a liking for us; there was nothing of the shyness and fear that most exhibited for a few days. Some of the other boys would laugh at him when he came up with a bright smile, perfectly fearless, to share with me some of the beans and nuts, or anything else that had been given to him, and when he could get a flower to present me with he was highly delighted. Slowly the truth began to take possession of his young mind; with him there was no sudden conversion, but rather a gradual taking in and understanding of the truth; but the change in his life was no less decided, and when he was fourteen years of age, there being no doubt in our minds as to the reality of his conversion, he was baptized and received into church fellowship. He continued his studies for a few years longer, and it was in the meantime, while still considered a schoolboy, that he went to Bing-yie, and was the means of the conversion of the old man, worshipping in the temple, mentioned before.

For fourteen years afterwards he was a consistent, godly, and earnest Christian, and for nearly ten years of that time a faithful preacher. He contracted disease of the lungs, and in spite of every effort to save so valuable a life, God took him when he was about twenty-eight years of age. Eternity alone will reveal how many he was the means of leading to Christ, for winning souls was almost a passion with him.

When he was about twenty-five years of age, his

parents, without his knowledge or consent, betrothed him to a young girl of fourteen, and at this we were greatly grieved, for we had hoped he would have married a Christian from the school, and thus be helped in his work. However, engagements entered into by parents are not to be set aside, and there was nothing for it but to try and get the girl into the school, and to seek by God's blessing to win her to Christ. The parents on both sides being willing she was brought, under a written agreement, to remain with us for five years; when she arrived from the country she was taken first of all to her future husband's home, and introduced to the family as their daughter, and by them brought to us. She was a very pretty girl, bright and more obedient than most were when first they came to us. We were therefore the more surprised when three or four days afterwards she disappeared; we searched everywhere, sent to the young man's home, but no trace of her could be found. A messenger was sent to her own home, where she was found quietly doing household work; she had run off, asked her way to the north gate, took her passage in a boat without any money to pay it, and arrived at her mother's house after six hours' journey. It was the most plucky thing I had ever known a Chinese girl to do, and when she returned with the messenger I decided to take very little notice of the escapade, thinking that fear of the foreigner was the cause; but when about a week after that she was caught in the act of running away a second time, we decided to take some action. I put her in a room and told her that, not having time to speak to her now, I must lock the door, as she was not to be trusted. It was more than an hour afterwards before I could return; I asked her to tell me plainly what her difficulty was; why did she run away? No answer. Was she afraid of me? She said "No." Were the other girls unkind to her? She answered "No." Why then had she run away, for no one had ever done so before? For a time she was silent, but I encouraged her to speak, promising, if it was anything I could remove, it should be done. She then opened up her heart quite freely. She said she had been engaged contrary to her own wish, and when she was brought to the young man's home, and saw how very poor they were, and that even their language she did not understand (they were Tai-chow people), she determined she would not marry him. But, I said, you don't know the young man himself, you have never seen him; if you did, perhaps you would change your mind. But she answered, "No; I would like to stay here, and if you will promise me I need not marry into that family I shall stay and do all you tell me." I pointed out how impossible it was for me to give such a promise, that the engagement contracted by parents on both sides was binding; "but," I said, "I can promise one thing, that if you will wait quietly for three years, during which time you will have opportunities of seeing the young man; if, then, after knowing him better, you are still of the same mind, still unwilling to marry him, I will use my influence with him, and I have little doubt but that he will release you." At that her face brightened; she said, "If you will promise me that, it will be all right; you need not lock the door, for I shall not try to run away again." And from that time she scarcely ever gave me an anxious thought, being both obedient and affectionate, learned quickly, and became a true Christian. Before the three years were over the young man's mother died, and she of her own accord put on mourning for her, thus showing that she had accepted him.

When we left for England in 1887, Z-nüe was evidently dying of consumption, and we, fearing his father might sell her to some other man, obtained, with the girl's consent, a document from him handing the girl over to us, we on our part promising to return the betrothal money paid by his father; so that after his death she was perfectly free. She was later on married to a Christian young man.

Another interesting case was that of Ling-ah-chang, who lived outside the east gate; he was an ironbeater by trade. I cannot now recall the incidents of his conversion, but he became a very earnest, useful Christian. He started a meeting in his mother's house, so that the neighbours around might hear of Christ, and became quite eloquent in preaching. His mother and brother were converted through his instrumentality. After two or three years he became a useful local preacher. In 1888, when we were in England, Mr. G. engaged him first as an evangelist and afterwards as pastor of a small church, and from that time he has been doing good and earnest work. His dear old mother died last year, a most triumphant death, rejoicing in the prospect of being with Christ, which she realised was "far better." He married one of the girls from the school, and she has been a great help in work amongst the women.

Mr. Tsie was a native of the Dong-ling district, where he worked at his trade, that of a shoemaker. About seventeen years ago, when twenty-two years of age, he first heard of the "foreign doctrine" through a Christian relative of his who lived near by. This Christian at last persuaded him to attend the Sunday services held at our chapel ten miles off. Mr. Stott went there once a month to instruct the converts, and, assisted by good native preachers, faithfully told out the gospel story. The young man attended pretty regularly for about two months, but understood very little. Nothing of the precious truth seemed to enter his heart or find any lodgment there. He would sneer to himself as the believers sung the hymns which sounded so outlandish to him, and would say to himself, "Well, those are barbarian sounds; those who believe this foreign gospel will turn rebels soon, and we shall have a rebellion in the country." After that he relapsed into his old ways, and absolutely refused to accompany his relative to the services. Some months passed, when, without any apparent preparation or cause, a great change came.

One day he was sitting outside his door mending shoes. In front was a large tree; and, as he looked at it, he began to consider the trunk, branches, and leaves. There they were, sure enough, but where did they come from; there must be a root, even though unseen by him. Then it flashed across his mind that that was just like the world. Here was he; here were his neighbours and friends, and before them their fathers and grandfathers and more distant ancestors; but, surely, to all, there must be a root—some great ancestor above them all. There and then he realised the truth that there is a God from whom we—every one—have our being.

From that day forward all was changed. When he wakened in the morning he felt like a new man, and forthwith, ignorant as he was, he began preaching the great truth that had taken possession of his heart. It was some months after this change before he got assurance that his sins were all forgiven; but he dates his conversion from that day, when, as it were, God commanded the tree to preach a parable to him. He understood little of the plan of salvation, and could not read a character in the Bible, but he spoke out what he knew. He told of the one true God— of how He has given us all good things we possess, and yet we daily sin against Him; and how we all were deserving of hell fire, but that God would hear us when we pray to Him, and if we trust Him fully He would save. On and on he preached in this strain as long as any would stop to listen, and afterwards he said it was one of the strangest things to him that, when able to read the Bible for himself, he found it tallied exactly with many things he said in those old days, thus showing that the Spirit in the Word and the Spirit in the heart is one. His old relative was delighted, and soon after the preachers and other Christians, who heard of his changed life and earnestness, sought to teach him more clearly about the things of God. It was not long ere all the Christians in his village suffered severe persecution, but though he had never heard that the Scriptures exhorted to endure persecution joyfully, still he and all did indeed rejoice to suffer for Christ, and in the midst of the fire sang hymns, prayed, and praised that they were counted worthy to suffer for His dear name's sake. In after days he often expressed the wish that he had now the same deep earnestness and longing to lead others to the light which he had in the beginning of his Christian life. Wherever he went—walking on the roads, in boats, inns, or in houses—he told the story. To him it was so wonderful, he thought he had only to tell others and they too would believe.

Later on, Mr. Stott, hearing what a promising young preacher he seemed to be, invited him to the Mission House in Wenchow, to study. He made very rapid progress both in his Christian life and studies. Since then he has been an earnest and true Bible student. For a few years he continued at his trade, but at the same time doing all in his power to help forward the work, and took regular services in his native village.

In course of time he married one of our Christian schoolgirls, who has been a true helpmeet to him, helping in the work amongst women and children, besides keeping her home in such cleanly comfort as is seldom seen in China.

In 1887, when the out-stations of Bing-yie and Dong-ling were given over to two young missionaries to be henceforth worked as separate stations, Mr. Stott handed over to them Mr. Dzang and Mr. Tsie as two of our most efficient helpers. For years he did valuable work there, until about four years ago, when he came to help me at Wenchow. He has been my right hand and greatest comfort since, for though others have done good and valuable work, he, by his deeply spiritual character and knowledge of the Word of God, has been a most valued teacher, as well as pastor of our large Wenchow church.

Sa-löe-sz-mo, our Bible-woman, has a bright round face which beams upon you at all times. I have often wondered, in looking into that face, whether her sad life's history, which she had often told, could indeed be true. Not only has the past been full of sadness, but even now there is nothing in her home surroundings which can account for her cheery, happy smile. Truly God has given her His own peace and joy, which the world can neither give nor take away. She was only a little child when she was betrothed to a man twenty years her senior, and taken to her future husband's home to be henceforth completely under the rule of her mother-in-law, who seems to have been a hard, unkind woman. The child was both hot-headed and warm-hearted. A little love would have brought out her better qualities, but with hard words and harder treatment she grew reckless and disobedient, ever ready to answer back if found fault with. Of course this only made her mother-in-law more unkind and bitter. It was most pathetic to hear our little woman tell of how desperate she used to get, and how, after being scolded and beaten, she longed to put an end to her miserable existence. Sometimes she even went so far as to try to strangle herself; but, feeling the choking sensation, would get frightened and let herself go in time. How wonderful was God's goodness in restraining her. She little knew then that she was His chosen vessel to bring cheer, gladness, and life to many a heart as sad as her own; for, alas! hers was no uncommon case—only a specimen of the many, many little daughters-in-law living a life of slavery, receiving as reward scoldings and blows.

About ten years ago, not very long after her marriage, a young neighbour woman became interested in the gospel. Soon this woman was converted and became earnest in telling others the good news. After her conversion she was visited by Christians and preachers, who were ever glad of an opening to tell of Christ's love to those neighbours whom she had gathered and whom she was anxious to interest in her new-found treasure. After the first curiosity was appeased very few cared to listen, and only into one heart prepared by the Holy Spirit did the seed seem to fall and take root, and that heart was Sa-löe-sz-mo's. Impelled by some, as yet, unknown power, she would go whenever possible, either to hear her neighbour's visitors, or to talk over the strange new things with her friend privately. As soon as her husband and mother-in-law found she was truly interested in what they called the "foreign doctrine" they tried to prevent her going out, complained of her wasting time, and forbade her to listen any more. Her only chance, then, was to steal out in the evening, when her day's work was done, to her friend's house, and there talk quietly, ask questions, and learn to pray. For many months things went on thus, but as she became more and more interested she longed for more spiritual food and begged to be allowed to go to the chapel on Sundays. The very mention of this desire brought down upon her a storm of petty persecution; but by that time she was slowly learning to restrain her tongue, and instead of answering back, as formerly, would retire to pray and to ask the Lord to open up a way for her. She tried very hard every day to be specially good towards her ill-tempered mother-in-law and to do more than her usual amount of silk spinning. By Saturday evening she had succeeded so well, that when she asked, with fear and trembling, to be allowed to go to chapel next day, she was surprised by a favourable reply; and thus, by dint of great effort and industry, the little woman used to get permission to accompany her friend to the Sunday services, and it was not long before she was truly converted. After that she had to endure bitter persecution. Her husband often beat and ill-used her for believing "the doctrine," but her manifest change of behaviour, her industry, patience, and brightness at last conquered the prejudices of both mother and husband. Not long ago, when some of the neighbours laughed at him for his weakness in allowing his wife to leave the worship of their forefathers, he answered, "A religion that is able to change and make her a much better wife must be good, and I shall not be the one to hinder." The mother-in-law is now dead, and the husband, though unconverted, allows her to do as she pleases. She has been an earnest, active Bible-woman for four years, and has been the means of leading many of her dark sisters into the light of God's love. She has unbound her feet—which means a good deal to a Chinese woman —so that she may be better fitted for country work, as she has often to walk ten or fifteen miles in the day. Often when we have been out together I have retired quite worn out with the day's labours, while she, who had done so much or more than I, would continue till midnight teaching the Christians and inquirers.

During the two hottest months, when it is impossible to go out much, she refuses her salary, preferring to support herself by tea-picking, silk-weaving, or otherwise. She is only thirty years of age, and thus rather young, according to Chinese etiquette, to go about alone, and when not accompanied by myself or one of the young ladies, I always send an elderly woman with her; but her conduct is so wise and discreet that no one has ever hinted that her youth was any barrier to her usefulness. Her cheery helpfulness makes her a favourite with the women, while her sturdy independence calls forth the respect of all. Her words carry conviction, so that even rough country men are compelled to listen to her quietly and respectfully. Her loving sympathy opens up the hearts of the people, and prepares the way for any straightforward words she may have to say about things which are not right in the lives of any of the Christians. She is not afraid to speak out, though doing it in such a manner as rarely produces any bad feeling. We look upon her as a God-sent gift to the Church.

One of our most devoted and intelligent women is Ling-di-na, who had formerly been a great opium-smoker; she was now a widow, but she had begun that pernicious habit while her husband was alive, he too being a victim of the drug. She was a silk-weaver, and the constant sitting over her work, together with poor food, brought on a painful internal trouble, for which she sought relief in opium, and thus the habit was formed. Soon work, home duties, and everything good and true was given up, and she lived only to smoke and enjoy the soothing after-effects; as she herself said, " all pride and self-respect were lost." The confirmed opium-smoker will not work if he can get the drug without, and, when reduced to poverty, will pawn or sell everything he possesses, even wife, child—all must go to procure that which has become to him more than life. By and by her husband died, and some time later a friend, by no means a bright Christian, persuaded her to accompany her to hear the gospel. She attended regularly, when one day her only son was taken ill and died. In her grief she refused to be comforted, and would not go near the chapel. The Christians, however, did not forsake her; they held a little service over the child, and tried to persuade her to stay in our compound and break off the opium. She half promised, and that night knelt down to pray for the first time. She told God what they wanted her to do, but that now her baby was gone she did not care what became of her; if only she could see her child again she would be comforted. They had told her it was in heaven with Jesus, and that, if she believed, she would go there and see it by and by. If that were true, and the Lord would give her some evidence that her child was indeed living, she would go next day to get the opium medicine and become a true "Jesus disciple." She went to bed, and that night was granted to her a wonderful vision: the room was flooded with light, and scene after scene was presented to her. I cannot recall all she said, but in one scene she saw our two young ladies dressed in white. "Ah, they are in heaven," she thought; "but my baby is not there."

Again she saw a beautiful boy : "That must be the Lord Jesus when at twelve years of age he was lost in Jerusalem." Then she saw a beautiful golden city, so bright and glorious that she knew at once it must be heaven ; but still her child was nowhere to be seen. At last she recognised him sitting on the golden pavement, as he had often sat on her mud floor, and her heart bounded with a great joy : "Yes, he surely was there, and she would believe, so that by and by she might meet him again."

The next morning saw her early at the C.I.M. premises, asking medicine to break off the degrading habit, though she knew it meant much suffering. This was eight years ago, and her Christian life has been without a shadow. When we were without a doctor, and Miss Bardsley was doing what she could to relieve some of the suffering around, this dear woman voluntarily gave up two mornings a week to preach to the women who came for treatment. In this and other ways she has been ever willing to do what she could for the spread of the gospel. She is well fitted for the work of Bible-woman, but physical weakness prevents her doing much country work, though she is always willing to accompany one or other of our young ladies when visiting nearer places.

CHAPTER XI

"When thou passest through the waters I will be with thee ; and through the rivers, they shall not overflow thee."—ISA. xliii. 2.

IN 1886 we were joined by three new workers, Miss Oliver, who arrived in May, Mr. Grierson in June, and Mr. Sayers in July. My husband and I had both felt that the work had grown too heavy for our shoulders; I wanted some one to relieve me of the girls' school, and he wanted young men to do more of the country work. In the autumn of that year, Mr. Stott handed over the two churches of Dong-ling and Bing-yie to the charge of the two young brethren; they were to live at Bing-yie and work in the surrounding districts, so what was an out-station before, became a new centre, from which stations were opened, these ever since having been a separate work. Mr. Sayers, after a few months, left for Chü-chow, where he was privileged to labour only a few months, for he was "called home" in the autumn of 1888. Mr. G. still continues in the charge of the Bing-yie work. In 1887 we felt it necessary to take a change to England, Mr. Stott being considerably run down in health; Miss Oliver, who had taken charge of the girls' school, was then engaged to Mr. G., in whose care the Wenchow church was left during our absence. They were married in 1888, and on my return went back to their own work at Bing-yie.

Mr. Stott's health began to fail almost as soon as we left China, and by the time we reached England he was very ill; congestion of the lungs, combined with weak action of the heart, caused such difficulty of breathing that to lie down was impossible. Night and day he sat in patient suffering for a year and eight months, although for most of that time he was able to go about and enjoy nature in all her lovely forms. After three months spent with dear friends in London we went to Dartmouth, and remained the winter and spring of 1887 and 1888 with the Misses Teage; there he was surrounded with every comfort that love and kindness could devise. He had a donkey-carriage and drove himself for miles round the lovely country, while I walked and talked by his side. That winter was a memory he loved to dwell upon, the dear friends making a deep impression upon his heart.

Being in Scotland in the summer of 1888, we were invited to join Drs. Gordon and Pierson in a missionary tour, and as an eminent physician encouraged us with his opinion that frequent change of scene would benefit the dear invalid, we accompanied them. We had most remarkable blessing during the six weeks in which we visited all the principal cities and towns in the north; large numbers, attracted by the eloquence of Drs. Gordon and Pierson, left deeply impressed by the wonderful story of what God had done among the heathen. Mrs. Gordon and I conducted ladies' meetings in each place, I frequently speaking in the evening meetings as well; but while it was my privilege to engage in this more public work in my husband's stead, helped by his encouragement, sympathy, and prayers, he was doing a no less blessed work, for, though unable to attend any of the meetings, the holy, sweet influence of his life was telling most powerfully on those around him. Everywhere our kind entertainers were deeply impressed with his not only patient but cheerful suffering, and many were won by him then who have been my warm friends ever since.

At the end of this tour the doctor said Mr. Stott was decidedly better, and if he would spend the winter in the south of France he might yet recover. So in November we left for Cannes, where we spent several months in a bright sunny home for invalids; but, in spite of care and doctors' skill, the disease gained upon him until, on April 21, 1889, Easter

Sunday, he most triumphantly entered into the presence of his Lord.

As he was evidently, though slowly, growing weaker, I asked the doctor if the place were suitable, or if a change of climate would be of any use. He answered he would like a consultation before giving me an answer, for if it was as he feared no change would be of any use. After the consultation, my husband, looking the doctor full in the face, said, "Do you think I shall be able to return to China?" The doctor, not wishing to tell the sad truth, turned the question aside. Mr. Stott, seeing the evasion, said, "Don't be afraid to tell me the worst, for there is no worst for me, thank God. I have had twenty years' service for Him in China; I did wish to go back, but if He says no, why should I desire it? I am willing to stay and suffer if it is His will; willing to go to China if it be His will." And then with a bright smile he added, "Why, I believe I am willing to go half-way to China and then go to heaven, if that were His will." The doctor looked at him earnestly and said, "I envy you." He then told him plainly there was no hope of recovery. Not a shadow crossed the face; he knew where his home was and longed to go. I was not unprepared; I saw the daily weakening of the poor body and feared there could be no return of strength; but it was more difficult for me to submit to God's will. To

"WHEN THOU PASSEST THROUGH THE WATERS"

him God's will had ever been first, and he had no hard lesson to learn.

I remember a lady, who was strongly impressed with faith-healing views, talking with him during his first few months of illness. She said it was only a matter of faith; he might be better if he would; it was so easy just to have faith in God, and it would be done. She asked, "Don't you think God could heal you and send you back to your loved work?" He replied, "My difficulty does not lie there; I know He could; but God once gave the desire of the heart and sent leanness to the soul. I do not want that. He knows if He gave me strength it will be used for His service, and if weakness, it will be borne for Him. I want Him to have His own way with me all through." The lady had nothing to answer; I think she must have felt as I did, that it was better to lie passively in God's hands than to refuse to suffer.

But I did not learn the lesson so quickly; for a long time I wrestled and struggled for his life. For a while I hid from him my distress; but one night, unable to bear any longer, I sobbed out that I could not let him go. Calmly and quietly he said, "Not yet, dearie, not yet; God will make you willing when the time comes." Three days after, God caused me to triumph in Christ, my will was swallowed up in His will, and all was peace. That evening, kneeling by his side, I was for the first time able to ask God to take him home, gently, quietly, and painlessly, and to take him soon. While I was praying he gave a sigh of relief and said, "Thank God." When I had finished praying he said, "You don't know how much good these words have done me ; I knew God would bring you to that point before He called me away. I was only waiting to hear you say such words as these ; I have nothing more to desire — all is well."

For six weeks after this we lived together on the borderland; not for one moment did I ever wish to keep him back. We talked and prayed much, and almost went into heaven together ; we made my plans for the future, even to the month in which I should start for China ; all had been talked over, and I was able to carry out the arrangements made by him even to the letter. It was a great joy to him to know that I was going back to take up his work, and to be both father and mother to the people he loved so dearly, for we had been as one in the work. When I asked if he had any instructions for me, he said, "No, you know the people and work as well as I, and will do just as I have done—I have no care about that ; only give the native Christians my love, and tell them I would have returned to them if I could, but I shall wait for them, and by and by we shall meet."

The very wonderful way in which he realised the Lord's presence is related in a small pamphlet entitled, "In Memoriam: George Stott," published by Morgan and Scott. From this I quote the following letters, written to our C.I.M. secretary:—

"MAISON BLANCHE,
"ROUTE DE GRASSE, CANNES,
"*April* 23, 1889.

"DEAR MR. BROOMHALL,—It was my privilege to be with our dear departed brother, Mr. Stott, during his last night on earth, and a few particulars of the closing scene will, I know, be acceptable to you. Slowly, during many weeks of pain, the earthly house of this tabernacle was being dissolved, and on Saturday evening, about 9.30, one of the sisters came over to say that his sufferings had become more intense, and the end seemed approaching. I was in the act of reading in the Christian classics, 'De Incarnation Verbi Dei,' the account by Athanasius of the triumphs of the early Christians and martyrs over death, due to their Lord and Master, who, by His Cross and Resurrection had vanquished death, so that they no longer feared but despised it. 'For,' says he, 'as when the sun rises after the night has passed, and the whole globe is illuminated by it, it is not at all doubtful that it is the sun which has shed its light everywhere, and has driven away the darkness and enlightened all things; so death being utterly despised and trampled down from the time when the Saviour's saving appearance in the body, and end upon the Cross took place, it is perfectly clear that it is the Saviour Himself, who appeared in the body, who brought death to naught, and daily exhibits trophies against it in His own disciples. For when one sees men, who are by nature weak, leaping forth to death and not cowering before its corruption, nor displaying fear at the descent into Hades, but with zealous soul provoking it; and not shrinking from tortures, but for Christ's sake preferring rather than this present life to rush upon death; or, too, if one be a beholder of men and women and young children rushing upon and leaping forth to death for the religion of Christ; who is so simple, or who is so unbelieving, or is so incapacitated in mind, as not to perceive and draw the conclusion that Christ, to whom the men bear witness, Himself bestows and gives to each the victory over death, rendering it utterly weak in each of those who hold His faith and bear the sign of the Cross?' It was thus, I thought, sixteen hundred years ago, but how many times, in common with all Christian workers in this land, I have heard the popular dictum, *Le Christianisme a fait son temps*, 'Christianity has had its day,' 'It is used out'? And as I went forth to witness for the first time a death-bed scene, this thought was uppermost, 'Will it ratify the affirmation of Athanasius, and show that after sixteen centuries the virtue of the Cross and Resurrection is in no degree diminished?'

"Entering the chamber, I saw our dear brother sitting up in the armchair, supported by his dear wife and one of the nursing sisters. It was one of the distressing features of his illness that he was unable to lie down, and all these weary weeks of pain had been passed sitting, with no possibility of supporting the poor head or giving the body relief, only by occasionally leaning forward. The strong man was bowed, and poor nature was in a pitiable plight. The props of the tent were being taken away, and the suppressed groans of the sufferer told of the silver cord being loosed, and the links being broken which bound the spirit to the earthly tenement.

"When he knew I was present he expressed a decided wish that I should stay with him, which I was only too glad to do; and as I look back on that night, I feel that not for any consideration would I have missed that scene of suffering and holy triumph. Never before did I know how truly death is a vanquished enemy, its empire overthrown and its sceptre destroyed. During eight hours we witnessed the King of Terrors doing his worst. The combat was a fierce one, blow after blow was dealt, strong pains were tearing at the vitals; the anguish of dissolution was there, but not for one moment did the spirit falter. With every moment's respite from pain he collected his little strength to give forth some word of testimony that the Lord was near, and doubt and fear far away. 'It is only the poor body that is suffering,' he said; 'the soul is happy.' Early in the evening he said, 'I bless God that thirty years ago He washed me from my sins in His precious blood, and now the sun is shining without a cloud'; and thus with unfaltering faith, and with unwavering hope, he went down into the valley of the shadow.

"Before leaving my house it came to my mind to glance at the portion for the evening in 'Daily Light,' and there indeed was a highway 'cast up.' Beautiful and appropriate it was, beginning with the words, 'It is I; be not afraid. When thou passeth through the waters I will be with thee; and through the rivers they shall not overflow thee; when thou walkest through the fire thou shalt not be burned; neither shall the flame kindle upon thee: for I am the Lord thy God, thy Saviour. Though I walk through the valley of the shadow of death I will fear no evil: for Thou art with me; Thy rod and Thy staff they comfort me. Who shall separate us from the love of Christ? Shall tribulation, or distress, or persecution, or famine, or nakedness, or peril, or sword?' I took it with me, that dear Mr. Stott might have a word like apples of gold in pictures of silver. In this 'royal road' we saw him advance, treading down with triumphant faith the powers of sin, and death, and hell.

"The words he repeated the most were, 'Come Lord Jesus, come now, come now,' often reaching out his arms to welcome the Lord, whom he felt was indeed drawing near. Once or twice, in moments of extreme pain, his cry went up, 'O Lord, help me; Lord, have mercy upon me.' The Lord heard him in the day of his distress, and strengthened him in the dire conflict. We sought to supply stones for his steps, as he forded the dark stream; words of life came spontaneously to our lips, and it was grand to see how his faith appropriated them. When his dear wife reminded him that he would soon hear the Master's 'Well done, good and faithful servant, enter thou into the joy of thy Lord,' his soul seemed to revel in the thought. 'Enter thou into the joy of thy Lord, of thy Lord,' he repeated again and again; then turning it into a prayer, and stretching out his hands, he said, 'Let me enter now, enter now, into the joy of my Lord, the joy of my Lord.'

"He had feared lest in his weakness and suffering some impatient word should escape him, and he should thus dishonour his Lord: he had begged his dear wife to put it down to nature's weakness; but her prediction was verified, the Lord's grace was all sufficient; no murmuring or impatient word passed his lips; while his deep gratitude and affection for the smallest service rendered him were touching and beautiful to see, and every one felt it a privilege to wait upon him.

"And thus the hours passed, he fighting the last battle; his dear wife, worn with many watchings, wearied out physically but wonderfully supported in spirit, with words of faith and hope cheering him as he breasted the billows, and watching for his release.

"Prayers from many loving hearts in England, China, and France, were being answered that night. There could be no doubt about it. And the word the memory of that scene calls up spontaneously to my mind is 'Mahanaim,' for that chamber of death was then the rendezvous of the hosts of God.

"It was six in the morning; nature outside was awaking in the first fresh joy of morning light. The sun had risen in a sky of cloudless blue. The birds were singing their morning song just outside the slightly opened window, while the carillon of the Easter bells came sounding joyously through the air Within we were standing on the borderland, close by the gates which were opening to another who, having fought the good fight through Christ, was more than conqueror. The change had come, the contracted features and glazing eye told that the last struggle was entered on. A hurried 'He is going' escaped us. I did not expect to hear him speak again, and, as consciousness seemed fading, I said, 'The Master *is* come, and calleth for thee.' He took it in, and to my surprise, with a last effort, said, 'Then lift me up, that I may give another note of praise.' Putting my arms around him, I drew him gently forward. Then as fast as his poor breath came he turned it into praise. 'Praise the Lord, bless His holy name,' he repeated again and again.

"It was wonderful to listen to, and I could not help saying to the dear companion of his life and labours, who on her knees, with only half-suppressed cries from the pangs which were rending her own heart, was holding his hands and watching the shadows of death as they passed over his face, 'This is a precious legacy he is leaving you.' They were like words of triumph coming out of the very realms of death. 'Do you know me, precious one?' she asked. 'Know you, Gracie? it would be strange if I didn't know you,' was the reply. Then with a strength that surprised me, he added, 'We have rallied together around that dish of fruit'—one of their last conversations had been about the fruit of the Tree of Life—'many a time, and the King in His beauty was there. Farewell, Gracie; don't speak to me again, I am going to see the King.'

"Those were hallowed moments. Sœur Achard, the directress, and another of the sisters had joined us. Most tenderly and faithfully had they done 'what they could' for him. M. Louis, the manservant, was helping me to support him; while before him, kneeling, was she from whom the desire of her eyes was being taken. Our tears were flowing fast, though we hardly knew why. He was looking on things which to us were invisible, and hearing sounds our dull ears could not catch. We could hear him say in a low whisper, 'Come, Lord Jesus—Lord, take my spirit;' then he said, 'Coming, coming—come, come.' With these last words our beloved brother, George Stott, went in to see the King in His beauty, on Easter morning, at half-past six.

"Nature's pent-up grief broke forth in brief cries and sobs, but they were happy tears. 'I don't mourn for him,' said his dear wife, 'I mourn for myself. He is happy—he is at rest now.'

"And so we knelt together to praise Him who had given us that night to see that death has no sting, and the grave no victory. 'As then,' says Athanasius, 'it is possible to see with the eyes that these things are true, so when death is mocked and despised by the believers in Christ, let him no longer doubt, let no one be wanting in faith that by Christ death was brought to naught and its corruption destroyed and put an end to.' Having seen with our eyes, we set the seal of truth to this testimony.

"We buried him yesterday in the Cannes cemetery. The Rev. P. W. Minto conducted the service. A number of Christian friends were present. All who knew him loved him as a true man of God, and a faithful servant of Christ. Among those present was Mr. W. T. Berger, his lifelong friend, from whose house, twenty-four years ago, he had started for the scene of his life's labour in distant China. In a few brief but beautifully appropriate words, Mr. Berger spoke of the zeal and love which had animated him in his work for Christ. He addressed words of loving sympathy and consolation to the widow, and reminded us all, for each of us the day was hastening to its close, and that we should work ere the night cometh. Then we laid him to rest, singing over his grave the Christian's 'Good Night':

> 'Sleep on, beloved, sleep and take thy rest;
> Lay down thy head upon thy Saviour's breast;
> We love thee well, but Jesus loves thee best.
>   Good-night! Good-night! Good-night!
>
> Until the Easter glory lights the skies,
> Until the dead in Jesus Christ arise,
> And He shall come, but not in lowly guise.
>   Good-night!'

There we left the body, sleeping in joyful hope of the resurrection, 'till the day dawn and the shadows flee away.'

"I remain, dear Mr. Broomhall, with Christian love,
"Yours sincerely,
"H. WEBBER."

CHAPTER XII

"The memory of the just is blessed."—Prov. x. 7.

ANOTHER testimony must be given, for it comes from one whose kindness ought to be mentioned as an example for the imitation of others.

"DEAR MR. BROOMHALL,—My acquaintance with our dear departed friend, Mr. Stott, began in, I think, the year 1868. My brother-in-law had convened at his house a meeting of friends who were interested in foreign missionary work. There was a good attendance, and it was agreed that each one present should put themselves in communication with some labourer in the foreign field, and that later on another meeting should be held, when replies received should be read. I cannot help thinking such a plan, if more often adopted, would be the means not only of bringing refreshment to our fellow-labourers in the regions beyond, but would also enable those at home more

"THE MEMORY OF THE JUST IS BLESSED" 161

definitely and intelligently to remember them at the throne of grace.

"I was unable to attend the meeting to which I refer, until just at the close, when I found that the name of Mr. George Stott, of Wenchow, whom I had never seen and whose name in connection with the newly formed C.I.M. I barely knew, was allotted to me. I at once wrote, and was very gratified in due course to receive an appreciative reply. I regret a second meeting was never held and, so far as I know, none present at the first continued their correspondence. But Mr. Stott and I regularly wrote to each other for nine years, when it was my privilege personally to become acquainted with him and Mrs. Stott on their visit to England. The correspondence continued without interruption ever after, and it was a great pleasure to receive them into our home, although he was in such a weak state when they arrived from China, *viâ* U.S.A., eighteen months ago.

"I cannot tell you the blessing this long friendship has been to me; and the pleasure of the service, which many might easily undertake and maintain, is one I would willingly commend to others. The insight which dear Mr. Stott's letters have given me into his patient self-denying labours (which by God's blessing have been attended with so much success) have taught me many lessons which I trust never to forget, and my earnest desire for myself and all who have known and loved him, is that we may by grace be enabled to follow him as he followed Christ (1 Cor. xi. 1). Our sorrow is not without hope, and the thought of our own loss is outweighed by the contemplation of his great gain, who has now been called to enter into the joy of his Lord.

"Believe me, my dear Mr. Broomhall,
"Yours faithfully,
"JOHN F. ALLEN."

Mr. Broomhall adds: "It is not a little remarkable that one who had to do with Mr. Stott's going out to China in 1865, who had been his faithful friend and correspondent all through his missionary life, should be residing at the place of his death and have the opportunity at his graveside to bear testimony, such as from fulness of knowledge but few others could bear, to the faithful service of his life; but this was Mr. Berger's privilege, and that which was the peculiar privilege of the living was the special and deserved honour of our departed brother."

Mr. Berger wrote as follows:—

"VILLA TALBOT, CANNES,
"*April* 23, 1889.

"DEAR MR. BROOMHALL,—Who can estimate the issue of a single grain of wheat falling into the ground and dying? Many lives will surely spring up therefrom and in consequence thereof. It has pleased God to take to Himself His faithful servant, George Stott, late of Wenchow, China, than whom it would be difficult to find one more devoted and steadfast in prosecuting the work he believed the Lord had given him to do. We committed his remains to the tomb yesterday afternoon, to await the voice of the Son of God calling those who shall hear it (His sleeping saints) to come forth from their graves, that they with the changed living ones may together ascend to meet and be with the Lord for ever.

"We have reason to believe that Mr. Stott's twenty-three years' labour in China has been greatly owned and blessed, he having left in existence in Wenchow and its neighbourhood (where, if I mistake not, no foreign missionary had previously laboured) three native churches, numbering in all about three hundred members besides as many attendants, to say nothing of the schools he inaugurated. You will pardon my entering thus into details, when I tell you that I made Mr. Stott's acquaintance prior to his going to China in the year 1865, he being one of the five who went out when the China Inland Mission was but in its incipient state. His works do follow him. In thus writing, we do not glory in George Stott, but in the Lord, who wrought the works by His servant.

"Of his devoted wife I must abstain from writing, but ask that much prayer may ascend to God on her behalf. Her heart seems set on returning to China to carry on the work she left as far as it may be in her power to do so. After twenty-three years' correspondence with Mr. and Mrs. Stott, I look back with the most pleasing remembrance of the same, and rejoice if in any measure I can be considered as having had partnership in their labours.

"I remain, dear Mr. Broomhall,
"Faithfully yours,
"W. T. BERGER."

A lady who had spent the winter at the Asile, and had thus become acquainted with Mr. Stott, now herself in the presence of the King, wrote:—

"ASILE EVANGELIQUE,
"ROUTE DE GRASSE, CANNES,
"*April* 25, 1889.

"DEAR SIR,—As one who had the privilege of spending this winter with Mr. Stott at the Asile, I feel I should like to send a few lines to tell you how bright a memory he has left behind with us of faith and patience and cheerful acquiescence in God's will; indeed, that will was evidently his delight, whether it meant doing or suffering. When speaking about plans for the future soon after he came, he said 'if it were the Lord's will he would like either China or heaven.'

We were struck with the way in which he entered

into and enjoyed everything, notwithstanding his weary nights, always spent sitting up in his chair; and his graphic descriptions of his life and work in China (work so dear to him) were an unfailing source of interest. He was quite the life of our little party here, until extreme weakness and suffering made speaking too great a fatigue.

"I was prevented by illness from intercourse with him for some little time, and when able to see him again found a great change for the worse had taken place. Dropsy had then set in, and, after a consultation, the doctors gave no prospect of recovery or of his being able to return to China. He took this decision calmly and cheerfully, comforting his dear wife with 'Never mind, dear; nothing can really hurt us, you know.' One day, when I spoke of the discomfort his swollen leg must cause him, he said, 'Oh, it is all quite right, my mind is kept continually in peace night and day, and as far as I know myself, I can say I am ready at any moment the Lord shall call me.'

"Several weeks of great suffering and weakness followed, borne with such Christian courage and patience as we can never forget. Sick people in the house were enabled to bear their burdens more cheerfully on hearing of him and servants and all who had to do with him, spoke of the wonderful way in which he bore his illness. There was not an approach to a murmur in his most painful moments, and always a word of welcome to those who entered his room. His gratitude for the least service or attention was very touching. He was loved by all.

"The Friday before his death, I went in to see him for a few minutes. He said, 'I am getting very near the kingdom now;' and then as I took leave of him, 'God bless you; perhaps the next time we meet will be in glory.' The following evening we knew that the last struggle had begun; but even during that Saturday night he was full of praise to God, and was able to rise in a remarkable way above the bodily distress. 'It is only the poor body that suffers,' he said, to those who were watching, 'my mind is full of peace and joy.'

"Almost his last breath was spent in praising God. He asked to be raised up a little in his chair, saying, 'I want to sound one more note of praise,' and then began, 'Bless the Lord, O my soul,' and shortly afterwards he said, 'Coming, coming, come,' and fell asleep in Jesus.

"It seemed, that Sunday morning, as if the gates of the heavenly city had been thrown open so wide to receive him, that we, too, had a foretaste of its peace and joy. We sorrow with dear Mrs. Stott in her great loss, and pray that the Lord may be very near her in her loneliness, and that He will strengthen her to carry on the work for Him in China, which she loves so well, for the 'little while' until they meet again in His presence. For us, amongst whom they have been this winter, their sojourn will be a precious remembrance of God's power to sustain, strengthen, and cheer in the time of trial.

"Believe me, dear sir,
"Yours sincerely,
"ELEANOR H. MOOR."

Miss E. R. Teage writes:—

"It is so blessed to think of our dear friend at rest. What a 'resurrection morning' it must have been for him! but one feels a great blank left. He endeared himself to all who knew him by his patient, bright spirit. You will, I know, feel much the loss of dear Mr. Stott from your Mission; he was such a faithful and earnest worker, and has been one with you from the earliest days of the Mission. We feel so thankful to the Lord for giving us the honour of having him under our roof. He was such an example of real, childlike faith, and so happy. . . . We desire to add our testimony to that of many others in bearing witness to the blessed influence he had over those among whom he stayed during the past eighteen months, since his return to England. Days and nights of weariness and suffering were appointed to him, and although for nearly two years he had been unable, owing to the difficulty of breathing, to lie down and take a night's rest, yet his bright spirit and childlike confidence in all the will of God concerning him seemed never to have been clouded for a moment.

"His heart's desire was to return to the people among whom he laboured for more than twenty years, and greatly will he be missed by those dear native Christians, to so many of whom he was made the honoured instrument in leading them to the Saviour. He has now been called to 'rest from his labours,' but we may truly say, 'his works do follow him'; for the little church in the far-off heathen land, which through God's blessing is the result of years of patient toil and tested faith, stands as a living witness to the grace and love of God in using 'a poor weak instrument' (as he himself would often say) to His glory.

"It was at about the age of eighteen that, owing to an accident, he was obliged to undergo the amputation of one leg, and soon after this time of affliction he was led to rejoice in Jesus as his Saviour. He then gave himself to the Lord for service, and was one of the first who went out with the China Inland Mission, to live among the people for whom he has since laboured so earnestly. His testimony to the end has been very bright; for, though suffering and extreme weakness have increased day by day, his spirit has been rejoicing in his Saviour, and his soul full of trust. 'Faint, yet pursuing' was the message he sent not many days since to some friends, and again, only four days ago, he said : 'I cannot speak, cannot sing, cannot pray, can hardly think, but Jesus is my all in all.' And now the race is run, and he has heard the welcome call, 'Enter thou into the joy of thy Lord.' In closing, we would add a verse of one of his favourite hymns as being so appropriate to his last moments :

> " For me be it Christ, be it Christ hence to live.
>   If Jordan above me shall roll,
> No pang shall be mine, for in death, as in life,
>   Thou wilt whisper Thy peace to my soul.
> ' It is well, it is well, with my soul.' "

I also append two letters written by his former school-boys, which show more than any words of mine how much he was loved and honoured.

Translation of a Letter written by Tsiu-die-ch'ing

" Our pastor, Mr. Stott, came to Wenchow twenty-four years ago to preach the gospel of Christ. At that time the good news had not yet been heard in Wenchow, the Light of God had not then shone upon the people. No one knew where they came from, nor where they would go to after death ; all men were dark and without understanding. Buddhism and Taoism had spread all over the place, and men worshipped only the gods they could see.

"Seeing this, Mr. Stott's heart was pierced as with a knife; in private he laboured in prayer that the good news of the gospel might spread far and near, nor did he begrudge time or money. For this end he opened schools, calling in the children of the poor to learn to read about God. Morning and evening he himself taught them from the Word of God, to know that they had souls which would never die. He told them also that they had sin, that sinners could not enter the kingdom of heaven; also that God loved them and sent His Son into the world to save sinners.

"Preaching the gospel then was not easy, for when Mr. Stott first came to Wenchow he did not understand the dialect, and had only a Ning-po man to help him rent a house and chapel. In the morning he taught the boys he had gathered into the school, and in the afternoon he preached in the chapel; this he did every day.

"One morning early I remember a rowdy named Ah-doa came to the gate, and, battering it with stones, demanded entrance. Mr. Stott asking him what he wanted, he answered: 'I want to sport inside' (aimlessly amuse). He was told to come in the afternoon. He replied: 'I must get in now.' Mr. Stott went out to exhort him, when Ah-doa threw a stone, and had not Mr. Stott put his head a little on one side, it must have felled him to the ground.

"Many were the dangers and trials he passed through, willing to bear all if only souls were saved. I was the first boy in school, and learned there for five years, and afterwards, through the grace of God, became a preacher.

"When I first entered the school Mrs. Stott had not yet come to Wenchow, and Mr. Stott suffered much during the winter from neuralgia in his leg, but as soon as the pain was gone he was out preaching again. Seventeen years ago he opened a chapel at Bing-yie, but as soon as opened the people gathered in crowds, and tried to get up a riot to drive out the foreigner, forbidding him to preach. They did not know that Jesus would get the victory; for now there are over one hundred Christians in that place, and altogether in and around Wenchow there are now over three hundred converts. A little over two years after Mr. Stott came to Wenchow, Mrs. Stott arrived, and began work among the women and girls; as soon as there were converts she instructed them in the Word of God, and taught them how to help others, forming them into a missionary band.

"I remember six years ago that the Wenchow chapel and house and school were burnt down by a riotous mob. All the foreigners were driven from the city, and the disciples scattered; but only a few weeks had gone by when Mr. Stott returned, and began to re-build, and during the five months the buildings were being erected our pastor had too much to do in attending to all the work himself. Then they had to live in the new house before it was quite dry, and thus, alas! he caught disease of the lungs.

"Three years ago Mr. and Mrs. Stott left for England, hoping to return shortly, but the disease which took our pastor to heaven only developed. For two years he suffered without complaint, glorifying God, then joyfully ascended to heaven. Mrs. Stott has returned to Wenchow, remembering that the sheep were without a shepherd. She would not leave nor forsake the disciples, and seeing some of them blind, poor, and old, she has opened homes to receive such that they might not suffer cold and hunger in their helpless state. Seeing that Mr. and Mrs. Stott have so earnestly done the will of God and kept all His commandments, their future reward must be great indeed."

Translation of a Letter written by Lui-sie-kwai.

"I wish to write a few lines about our pastor, named Mr. Stott. His native place was Scotland, where he was educated. He was sent out to China by the China Inland Mission to preach the gospel. His disposition was straight, and righteous, and very intelligent; in that respect there are few men like him. To look upon him was to feel awe, but to know and come near him he was gentle and gracious. In

"THE MEMORY OF THE JUST IS BLESSED" 173

all matters he thought all round first, and then acted. His words were few, but his wisdom was great. Whatever he said he always did; his power and influence were felt by all. He might well be called the pillar of the church at Wenchow; every one aimed and desired to be like him. Our pastor for many years gave himself to teaching and instructing. He loved much to go out and preach the gospel to others. He came to Wenchow twenty-four years ago, and two years later Mrs. Stott joined him. Together they worked the will of God, happy that they were chosen for such work, leaving friends and relations and native country for distant Wenchow, learning our native dialect so that they might understand our language. They organised churches, opened and maintained boarding-schools, not regarding time nor money, receiving orphans and other poor children, teaching them to read and understand the Bible. Not afraid of toil and suffering, he went out to near and distant places preaching, selling books, and helping the distressed. All this he did that the gospel might spread abroad.

"Alas! the district of Wenchow is given up to the worship of idols more than many other places; learned and unlearned alike worship idols. Mr. Stott seeing things in this condition, his heart was stirred up like a fire. He prayed, with sorrow and distress, that God would look down and pity the people. Soon God gave the answer, and the gospel spread to different places. Three churches were formed at Wenchow, Bing-yang, and Dong-ling. At each chapel there was a native preacher. Our pastor was not afraid of toil ; every month he went himself to those stations preaching, teaching, and examining converts. In all this work Mrs. Stott was his helper, she also teaching and instructing women and girls ; and when souls were saved she taught them how to help others, and formed a 'Native Women's Missionary Band,' caring for the helpless and sorrowful, the cold and the hungry. All that was good connected with the church they earnestly and devotedly attended to, spending their whole strength in the work. For many years they thus worked, and are the foundation of the church. Now there are over three hundred converts. Is not this good?

"In 1887 Mr. and Mrs. Stott returned to their native land to visit once more their relations and friends. They had only gone a few months when Mr. Stott developed disease of the lungs. The best doctors in medicine were called in and used, but it was God's will to call him home, and after nearly two years of suffering he fell asleep, joyfully entering the happy land. When the news reached Wenchow the church members wept bitter tears, our hearts were heavy and sad ; but, reflecting on our pastor's virtues, old and young gave grateful thanks for his grace in teaching them. All who knew and received this grace feel deeply that they are separated from him, and are very sad. Thinking of the words and actions of our beloved pastor, I cannot tell nearly all his goodness, but send these few lines. Let those who read not despise my simple words."

The above was sent to the Chinese Christian paper for publication.

CHAPTER XIII

"He will be very gracious unto thee at the voice of thy cry; when He shall hear it, He will answer thee."—ISA. xxx. 19.

DURING the last few weeks of Mr. Stott's life he frequently prayed that God would raise up one who might be as a daughter unto me, in whom my lonely heart might find comfort, and one who at the same time would be a real help in the work. So sure did I feel God would answer his prayer that I was not in the least anxious about the matter, knowing that at the right time God would manifest the one He had in keeping for me. I was to sail in November, but up to October was without guidance in the matter. When at Keswick Convention in July Miss Bardsley was introduced to me as a young lady going out to China in the autumn, how little I then thought she was the one God had appointed. From Scotland I wrote to Mr. Broomhall to have my passage taken for November 28th. Friends thought I was too rash in deciding the date of my sailing while as yet no companion had been found; but God says, " He that believeth shall not make haste," and He kept me at rest.

Returning to London in October to spend the remaining six weeks with dear Mr. and Mrs. Broomhall, who had ever been father and mother not only to the young candidates, but also to the returned missionaries, I found there was a party sailing the following week of whom Miss Bardsley was one. The arrangements had all been made, passage taken, " Goodbyes " said, and it seemed as though it were too late to suggest a change; yet I felt sure she was the one whom God had chosen for me. On mentioning this to Mr. Broomhall, and afterwards to Mr. Taylor, the suitability was also apparent to them, and they kindly suggested she should be kept back, while her place was filled by another; and, what was more remarkable still, upon my asking Miss Bardsley " whether she would like to accompany me as a friend and companion?" she unhesitatingly replied " Yes," and at the same time told me that it was the expressed desire both of her father and mother, who had met me months before. Thus on all sides God's will was manifested. And now for six years she has been all my husband prayed for—a loving, helpful daughter.

On November 28, 1889, I sailed on my third voyage for China, accompanied by six young ladies going out for the first time. We had both a pleasant and profitable voyage. We of course went second-class, and had a full complement of passengers, and for that reason we had first-class cabins apportioned near the officers' quarters. The one Miss Bardsley and I had was a three-berth cabin, large and airy, with two windows, which kept it delightfully cool, and into which we packed daily ten for reading and prayer as soon as the first days of sea-sickness were over. The captain was a nice, kind man, and the chief officer a decided Christian. One day while the former was on his usual tour of inspection, he seemed amused at seeing so many of us. I laughingly said: "We are not always so packed, captain; we have only gathered for a little prayer," and asked him to see how beautifully we had managed. He turned to the purser who accompanied him, and said: "You are not taking in more passengers, are you?" He replied: "Yes, sir, at Naples." He then said: "Not here; they are full." In this kindly way he gave the hint to let us have the cabin to ourselves, though it was fitted up for three.

Amongst our passengers there was a Christian colonel of the Bengal Army who was a great help to us, and he, with the captain's permission, began Bible readings at 10.30 in the second saloon, which were attended by a fair number of our fellow-passengers. One day he asked "if I had pluck enough to give an address, and repeat some of the yarns I had told him?" Of course I promised, and a goodly number attended. The following Sunday after prayers, read by the captain, a request came from the passengers that I should give a little account of the work in China. The captain had the decks prettily arranged with awning, acted as chairman, and kindly introduced me. There were about thirty present, and before separating they asked for another similar meeting. These little services, though unsought on our part, were gladly welcomed. One of the passengers, in conversation, said I had just described his case; he had once come to the point of almost deciding, "and went slowly back," and he seemed much concerned. Our Christian colonel gave two most interesting addresses on "The Tabernacle"; the captain, one or two officers, and a goodly number of the first-class passengers attending. The young ladies held meetings among the sailors, and two or three professed conversion.

We were sorry to leave our good friends at Colombo, for we could not help noting the change that had come over many of our fellow-passengers; dancing and noisy fun had been discarded, while a few sought conversation on spiritual things, though at first we had been avoided. The captain expressed his regret that he could not take us on to Shang-hai, and in this regret we all shared.

At Colombo on Christmas Day we transhipped to

the S.S. *Clyde*, where we were delayed four hours longer than we expected. We had said all our "good-byes," but the chief officer returned, as he said the temptation of another sight of us, and good-bye, was too great to withstand; he had been so much cheered and helped by our intercourse. As we passed the S.S. *Rohilla* and waived an adieu to our old friends, the sailors gave us three ringing cheers, and we felt rather like leaving home again.

We had a rough passage from Singapore, and reached Shang-hai on January 13, 1890, where we were lovingly welcomed by many old friends. Ten letters from different parts of China awaited me, full of tender sympathy; but the sorrow and loss pressed heavily on me, yet above all I could hear His whisper, "Like as a mother comforteth . . . so have I comforted you"; and it was blessed to feel able to say "My will is the will of my God," without even wishing that it should be otherwise. Miss Whitford, one of our party, desired, if possible, to work with us in Wenchow, and as Miss Judd, who had then charge of the girls' school, was alone, the way seemed opened for her, and Mr. Stevenson willingly consented, so she accompanied us.

We reached Wenchow in the morning of February 4th. As soon as we had anchored, I saw Mrs. S., of the Methodist Free Church, coming (Mr. S. was in the country); then Mr. and Mrs. G., and Miss J. of our own Mission; but the first to meet me were my two faithful servants. For many years they had served me with a devotion rarely met with in this country, and for a moment they seemed to forget their loss in the joy of seeing me again. All along the road the Christians were hurrying to bid me welcome, and by the time I had reached the house many others had gathered. The news seemed to fly, for by the next day some had come twenty miles to show their love. I know not how I got through the first two days; the sorrow of our dear people made my heart bleed afresh, and often as they went into the study, to see the large portrait of their beloved pastor, tears would flow as they sobbed, "It is himself, but he cannot speak to us." "If only he had come back to us for a few years longer," came from many lips. Dearly was he loved, and much missed by his people. "O God, give me all the wisdom and strength needed, to be a mother to this shepherdless flock," was my daily prayer. An extract from a letter of Miss Bardsley's will be interesting at this point:—

"I shall never forget the scene on our arrival. The native Christians had heard the whistle of our steamer, and surrounded Mrs. Stott at once, and when we got into the house a few minutes later we found the sitting-room half filled with them, many crying bitterly, Mrs. Stott sitting in the middle of them. It was most touching to see them take her hands and weep over them; this continued all the week. It was a heartbreaking week. The native Christians came in from all the country round, many of them walking ten and twenty miles; they all went into the study to see the life-size portrait of Mr. Stott, and at the sight burst into tears. You have no idea how they love and honour Mrs. Stott, and they are a nice lot of people too; you can see they are Christians by their faces."

Two days after our arrival, Mr. and Mrs. G. left for their own station, Bing-yie, about thirty-three miles south of us. Carpenters and bricklayers had soon to be called in, to repair the damage done by white ants, as part of the floors were quite eaten through, and the house needed to be cleaned throughout; but in three weeks we were in order again. The Christians were all eager for me to visit them, so beginning with the nearest places first, I went to a village seven miles distant from the city, to the house of a man who had been for years the only Christian in that place. My delight was great to find ten converts now, and nearly as many inquirers. After supper, twenty persons with Testaments and hymn-books gathered for evening service. I spoke from John iii., "God's love," and was followed by two of the converts, who gave such addresses as showed how they had grown in grace. In that village there are now twenty disciples, and a Bible reading has been conducted by one of the young ladies every Thursday afternoon. It takes her two hours to go and the same time to return, but it is labour well spent. This man who was at first and for years the only Christian, and who endured no small amount of persecution, has had the joy of seeing his wife, and wife's mother, his four children, two sisters-in-law, and a nephew all brought into the fold; indeed, one of the encouraging features of our work now is, that so many families are one in Christ Jesus, although years often elapse between the first and the last convert. I had with me a dear woman who has ever since been a very faithful and much-used Bible-woman. She with many others had been brought to the Lord during our absence.

The following Saturday, Miss Bardsley and I went to Dong-ling. The members there were most urgent for me to visit them, as many could not come to the city. We arrived about 6 p.m., the journey taking six hours, although only twenty miles distant; Mr. and Mrs. G., from Bing-yie, joined us. As the people knew I was coming they turned out in force, the chapel was crammed from end to end, many standing outside. This was the new chapel which had been rebuilt in place of the one burned during the riot in 1884, and seated about one hundred; but there were quite one hundred and fifty present at both meetings. I took the afternoon service, and with tears gave them the last message of their beloved pastor; they were all deeply affected.

It was at this time I began the homes for the blind men and old widows. We had in the church seven or eight blind men unable to work for themselves, and without sons to care for them : my heart was burdened week by week as I saw them led into the chapel, and I felt sure God would have me do something for their relief. There was one dear old saint about eighty, not blind, for whom I was especially anxious to provide, and when we got a little house for their accommodation this old man could hardly be persuaded to take sufficient food; when urged to take advantage of what had been provided he replied, " I could not get two meals a day before, why should I eat three now?" A few widows in similar circumstances were also housed in our compound, and for the support of this, as well as every other branch of the work, the Lord gave abundantly. Money goes further in China than in England; £4 10s. being ample to support a man or woman for a year.

From one cause or another, the few whom my husband had formed into a Volunteer Preachers' Band had been scattered; one had died, two had been made preachers, the others had lapsed; this branch, therefore, had to be re-organised. Villages were crying out for preachers; we had none to send, and I was averse to employing any but, as far as I could judge, "God-given men." I therefore appealed for volunteers, impressing upon the church members the responsibility

Group of Wenchow and Bing-yang Preachers, sixteen of whom are unpaid. Left hand, Mrs. Stott and Mr. Woodman ; right hand, Mr. Grierson, Mr. Menzies, and Mr. Hibbard.

of souls, and urged that as God had sent the gospel to them, "without money and without price," it was their privilege as well as duty to give it to others. I promised to defray travelling expenses of any who would freely give up the half of Saturday and the whole of Sunday to gospel work. Four responded to the first appeal, they were formed into a class, and districts given them. We had a meeting for prayer once a month, when they gave me their reports, mentioning any cases of interest that had occurred. As calls for teachers from other villages came, preachers were forthcoming, until now we have fourteen who freely give their time to the Lord on Sundays, while working at their trades and farms during the week.

We felt something must be done for the teaching of these men, as they were deprived of the Sunday services, and a few could hardly read, and thus draw the water of life for themselves—to them the well was deep. After much thought and prayer, we decided to invite them for a month's Bible study, during which time I offered them hospitality, but no remuneration. This invitation was gladly responded to. I gave up myself entirely to them during that month, and the advantage of two Bible classes daily were keenly appreciated; the intervening time they spent in learning to read better.

After the first year or two, being anxious to know how these men preached, I proposed that the afternoons should be devoted to this, that they should preach as though to a congregation, and allow the native pastor and myself to criticise, we explaining that our object was to help them to understand and handle the Word of Life. At first they were a little nervous, but before the classes closed they begged for another week in the autumn of such helpful teaching, so we have now five weeks in the year devoted entirely to their instruction. It would be interesting to add a few notes of some of their addresses.

Feb. 18.—In morning, Tsie spoke on Matthew iv. 18–22. These four fishers left all to follow Christ. We teach new believers that they must leave all lusts of flesh, &c. As to us older Christians : in fishing we use our own nets, but in catching men must leave our own nets, our own ways, wisdom, &c. Yet we must have a net, *i.e.*, the gospel. Glory, eternal glory, to be obtained by catching men. Fishermen sometimes have no work, so go off and do something else. Christ calls us to always be fishers of men (2 Tim. iv. 1, 2). We have proof that three of these disciples were truly faithful unto death. We must pray for those who are not going out preaching this year [two had just withdrawn]. Peter faltered and went back, but only for a short half-hour or so. If we are truly chosen of God, have received our office from Him, we must be careful not to go back. To catch men is harder than to catch fish. In fishing we fear cold and exposure; in catching men must fear coldness of heart. Even in fishing for men the disciple may be called upon to suffer cold, hunger, persecution, &c. Peter, James, and John followed Christ most closely, and were most dearly beloved, and yet they suffered most. Their one desire was to "catch men"; snow, rain, cold, nothing prevented them. If father or master tells son to go out and fish in the evening, on return first question will be, "How many fish have you caught?" Even though there is not a word of fault-finding at the few caught, that son or servant will be ashamed. To catch men is most difficult, because we have to get to their inner heart. Have to use different nets to catch different kinds of fish.

O-dzing Ah-lie spoke on Matthew v. 1–7. He was very nervous at first, but gained more confidence later on :—The "poor in spirit" in Chinese is *Shu-sang* ("shu" means empty), so it is only when we come to God as beggars, realising we have no goodness, no merit of our own, that He will be willing to receive and bless us. Example, the prayer of the Pharisee and publican.

"They who mourn"—mourn for their own sins, the sins of their relations, friends, and others unconverted. Example: Mary weeping at the Lord's feet, mourning her sins, and how He comforted her. 'The meek," not only those who treat their friends well, but those who when ill-treated bear no grudge and do not get angry; they will be blessed. Example: the contention between the herdsmen of Abraham and Lot. Abraham willing to divide off and let Lot have choice of land: that was true meekness. Abraham's descendants received Canaan, but we shall receive an incorruptible inheritance. After a long journey over mountains, how good a drink of water tastes, and how we enjoy our food. We should have just such a hunger after hearing the word of God, and after righteousness. God has promised to fill.

Feb. 25.—Chung-dzi spoke on that subject which is unfortunately so fruitful to the Chinese mind in similes and symbols, the Good Samaritan. . . . Jerusalem—heaven, Jericho—earth. Our soul originally comes from heaven; when we are born into this earth we suffer from soul's enemy, sin, &c., robbers. Clothes—our good deeds. Priest—Jewish priests, or Confucianists, Taoists, vegetarians, &c., nowadays, or Roman Catholics, who say they forgive sins, but cannot heal our souls. Levite—those who teach law; it cannot save our souls. Samaritan—Christ, who saw us injured and half-dead as result of sin, and had pity. Oil—Holy Spirit; if we haven't Him to open our hearts, we will not recognise God or Christ. Wine—Christ's blood. Beast—Christ's grace; if we haven't this we will never be able to get along on the heavenly road. Inn—chapel; there we get food and help in various ways. Innkeeper—pastor.

Pastor Tsie in commenting on the above, spoke of how, in interpreting parables, we must keep to the point of what Christ originally meant to teach by it. For example, here Christ gave the parable because of the scribe's question, "Who is my friend?" Besides this meaning we may afterwards get other meanings, as Chung-dzi did. Jesus—our conscience. If we all acted according to our conscience we would meet no trouble or danger. Leaving our conscience we "go down." When the Samaritan came along the man was unconscious; so were we when Christ came to save us.

Feb. 26. — Tsing-kwai spoke on Matthew xv. 21–29, well and to the point: lessons of faith, unceasing prayer, humility. In the afternoon, Koe-yi [Nga-yue's husband] on Hebrews v. 11, &c.: Melchisedec a priest (Heb. vii. 3), God alone is without father, &c. (v. 12). An apprentice learns three years or so, afterwards becomes workman; first is given easy things to do. Though he spoke very shortly it was to the point, and on the whole good. He is evidently profiting by his wife's knowledge of the Scriptures.

Another day—the 5th, I think—the pastor spoke on the best ways of preaching the gospel, taking as examples Christ and the apostles. Christ fitted His preaching to the kind of listeners He had. To the Samaritan woman he spoke in one way, suitable to her occupation of drawing water. To the country people who came to hear He spoke of the sower, mustard-tree, &c. To the Pharisees, &c., He used the Old Testament and Law (Luke iv. 16–22). To His disciples He preached the mysteries of God's Word and kingdom.

The pastor certainly has the gift of teaching, and also is a thorough critic. These meetings were really quite helpful to us foreigners as well as the natives, and often created subjects for discussion and pretty deep thought.

We had all this year (1890) in our compound the poor persecuted people from O-dzing to feed and care for, as the magistrates refused to allow them to return until the case was finished. One family consisted of father, mother, two sons, the wife, and only child of the eldest (the betrothed wife of the younger son had returned to her home, but her parents fearing they might be implicated sent her back, so she, too, made her way to the city, and they were married at once). Three of this family, who were only enquirers before, came out decidedly on the Lord's side, and after some months of testing were baptized. The poor little baby sickened and died, but though they all felt the Lord's hand was heavy upon them, their faith failed not, giving glory to God. They gained much Bible knowledge during the year, indeed it was wonderful the progress they made; daily at morning prayers their faces fairly beamed. The Lord was preparing them, during this long waiting, for service in their own village by and by, and they were thus better fitted to be teachers of others. The second son is now one of our most devoted unpaid preachers. Every Sunday morning he starts about 4 a.m. for a village ten miles from his home, where he conducts two services, returning in the evening.

During the time of weary waiting, many were discouraged and disappointed that we had not more power in compelling the magistrates to bring about a settlement. Our hope and help were in God alone, and we decided to spend three mornings in prayer. One of the meetings has been described by Miss B. in a letter to her friends, from which I give extracts:—

"*June* 24, 1890. — It was decided to meet Saturday, Sunday, and Monday forenoon, June 21st, as on those dates we expected many of the Christians from the country districts, who come in once a month to remember the Lord's death. We had had continuous rain for some days, and by Saturday the roads were flooded, and it was impossible for many to get in. The first meeting was at 10 a.m. Saturday; there were about thirty present. After the opening prayer the pastor read the parable of the unjust judge, and said that God did not answer prayer simply to be rid of people's prayers, for He has their good at heart, &c. He afterwards said that there were many passages in both Old and New Testaments proving that God heard and answered prayer; had they ever experienced any answers to their prayers? At once one of the blind men said: 'Three or four years ago, when I was a young Christian and knew little of God, I was much tried about my son, who had become careless and idle in his habits, had left his work, and nothing I said seemed to influence him. I took the matter to God, told Him I was helpless and ignorant, not knowing how to pray aright. I told Him how disobedient my son was, and asked Him to influence his heart and make him go to work again. My son had gone out in the morning and I did not know where he had gone to; but just after I had prayed, a neighbour came in and told me my son had gone to his work. Thus the Lord heard and answered while I was praying.'

"The preacher then asked if any one had anything else to say, and another of the blind men began: 'You all know I was an opium-smoker before I trusted in Jesus. I knew I could not be a follower of Christ and smoke opium. I prayed God to give me strength to break it off. It was a hard struggle, for I had smoked for twelve or fourteen years. The first day in the morning, the desire for opium came upon me. I had decided not to take any medicine, but trust in the Lord, so I knelt down and prayed. I told the Lord how bad I felt and how the desire for the opium was tormenting me, and how helpless and weak I was. While I prayed the desire left me, but about mid-day it came back again, and again I resorted to prayer, and was relieved. And so for three days, three times a day, the desire returned, and was each time relieved by prayer alone. *Then I got the final victory, and have never had any desire for the drug since.*'

"The pastor then gave his experience, and told a truly remarkable story. He said, 'Some years ago, when I was at the station of Bing-yie preaching, the little chapel was crowded. Amongst the audience was a man making a great noise, talking incessantly, so that I could not get the attention of the people. I asked him to be quiet, but the people answered, " It is no use talking to him, he has been out of his mind for some years." The man continued noisy, so, not knowing what to do, fearing to turn him out, I lifted my heart to the Lord for strength. Pointing with my finger at the man, I said with a loud voice, " In the name of Jesus Christ of Nazareth, come out of him." The man sat down quietly, shut his eyes as if asleep, and I continued preaching. By and by I told the people I was going to pray to the God of heaven, and asked them to kneel down with me. The man who had been possessed knelt down with them, and after prayer came up to me, and in a quiet voice said, " Many thanks, many thanks. I have been out of my mind for ten years ; now I feel quite well ; I will go home to my friends and to my work." ' The pastor added, ' I do not know where he is now ; he did not attend the chapel nor become a Christian, but some months afterwards I heard he was still in his right mind and at his work.' He told this story to show what power there still is in the very name of Jesus. The meeting closed after six or seven had prayed.

"The second meeting was held at three o'clock in the afternoon. The passage read was Peter in prison, and the church praying all night in the house of John, and as they prayed Peter was released by a miracle. After that the pastor asked if there were any more testimonies to answered prayer. The elder of the O-dzing women who was so cruelly beaten, ill-used, and driven from her home, said, ' I have got something to tell.' She looked as though she had too ; her face beamed with joy. She has a beautiful expression ; I wish you could see it as, morning by morning, she drinks in the words when Mrs. Stott is explaining the Scriptures. I love to watch her, and to think of the bright smile of welcome and the 'Well done' that is awaiting her from the Lord she loves so well and has suffered so much for. She said, 'It was only the beginning of last year that the gospel reached our village, and after I had believed I wanted to have preaching on Sundays, that the neighbours, too, might know of the love of Christ. My house is very small, and there is a family in the village who had a nice large room that I thought just the thing for preaching in. I began to pray that God would save that household, and turn the guest hall into a preaching hall. I continued praying two months, and at the end of that time all were brought to the Lord'—she did not say how many persons were in the family—'and the room was given up as a preaching hall.' It was very touching to hear this woman praying for the persecutors by name, and in tears pleading that they might all become followers of the Lord Jesus, for the women as well as the men took part in prayer in these meetings. Time forbids me to go into details of all these meetings—they were very blessed times, as one after another poured out their hearts to God, several with tears. God grant they may be the means of much blessing in the future. The case of persecution is not yet settled, though the magistrate has himself been in the place, and we are hoping that something will be done soon.

"The pastor is now preaching every evening in the Street Chapel at the Blind Men's Home. He has had large crowds; as the novelty wears off the numbers will decrease; but those who are really interested in the truth will continue going. Will you join us in prayer that many may pass from 'death into life' in that room, that God may thereby be glorified."

CHAPTER XIV

"And both Jesus was called, and His disciples, to the marriage."—
JOHN ii. 2.

ABOUT this time one of our school-girls was married; they had waited my arrival, and as it was the first Christian marriage Miss B. had ever witnessed in China, she gives the following interesting description :—

"There was a wedding here yesterday of more than usual interest, for it was a real love affair, which is not often the case in China, where, as a rule, the young people do not see one another until after marriage. The engagement is contracted by the parents when the children are both little, and the poor girl never has any voice in the matter. On the wedding day she is taken to her husband's home to live with his parents, whom she has probably never seen before. The bride was one of the school-girls, a fine girl and an earnest Christian; the bridegroom was brought up in Mr. Stott's school with his elder brother, and when old enough, Mr. Stott apprenticed them to a tailor to learn that trade. They have both been diligent, and have now a good business of their own and a nice house too, so the bride will have every comfort, though she does not go to a home of her own exactly, for his mother, two brothers, and their wives live there; but as that is the custom in this land, I suppose they will not mind it as much as we should.

"This young man came to Mrs. Stott five years ago to ask her to give him a wife, and said he wanted Vong-yang (the one he has married). Mrs. Stott told him she was much too young, and she could not think of it. He was not a Christian, and that was the great barrier, for Vong-yang was; but she did not give that as her reason, or he would have soon become one in name, and that was what she wished to avoid; there is far too much of a nominal Christianity in England for her to wish to see it here. About two years after he came again to Mrs. Stott, saying his brother was very anxious for him to marry, and that if she would only promise him Vong-yang he would wait for her, and his brother would be satisfied. She told him that though she would not promise him this girl, if on her return to China (she was just about to leave for England) she heard a good report of him, she would give him a wife.

"I ought to have told you that before this he found some means of communicating with the girl, and told her he would wait for her, and never marry any one else, begging her to refuse to marry any one who should ask for her. The school-girls have a great advantage over all other Chinese girls; when a young man asks for one she is always told of it, and allowed to decide for herself whether she would like to marry him or not. During Mrs. Stott's absence the young man came out boldly on the Lord's side, and was baptized by Mr. G., and when he again asked for a wife he was not refused, and we all rejoiced at the prospect of their happiness. The preparations began a few days since, and as the marriage took place here, I have been able to watch the proceedings.

"The room where the ceremony was performed was draped with scarlet, that being the bridal colour, and the ceiling hung with all sorts and shapes of lamps, and very pretty they looked when lighted. Some of the chairs had scarlet covers, and cushions beautifully embroidered with gold; I have never seen such lovely work. All these things were hired, with the dresses of the bride and bridegroom; this is the custom here, as the clothes are never worn on any other occasion. Our cook gave up his room, for after the marriage they did not go away, but stayed here. The ceremony took place at 7 p.m., and Mr. S. was asked to conduct the service. When we went in, we found the friends assembled; the bridegroom standing on a scarlet blanket, awaiting his bride. His dress was not very nice—to me it looked very like a dressing-gown; he looked much nicer the next morning in a maroon silk top garment; he wore a mandarin's hat, that is round, with a red tassel on the top.

"In a few minutes there was a slight stir amongst the people, and some one whispered, 'She is coming.' I looked in the direction of the movement, and saw 'something' being led in by two women, which turned out to be the bride; it was certainly necessary to lead her, for she could not see where she was going. I will describe the dress, beginning at the feet: scarlet satin shoes, beautifully embroidered entirely by herself; a bright green satin skirt, embroidered with gold; a scarlet satin top garment, also embroidered with gold, with nuts and fruit sewn on; on the head a sort of helmet, very large and heavy, set with green stones and figures of men and women all over it; at each side a sort of wing projecting, set with stones; and all over this a scarlet silk veil, so that the face was quite hidden. You would never have known there was a human being inside. She was led on to the scarlet blanket, and her attendant held her while we sang the marriage hymn. I will give you a literal translation of it; it will show you the idiom as well as give you an idea of the hymn; we sang it to the tune 'Duke Street.'

"'This day assembled, all, pleased,
According to God's holy command, righteous act of marriage,
Bridegroom, bride, two men made one,
One home, one body, one heart, one mind.

> Like this, during life, together walk one road,
> Mutual honour, mutual faith, mutual love, mutual help,
> > Heavenly Father, constantly protect and give peace,
> > Not have calamity, weariness, suffering.
> > Beseech heavenly Father, give happiness in the home,
> > > Give this couple happiness and joy,
> > Obtain influence of Holy Spirit, to love the Saviour,
> > > During life, turn their heart to serve heavenly Father.
> > Beseech heavenly Father, grant our prayer,
> > > Give this husband, wife, one pair till old age,
> Happiness together receive, suffering together endure,
> > Death after, two men together in heaven.'

The hymn being sung, the preacher prayed, then Mr. S. gave them a little exhortation, then another hymn and prayer, and the ceremony was over. The bride was taken to her room, which was close by, the bridegroom followed, and no more was seen of them that night. The bridegroom gave a feast to the men that evening, and the next day at 1 p.m. was the women's feast, to which we were all invited. When the meal was quite ready we were called, and had first to go and see the bride, who was sitting on her handsome wooden bedstead with another dress on, scarlet figured satin, trimmed with black satin. We each took a cup of tea (without sugar and milk, in real Chinese cups), after having drunk which, we made for the well-spread tables. There were three, but we foreigners had one to ourselves, and, during the first part of the time, the bride sat with us but did not eat anything; it is the proper thing for her to hang down her head and look miserable. The bride's attendant sat with us and saw that we did justice to all the good things. There were special dishes prepared for us, and very good they were too. Let me try and describe the table—ours was set for seven people. There was no cloth on; each had red chopsticks and a pewter ladle, a wee pewter wine-cup and plate, like dolls' things for size. There were twelve dishes in pyramid form, fancy meats, &c. There were four little bowls of vinegar and sauces, and by the side of each person a plate of monkey-nuts, shelled and roasted, and water-melon seeds also roasted. After taking all this in, I turned my attention to the other guests and found we were most improper, for we had gone to the seats given to us quite willingly, and at once; these other people had to be dragged to their seats, and made quite a little fuss about it, and that is the proper thing in China.

"At last we were settled, and Mrs. Stott was invited to ask the Lord's blessing; after which the first dish was brought in, placed in the centre of the table, and the attendant asked us to eat. We all with our chop-sticks made a dive into the dish and conveyed the captured piece of fowl to our mouths. It was great fun. We used our ladles for the gravy. There were thirteen dishes brought in, one after the other, and we were expected to eat of each kind, and in just the same way. The last few were sweet dishes, and they gave us each a piece of folded paper to wipe the table in front of us with, and one little bowl of water to wash our spoons in. We had still those twelve fruit dishes to eat from, but several remained untouched at the last. After all that, came bowls of rice and five or six other little dishes; it did seem too much, but I ate a little and then we were at liberty to go. We had been sitting there two hours and a quarter. During the meal the bridegroom's brother came several times and told us they had nothing for us to eat—that is their way of being polite, I suppose. As we were leaving, we were each presented with a box of cakes and two parcels containing the things we had left at the feast.

"I ought to have told you that all that morning the bride sat on her bed, with her attendant by her side; she was dressed in her wedding dress, with the heavy ugly helmet on, and the red veil over it, and she has to receive the visits of all who wished to see her, and hear their remarks about herself, or anything else they liked to say. To all who went were given nuts and fruit. The bridegroom came to us, bowed low three times, and so did we, saying, 'I congratulate you'; he replying, 'I have troubled you.'

"In the evening about seven o'clock, after a short service, the bride was taken to her husband's house, where he had gone before to be in waiting. I expected he would have taken her, but was told such a thing is never done in China: the husband never goes out with his wife; he may sometimes with his mother, but not his wife, and they do not eat together. Oh, how different it is in our own dear England. A wife has no name in China; she loses it on her marriage and is always called So-and-so's wife, or, if she has a son, the mother of So-and-so.

"We went to call on the bride this afternoon, for, poor thing, she has to be dressed up for some days after her marriage and, sitting on the side of her bed, receive visits from all who want to see her. She has a very nice room—we admired it all and took a cup of tea and cake, then a bowl of rice-flour balls in sweetened water. They tasted to me like flour and water boiled. After that we had another cup of tea, and rose to leave. I was sorry for the poor girl; at the sight of us she began to cry, and turned her face to the wall; her husband's relatives were much distressed lest we should think they were unkind to her; but she has been brought up in the school since she was a little thing, and it has been a happier home than she could ever have known elsewhere, and of course she felt leaving it. Mrs. Stott, and lately Miss Judd, have been like a mother to her; she is a very nice girl and a fine Christian; she is now in a home where she and her husband are alone in serving the Lord, and I want to ask your prayers for them. They will find many difficulties, but if kept faithful and near to the Lord they may be the means of leading others to a knowledge of the truth.

"It is no easy thing to be a Christian in this dark land where Satan has so much power; Christians at home know very little of what it is to really suffer for Christ's sake, and they have so much to help them onward, but these people have everything to drag them back and hinder. God is for them, and His power can keep them. Will you join us in prayer for all the native Christians that they may live Christ, and show by their lives that Christ does change them, and that they may go about more amongst their own people telling the good news of a Saviour's love?"

Six years have passed since then, and it is beautiful to see the love between these two; together they come to the chapel with their little child, and both have grown in "the grace and knowledge of our Lord Jesus Christ," though as yet no other members of the family have been converted.

How often we are called to "rejoice with those who rejoice, and weep with those who weep"! In May Miss Judd and I went to Shang-hai to attend the general Missionary Conference; there we met Miss Boyd, who had just arrived from her station at Kiu-chau. She had come with the hope of attending the meetings and finding refreshment of spirit as well as body; but the very first day after her arrival she was asked to go to Bing-yie to nurse Mrs. G.; there was no one else to send, and, with that noble unselfishness which characterised her, she decided to go, and left at once. The G.'s were then living in an unhealthy native house.

The weather became unbearably hot, and one day in the beginning of July we had a letter to say that Misses Boyd and Britton, with Mrs. G., had fever. Miss Whitford kindly offered to go to their help, to send Miss Britton and little Olive here while she remained to look after the other invalids. This step was of God, for the day after Miss W. arrived there, Miss Boyd was so ill they feared she might not get through the night. I had sent all the little delicacies I had, which proved a boon, but Miss B. continued to grow worse, and fearing if they remained there she and perhaps Mrs. G. too might die, they decided to run the risk of the journey (fourteen hours on the boat) as the lesser of two evils.

On the morning of July the 8th they arrived. Mrs. S. kindly received Mr. and Mrs. G., while Misses B. and W. came here. Miss Boyd was very low indeed, but we hoped that our cool, healthy house, with careful nursing, and doctor's skill, might save her. In spite of all efforts, however, the fever raged night and day, until the 13th, when she seemed decidedly better; the fever was gone, and she slept a little, which she had not done for several days and nights. In the morning I was able, for the first time, to send a favourable report to the doctor, but alas! it was only a flicker: at 10 a.m. the fever returned, and she became unconscious and remained so until 5 p.m., when she quietly fell asleep in Jesus. The other invalids recovered, and were able to go by steamer to Che-foo for the change they much needed.

During this summer and autumn we had much sorrow and loss, four of our native Christians died in one week, but we had comfort in them all. Miss J., who had charge of the girls' school, often ailing, now became seriously ill, and had to leave for England. Miss W. took charge of the girls' school, and although she had made very good progress with the language in the time, she was not able to talk much, so the school was practically thrown on my hands again, she doing the work, however, under my superintendence. But during all this time of persecution, sickness, death, and sorrow, wisdom and strength were given day by day. God had put me in that place of responsibility: 'the work was His," "I was His"; so "all was well," and it was sweet to feel His hand underneath, and His strength made perfect in weakness; without this strength, heart and flesh would often fail.

In the very midst of our own sorrows the steamer came in bringing heavy tidings—four dear missionaries (not of our Mission, but all known to me) died in one week, and six of our own were dangerously ill; these are times when one proves the power of God, and feels it all-sufficient. Joy blended with sorrow, as it usually does, for it is seldom our Father asks us to drink an unmingled cup—five persons, decidedly converted, were baptized and received into the church at this time.

A few notes taken down at the examination of these candidates will give an idea not only of the people, but of the kind of questions and answers asked, and given. They were all country people, three women and two boys, and came in a few days earlier to enable the pastor and myself to know them better; the youngest of the women was nineteen, and had been a professed Christian about three years, her father and brother also being Christians, and all who knew her spoke well of her consistent life. The other women were aged respectively sixty-eight and seventy, the eldest was blind, and her remarks about the Lord Jesus loving such helpless ones were most touching; she was a widow and childless, living with a nephew, who was not at all kind to her. On Saturday afternoon I sent for her to have a little talk, and on coming into the room she knelt to pray, not knowing any one was there. She thanked God that He loved blind people, it made her very happy, &c., and thanked Him for saving her through the blood of Jesus. I asked her when she heard the gospel first; she replied, "Last year, in the eight month, I heard God would receive the blind, and lame, and no one else wanted them." Q. Are you a sinner? A. I have committed many sins, but now all are gone. Q. How? A. Jesus washed them away in His own blood. Q. What induced Him to shed His blood? A. Because He loved us, and wanted to take us to heaven. Q. Supposing God were to call you away to-night, where would your soul go to? A. To heaven. Q. Why? A. Because Jesus saved me. Q. But you have not been baptized, and the Scriptures say, "Whosoever believeth and is baptized shall be saved." A. Baptism is by water; water can wash my body but not my soul. Q. Then of what use is it? A. It is a sign. Q. Of what? Here she did not know what to say, and I explained the true significance of the ordinance. She was examined in the chapel in the evening, but I need not give the answers here, though they were equally clear, and quite different from the above. The boys, fourteen and sixteen years of age, were examined by the native pastor: they were both bright lads and their answers pleased us much. Q. When did you first believe? A. Last year, the ninth month. Q. What is the Lord Jesus to you? A. He is my Saviour. Q. Where does God live? A. In my heart. Q. Where besides? A. In heaven. Q. By what means did Christ save you? A. He died on Calvary's Cross for me. Q. And after that what did He do? A. He rose again the third day. Q. What is it to believe on the Lord Jesus? A. It is to be a new creature. Q. Are you a new creature? A. Yes. Q.

What evidence do you give of that? A. I used to curse, and swear, and quarrel with the other boys; I don't do that now. Q. Suppose you were to die to-night, before you were baptized, where would your soul go to? A. To heaven. Q. Will baptism save you? A. No. Q. What is the use of it? A. To show that I have been saved. Q. Could you get to heaven by your own merit? A. I have no merit. Q. You are young and may have to endure much persecution for Christ's sake, what then? A. I will endure it. Q. But suppose the devil comes and tempts you to say and do wrong things, and tells you it is no use to depend on Christ for help, what then? A. I would pray and ask God to hold me up.

I thought such answers were grand from a boy of fourteen, who had never, until last year, heard the gospel message. We kept this lad a few weeks in order to give him further instruction in the Scriptures, and Miss B. taught him the Roman Colloquial along with the others (Mr. Soothill, of the Methodist Free Church, has translated the four Gospels and the Acts into the local dialect, and our young ladies have taught quite a number to use them).

Sunday morning the chapel was crowded, the country Christians having come in, to remember the Lord's death; the five were baptized before the usual service began, and it was a heart-stirring sight to see these poor women, just on the brink of the grave, confessing the Lord Jesus, after spending so many years in ignorance of Him, and the three young ones just beginning to serve Him; again we realised that "the gospel is the power of God unto salvation to every one who believeth." Nothing touches the heart like the story of the Cross; often have I noticed when we have been speaking of such subjects as "the blood," "the burnt-offering," &c., the tears of the women have fallen as we dwelt on the sufferings of Christ.

At this time we began the first of our united quarterly meetings of preachers, which continued two or three years. We met alternately at Mr. S.'s house and our own, and at the first meeting no fewer than twenty-six were present, though none of the Bing-yie or Dong-ling preachers were there. Much of the time was spent in prayer, and nearly all referred to the time, over twenty years ago, when Mr. Stott, a solitary worker, came among them, and none knew of God's love; and as we looked at those earnest faces and thought of them as preachers, again and again the tears would start, and the language of our hearts was "What hath God wrought." Mr. S. opened with an address, using as his text, "And without a parable spoke He not unto them," urging them to be simple, pointed, and short in their preaching; always to prepare carefully with prayer, and never to allow the thought that they had not time for that. He also spoke on 1 Cor. xi. 23-33, after which we all had dinner *à la Chinois*, the men in one room, the women in another. In the afternoon I spoke on Rom. xii. 1-2, first, "Present your bodies," &c.; second, Sanctified and sent (John xvii. 16-18); third, Communion and Testimony (John xv. 27; Acts iv. 13); fourth, Love to Christ before Service (John xxi. 15-17); fifth, Enlightened, therefore giving Light (2 Cor. xiii. 14); after more prayer, and further remarks by the preachers, we separated, all feeling we had spent a good day.

CHAPTER XV

" And the common people heard Him gladly."—MARK xii. 37.

EARLY in October, I went to Tung-tso, when I was accompanied by Miss Bardsley; I give you her description of the ten days spent there :—

"*October 2nd.*—We left Wenchow on our first country journey of the season. Our party consisted of two Christian boatmen, a native constable, an earnest inquirer, who will accompany us all the way, one of the young preachers, and our Christian cook. The first evening we went but a short distance, only crossing the river, which is over two miles wide, to the constable's village, where there are some inquirers and Christians. After taking our evening meal on the boat, we made our way to the constable's house, escorted by most of the village, to hold a service. We sat outside the house, and the people gathered round at once, some standing on forms and stools to get a better look at us. The young preacher, Chang-loa, spoke first. We had some books and tracts to sell, and he told a little about them, reading and explaining part of one, and after that Mrs. Stott spoke; the attention of the people was very nice; most of them answered the questions put most intelligently, showing they not only heard, but understood a good deal of what was said; then Chang-loa spoke again. The Christians present very much wanted us to have a service for them, but the crush of people made it impossible; when we went into the house they all followed, and Chinese etiquette forbade their being turned out; however, when we returned to the boat we were able to have a Bible reading with them and the inquirers. We slept on the boat, or rather we had intended to do so, but the rats kept us awake through their midnight gambols; fortunately we had our mosquito curtains with us, so they were unable to touch us. A preacher goes to this village every other Sunday.

"*October 3rd, Friday.*—We were unable to go ashore again on account of the tide, but had another Bible-reading on board. After that we set off, and the next calling place was at the hut of some Christians, who were once beggars. After their conversion, many years ago, Mr. and Mrs. Stott helped them to get a few tools, and they built a hut on a hill, and began to till a little ground; the original hut is now used as a chapel, and they have built themselves another house. After visiting them, we had a delightful four miles' walk through the rice-fields; it was a glorious day, the sun not too hot and a nice breeze blowing from the sea; on the one side of us were mountains as far as the eye could reach, and on the other the river flowing, mountains rising straight out of it in some parts. About two o'clock we reached a village where there are three Christians, and went there, hoping to hold services; but the people are a very rough lot, and though Mrs. S. and the preacher both tried to gain their attention, no one listened, and after visiting two houses, we left for the boat again. On account of the tide we were obliged to remain where we were till midnight, and had to be content with a short service on the boat again.

"*Saturday.*—On wakening, we found ourselves at Soa-diu, the end of our boat journey; and after an early breakfast and prayers, we set off at 7 a.m. for Tung-t'sö. I will try to describe our party: It was all so new and strange to me, and I want to give you some little idea of it now, as the novelty will have worn off before the next time. We had half a day's journey before us, across hills and rivers; we had one chair between us, and Mrs. S. started in it, we deciding to walk an hour and ride an hour alternately. Then there was the man with our bedding; we had a wadded thing as a mattress, two rugs, pillows, &c., these were fastened up in a Chinese mat, and put on one end of the bamboo-pole, at the other the cook's and the men's bedding were hung; this the man carried across his shoulders; after him came another man with a variety of packages, such as our rice-bag, basket with the food, one containing three fowls, and other parcels varying in size and shape; our cook came next, then the constable, preacher, and myself. It was a funny sight, so different from our mode of travelling at home. I hardly know how to describe the scenery, it was so grand; we both said we never saw anything like it. A cloudless sky of the deepest blue, mountains of all shapes surrounding us, some were bold and bare, others covered with the lovely dark green and light bamboo, some almost perpendicular and went to a point, others again were rounded, but all were grand. The river, too, was of the clearest crystal; once we stooped down to drink of its fresh waters, flowing from the hills; it winds in and out between the hills for many miles, and as we took shorter cuts we had to cross it four times. Being so entirely surrounded by hills all the way, we wondered how we could get out, and no sooner did we leave the one valley than we were in another; it was too grand to describe; we so often wish our friends could share it with us.

"We reached our journey's end, about 12 a.m., tired and hungry. In a few minutes we were surrounded by most of the village; being the first foreign ladies they have ever seen, of course we were great wonders.

"Bonney Corner," three minutes' walk from our Mission House.

We were hot, and longing to wash our hands and face, and on asking for water we had about a pint of hot water at the bottom of a bowl handed us, with a filthy face-cloth, which we politely declined, having our own with us. The Chinese process is to put your face-cloth, which by the way ought to be dirty to be proper, into the hot water, squeeze it out, and rub your face and hands—that is all, no need to dry it; such a thing is unheard of in China. We had to perform this in the presence of about one hundred people, then took our seats to be again inspected. Our dresses, boots, &c., were all touched and discussed; our eyes and hair, &c. This we endured until our dinner was ready, then went into the bedroom to partake of it.

"While we are having dinner you shall have a peep at the room. A mud floor with holes all over, in one corner a heap of stones reaching one-third of the distance to the roof; the partition boards on that side were supported by stones, between most of which you can put your hand, not one board fits its neighbour. The boards over our heads reach a little more than half across the room where the hay is kept, on the other side of the room is an open straw shed, where we can see the sky quite plainly, and as we eat our dinner boys and others have climbed up on the straw, and from all parts of the room are looking down on us. In one corner is an old truck with planks laid across for a bed, having a straw mat, the ends of which rolled up make a pillow, and the broken chair is the only other piece of furniture of which the room can boast. My first thought was 'a grand place for rats,' which experience has proved true; the boards are all thick with dirt, and dust is everywhere. Fortunately we are using basins and chopsticks, or the people would be more curious. We wanted to rest after dinner, but had to lie down with the gaze of many on us; they were even on the loft over our heads.

We had a service in the afternoon, Mrs. Stott, the young preacher, and his father, who is the preacher in this district, all speaking; after that we escaped to the hill for a little quiet, but were followed by quite a crowd. There was another service in the evening; the room was crowded, and probably all the village turned out. They listened very attentively as again the gospel was preached in all its fulness.

"*Sunday.*—Another glorious day; the air here is so pure and sweet. As we sat on the hill after breakfast for a little quiet time, our hearts rose in praise and thankfulness to God for being permitted to enjoy His handiwork in this quiet spot. The scene around us was one of unequalled beauty, and in the valley at our feet lay the village, looking so peaceful and picturesque; but oh, how full of sin and misery! and yet there are a few in it who know what it is to be born of the Spirit, and have the Spirit of God dwelling in them. On returning we had the service, and Mrs. S. had an interesting talk with an old woman of eighty-one years of age; she said, 'Oh, will you take me with you to heaven?' Mrs. S. replied, 'The Lord Jesus only can do that.' She answered, 'Well, I ask Him every day to wash me in His blood.' 'Has He done it?' 'I don't know, but it is the one thing I desire, and the one thing I pray for, and if you will only ask Him, He will hear you, for you are acquainted with Him.' The afternoon service began about 1 p.m.; the same persons spoke, one after the other, and when it was over, we escaped to the hill, and had three hours together there. It was a delightful rest after all the noise below. We climbed to the top of one of the hills and feasted our eyes on all the beauty around us; there, alone, we had a quiet time of prayer, and sang that hymn, 'How sweet the name of Jesus sounds.' May the Lord hasten the day when every valley and hill will resound with that precious name!

"In the evening the people would not go, begging Mrs. S. to speak again, saying her words were good. They understood every word, but she had used her voice so much that it failed her, and the old preacher, Mr. Pöe, spoke a long time; thus they heard the gospel three times, from three different persons each time. 'Paul may plant, and Apollos may water, but

God alone can give the increase.' Please pray with us that much fruit may be the result.

"*Monday.*—Mrs. Stott has been seeing candidates for baptism this morning while I write this. The three women she saw are all trusting Jesus, they say, but don't know whether they are saved. They will have to wait some time yet, and receive more instruction; these poor people are so very ignorant, they have everything to learn—we can have no idea of their darkness.

"After writing the above we went to the hill for an hour, coming back to dinner at 11 a.m. At 11.30 we all went to a village an hour's walk from here; it is beautifully situated between the hills. The people round the district followed us into the house of the Christian, and there the gospel was preached by Mrs. S. and the two preachers. The people took down doors and windows, and stood in all corners of the guest hall; there would be over a hundred present. Although I could not speak, I had to stand on a chair to be looked at; it was quite a new experience. Five women standing near us listened most attentively, as did others, but many in the crowd were too much occupied with us to listen much. It is very natural, for we are the strangest sights they have ever seen. I don't know what they think of us, but one person said to another that we were barbarians.

"One of the women who listened so attentively,

her face continually changing, led us to her house. We were followed by the crowd, and again they heard the gospel three times. The same woman then took us to the large ancestral hall belonging to the whole village, and from the theatre stage the gospel was preached By this time there would be quite three hundred people, and most of them listened very attentively, and at the close bought all the books we had with us. One little incident amused me rather. A man handed a dirty pewter teapot full of hot tea on to the stage, and we all took a drink from the spout; after we had drunk, it was handed to several in the crowd. We had been five hours out in the hot sun, noise, and excitement, and on our return we again escaped to the hills, returning again at 6 p.m. for supper, refreshed and ready for the evening service. I gave the little boys another lesson on the Romanised, which I had begun to teach them in Wenchow, and then we had the service. The room was full, and the people most attentive and very quiet. The preachers were all hoarse by the close, and tired out. We feel sure there will be blessing from these meetings, and all who are interested will be able to receive further instruction from Mr. Pöe. After we had retired to our room the Christians had a prayer-meeting; we counted twelve different prayers, several of which came from the lads, of whom there are said to be nine in this district who believe.

"*Tuesday.*—Soon after 11 a.m. we started for other villages, and after walking one hour and three-quarters arrived at the furthest, taking the nearer ones on our return. Again the good news was proclaimed at five different places, but the last was the most interesting of all. When Mrs. S. rose to speak, she asked the people to be as quiet as possible, as her voice was weakened by so much out-door speaking. They listened so quietly, and were so interested, that she was encouraged to give them quite a long explanation of the gospel. We were altogether six hours and a half out, and had hardly time to take our supper when the people arrived for the evening service, after which there was another prayer-meeting by the native Christians.

"*Wednesday.*—We left Tung-t'sö at 7.30 a.m., intending to stop at two or three villages on our way to Söa-diu, where our boat was waiting for us. The return journey, though different, was through lovely country. The first part of the way took us over a very high mountain path, where we had an extensive view; on the way down we met the woman to whose house we were going, and as she was the only Christian in the village and was unable to turn back with us, we decided to leave that visit to another time and push on to the house of an inquirer. There we had a very quiet and attentive crowd; Mrs. Stott spoke for a long time, and the young preacher spoke twice; his father, Mr. Pöe, had decided to stay the night there and give the people more instruction. The mother is the only one who seems interested in the truth, and she has not got very far, for the incense-pots were in their place, and in the bedroom (where we had dinner) there was a horrible-looking idol. About 1 p.m. we all set off once more, and reached Söa-diu about 3 p.m. The boatmen worked hard at the oars, hoping to reach a village, where there are three Christians, in time for evening service, but it was dark before we arrived and we dare not go to the house, as the people, not being able to see us in the darkness, would have got excited.

"*Thursday*.—Immediately after breakfast we went on shore and made our way to the house of the Christians. Very few people came to hear, and those who did gather were not at all interested. This has always been the case in that place; preachers have been sent before and all say the same. The Christians begged us to hold a service in the evening there, saying some wanted to hear who were busy during the day in the fields; Mrs. S. promised to do so, and then went to two more villages preaching; in each the people were very attentive, and some seemed interested. In the evening we went to have prayer in the house of an old man who was dying; he believes the gospel, has heard the truth from the Christians. After that there was another service; many men were present who were attentive and quiet; we trust the interest aroused will be the beginning of a work of grace in that village. On gaining the boat at 9 p.m., Mrs. S. was so tired out that she threw herself down, too tired to undress or to sleep, and on Friday morning, instead of spending the day at Köa-diu as she had planned, gave orders to be rowed straight to Wenchow; she had no strength for any more.

"We reached home about 8 a.m.; the servants were at prayers, and we let ourselves in at the back door. I shall never forget the feelings of delight as I gazed round the nice clean rooms, the natives looking in often say to one another it is like heaven, and I felt I could echo their words. Our letters were waiting for us, but we did not even open them until we had had a bath and changed all our garments. In looking back on the journey, we have very much to thank God for; in most of the places the people listened, and, considering we were the first foreigners they had seen, behaved well. We visited fourteen villages in the eight days, preaching twenty-three times, besides the daily Bible-readings with the Christians. The weather was delightful, and we were able to walk many miles a day from place to place.

"In Tung-tsö there are nine Christian boys, and we would very much like to give them some training; in the meantime, we hope to bring them here for two or three months during the winter, but should the Lord provide us the means we will gladly give them two years. We say two years, for in less time than that they could hardly get instruction enough to make them useful in after life in teaching others, while a longer time would separate them too long from their natural employments and more or less unfit them for returning to them. Our desire is to help them that they may help others, and not to make paid teachers of them; this is a matter that lies heavily on our hearts, we do not yet see the way to carry it out. Will you join us in prayer about this matter and also that fruit may be found from this journey?"

CHAPTER XVI

"In the morning sow thy seed, and in the evening withhold not thy hand: for thou knowest not whether shall prosper, either this or that, or whether they both shall be alike good."—ECCLES. xi. 6.

ON October 20th we went to Dong-ling to visit some of the older Christians, for although Mr. G. had now charge of that branch, they would not be satisfied until I had been to their homes, and indeed I was glad to see many of the old faces once more. Miss W. gives a description of our few days there, and, as it was her first country trip, she notes many details which will interest the reader which I am too much accustomed to to notice; indeed I am much indebted to these younger workers for accounts of journeys which otherwise would never have been written.

"*Tuesday, October* 21*st.*—Mrs. S. and I started this morning for Dong-ling about 9 a.m. We had about three and a half hours' journey up the canal between fields of rich grain just ready to be cut surrounded on all sides by high hills, some green, others rough and bare, but all equally beautiful. When we left the boat we had a walk of some ten *li* over the hills to this house, where we hope to stay to-night. I cannot attempt to describe the beauties of the country around; from the hill we could see the fertile plain beneath, and the hills terraced and cultivated, some with rice in various stages of perfection, some almost ready to be cut, and some still green; in other places the sweet potato plant with its pretty leaves was creeping up the hillside, interspersed with tea and indigo plantations. We saw them threshing some of the corn, which they do in the fields as soon as it is cut, using a very primitive machine; also the vats which they use for preparing the rich indigo blue dye for their clothes; they strip the leaves off the plant, put them in one of these stone vats to soak for some days, and drain off the clear water, leaving the thick blue dye at the bottom. We also saw the holes in the hillside where they put their potatoes for the winter; they store them all there, cover them with earth and put a stone at the mouth, and they keep sweet until the next year. These people upon the hills have very little except rice and these potatoes to eat; occasionally, some little fish they find in the mud, or some one comes their way with a little salt fish to sell.

"The man at whose house we are staying is the uncle of our milkman; he and his wife are Christians, and there is a numerous family of children. This afternoon we went round the hill to a little village; we next went into a house, and when the people had gathered round Mrs. S. spoke a few words, but they were too much occupied with us to listen very attentively, though one man seemed interested and bought a little book, he thought the doctrine was 'good, but difficult to observe.' Then we came back, and after washing our faces I sat down in front of the little house. (I am writing this with an old man deeply interested in the performance sitting beside me and occasionally puffing smoke into my face. I am writing five copies at once, which astonishes him very much). Close to me a woman has just been grinding some rice into flour in a manner very similar to that which our Saviour alludes to. She has the upper and nether millstones, a large tub underneath to catch the flour as it falls, and she turns it by means of a rope tied to the top stone and attached to a sort of swing; the rice is on the top stone, which has a hole in it, through which it falls as it is needed.

"*Dong-ling, Wednesday evening.*—By the time we had finished supper a goodly number of neighbours had gathered in for prayers. We sang, 'One there is above all others,' then Mrs. S. spoke on the parable of the lost sheep and prayed; followed by the Christian master of the house. Several were there who had not heard the gospel before; one man seemed interested and asked questions, and they went on talking long after we had gone to bed. I don't know if I can describe our bedroom: it had a mud floor, the partitions were partly boards and partly basketwork, the crevices all round affording ample ventilation and also opportunity for any one to inspect us who wished. We had a red candle stuck on the most primitive of supports to light us; our bed was somewhat hard, but notwithstanding that, and sundry mosquitoes and rats, I managed to sleep fairly well, though babies were crying and people talking until pretty late. I am afraid Mrs. S. did not rest so well.

"After an early breakfast, and prayers with the people, when Mrs. S. spoke from the story of Nicodemus, we started to walk here, a distance of about twenty-five *li*, or nine miles, stopping at one village to speak to a few people, and again at the house of one of the members, where we dined and rested a short time, then starting forward again we reached here about 12.30. This is a truly Chinese building, nestling in amongst the hills, apparently in a most out-of-the-way spot, but really within convenient distance for all the members. We received a hearty welcome from the young preacher Ah-chang, his wife (a former school-girl), and mother, and another preacher (who is partially supported by the Church), and all of whom live here; and at once they began to trace the route we should take, for the next three days, so as to reach as many of the outlying stations as possible. After a rest, we went out on to the hill for a little quiet reading before our evening meal, and thoroughly enjoyed the beautiful prospect spread out before us; the river on one side, and on the other the plains, filled with the rich golden harvest, dotted over with the reapers; and the hills on all sides stretching as far as the eye can reach.

"*Saturday, Dong-ling Chapel.*—After three days' travelling we are very glad to find ourselves back here again in our own little room over the chapel, and while Mrs. S. is resting I will try and tell you what we have been doing. We started from here about 8.0 a.m. to walk to the house of one of the members where we were to dine. Our road lay for some distance by the river, past fields of sugar-cane and rice. We passed several villages where there were Christians, stopping now and then to exchange a few words with the women; the men were all busy in the fields cutting the corn. Then we crossed the river (by this time very low and very muddy) in a dirty ferry-boat, to go to the place where we were to dine, in truly Chinese style of course, basins of rice and chopsticks. We had fried eggs and pork, done up with some kind of vegetable. After you have finished a meal they always give you some hot water to wash your face and hands, and then a basin of tea.

"I should like to tell you about these people; the house belonged to two brothers, the younger of whom was a gambler, and is now dead; the elder brother's wife came from a Christian home and was converted before she was married, and when she went to her new home none of the family were Christians, and the mother-in-law was bitterly opposed to her, and for several years would not allow her to attend the services, nor the Christians to visit her. But she, by her gentle submissive behaviour, and by speaking when she had opportunity, so won them over that her husband now regularly attends the services, though he has not yet been baptized; and the old mother has ceased to oppose and persecute, though not yet converted. She received us very graciously. After giving the gospel to those who gathered round, we started on our way again to the house of this young woman's father and mother (where we were to pass the night), which we reached about 4 p.m., having walked in all, I suppose, about ten miles. After a short rest we went up the hillside to visit a poor old woman whom Mrs. S. had known some years ago. We sat some time enjoying the quiet and the beauties around us and stopped to take a drink of the pure mountain stream, and to bathe our faces in its clear water; and finally reached the old woman's hut, a tiny thatched place, with scarcely room to stand upright in, and light only admitted by the door. The old woman (who is eighty years of age) looked doubtful at sight of a stranger, and then exclaimed, " It is

Sy-mo! Ah, my ears are deaf, and my eyes dim, and I couldn't see you, and it is so long since you were here,' and then she took Mrs. S.'s hand and led her in. Poor old thing! she is so deaf, she goes on talking, whether others are talking or not; she cannot hear anything that is said, and can scarcely see either; she has heard the gospel many times, but I fear has not received it; if such is the case she is beyond reach of it now, for she cannot take in anything. Her son was a Christian; he died quite peacefully last year, after only eight days' illness, we were told by his widow, who is also a Christian.

"We came down the hill again to our evening meal, a truly Chinese one—the usual dish of fat pork, fried eggs, and the native potatoes fried in slices. It is very nice just at first if one is hungry, but by the time I have got through half my basin of rice I feel as if I didn't want any more. The two preachers who accompanied us made the most of their time amongst those who crowded in to see, and by the time all were ready for evening prayers a goodly number had gathered, and the gospel was once more preached, after which we retired to rest. The natives, however, went on preaching till late, and began before we got up in the morning. The old people are both Christians, also their son, who, with his wife and two children, live there; the mother is a dear old woman, with such a bright, happy face.

"The people are astir at sunrise, so it is impossible to sleep much after 5 a.m., and about 8 o'clock we were ready to start off again. The first place we called at was the home of these people's second daughter, whose husband is a Christian; but she, having three children, does not often come to service now. The people did not gather there, so we walked on, and soon after again crossed the river. On the opposite bank was deposited quantities of sand, as far as we could see on either side, and for about half a mile inland. On inquiry we learned that last year this was all cultivated, but the river overflowed and left this deposit of sand, thus destroying hundreds of Chinese acres, and leaving many people in want.

"We soon reached quite a large village, where the gospel has not yet been preached, and spoke at some length to a large concourse of people, who seemed interested, and bought books and papers. We then passed on to the house of an inquirer in the next village, where we dined; the people there were so clamorous and noisy that we could scarcely get our meal; and they seemed almost ready to pull the doors down because they could not all see at once. However, when they were a little quieted, Mrs. S. and the preachers were able to again deliver the message of salvation; but not till at the people's request we had adjourned to an idol temple, where, on a platform surrounded by the most hideous images, the glad tidings were again proclaimed. We then started again, and passing through several places, stopping wherever the people seemed disposed to listen, reached the house of another inquirer, situated in a lovely corner of the valley surrounded by hills, and amidst the most beautiful vegetation, where we were to pass the night. Here the people were quite different, though they also had not seen foreigners before; they did not press and crowd like the others, and seemed anxious to hear the gospel. As soon as we were a little rested we began, and when the speakers were all tired out, told them to go home and have their evening meal, and if they returned they would speak again. They soon came back in larger numbers, and sitting outside, for there was no room large enough to hold them, Mrs. S. and the preachers again gave them the words of Life. The people of the house told me I need not come out, but I found the people came inside to look at me instead of listening; so I joined the throng, as to sit and be looked at was all I could do. Oh! how I longed to be able to speak too, and give them the message of salvation!

"The preaching went on long after we had gone to bed, and quite early in the morning we were asked to go to another house for breakfast; so about 6.30 we turned out in the cool, clear morning air, and after a short but lovely walk, mostly through bamboo groves, we reached the house of another inquirer, where, after taking our morning meal, the gospel was again preached. As we had walked about ten miles each day, and they told us to-day's journey would be longer than the preceding ones, we arranged to have chairs for the first part of the way, and accordingly were carried to the first stopping-place, the house of a Christian, where we had dinner, though it was only eleven o'clock, but we had breakfasted early, so were ready for some refreshment; there also we preached, but the people were not very attentive; and as we were anxious to push on, we did not stay very long, but started for this place about twelve o'clock, walking this time. We stopped at various places on the way, preaching wherever they were willing to listen, and now and then resting in a quiet spot, and reached here about 3.30, having walked, I suppose, six or seven miles.

"To-morrow is Communion Sunday here, so several of the Christians have already arrived, and others will be coming in to-morrow morning. We have just had the usual Saturday evening prayer-meeting, and the native preacher, Mr. Tsie (whose wife was also a school-girl), gave a very nice address on the parable of the unmerciful servant. One of his thoughts especially struck me; he said that if the servant had remained near his master, after his debt was forgiven, he would not have treated his fellow-servant so unkindly; so if we are not continually in communion with Christ, we are sure to fall into sin. We have an opportunity to-night of putting in practice the lesson of forgiving others; for the man who was to carry our beds from the place where we slept last night has not arrived (10 p.m.); fortunately, there is a bed here Mrs. S. can use, and I am going to console myself with two shawls; but we are minus towels, brush and comb, and other necessary etceteras. We suppose he got to the river too late to be ferried across; we are hoping he will arrive in time for us to make our toilet in the morning.

"*Sunday.*—This morning we were up pretty early, our beds not being particularly inviting as you may imagine, and on inquiry found our belongings had arrived about dawn; so were able to make our toilets in comfort, very glad to be out of reach of the curious eyes which have followed most of our movements for the last three days.

"Very early the Christians began to arrive from all directions for the service, and after breakfast it was quite interesting to watch the different groups converging from all sides to the one point; one party of twenty-two we saw just after they had crossed the river, and quite a procession they looked as they filed along, for the roads are so narrow it is impossible to walk two abreast. And so by twos and threes they kept on coming till about 10.0, when the service commenced, 120 to 130 having then gathered. Mrs. Stott gave them an address on the parable of the ten virgins, and their ready and correct answers to her questions showed the attention with which they listened. Some earnest words from Mr. Tsie followed, and then the communion service, after which their mid-day meal was discussed; each one brings his own rice, and five cash to pay for the vegetables, &c., that they eat with it; it is cooked altogether, the Christian families taking this duty by turns; an early afternoon service followed, and by four o'clock all had dispersed to their homes.

"*Tuesday, Wenchow.*—After an early breakfast yesterday morning we started about 7.30 to walk from the chapel to the canal where we could get a boat for Wenchow, a distance of about nine miles. Most of the Christians had gone home the day before, but there were one or two remaining with whom we had prayers before leaving. Many whom we had not visited were much disappointed the day before to hear that we were leaving so soon, and should not have time to get to their homes. But they are so scattered it would have taken another week to reach them all, and Mrs. S. was anxious to get back here, because of the O-dzing affair being not yet settled. Part of our way back lay through the same plains by which we had come on the previous Wednesday; but about half-way we turned off into a fresh road, and grand and beautiful as the former was I think this surpassed it. The valleys were narrower and the hills closer to us, and most majestic they looked, and their sides were not cultivated, mostly covered with young fir-trees.

"We ascended the Dong-ling hills by a gentle slope by the side of which a clear mountain stream leapt and sparkled over the stones, now and then falling in tiny waterfalls into a deep pool, sometimes close by our side, but generally far below in the gorge. We rested at the top enjoying the view; the steep descent on the other side was soon accomplished, and in a very short time we were seated in the little boat *en route* for home, and what a home it looked after the dirty, comfortless places we had been in! We found Miss B. looking very bright, and all seemed going on well. It was nice to see the dear familiar faces again, and not feel that every one was staring suspiciously at you, and wondering whether you were a man or a woman. I was so glad to get back to my girls and my regular work again, though I thoroughly enjoyed the journey and feel much better for the change. Perhaps the next time I go I shall be able to take a little share in the work; the constant speaking must be very tiring."

On our return from this journey we found quite a string of events had happened during our absence. One poor woman had died; three preachers were too ill to take the usual Sunday services, but unexpectedly one of the Bing-yie men came in and filled the gap;

how faithful our God is in every hour of need! "Boast not thyself of to-morrow, for thou knowest not what a day may bring forth." I had hardly sent off a letter to a friend, boasting that I was so strong, "fit for any amount of work," &c., &c., when I was laid aside with an attack of the famous influenza, which had at last reached this out-of-the-way corner of the earth. I was ill a week, and never remember being so weakened in so short a time, and we heard it was much worse in Shang-hai and Ning-po. So my next country trip had to be curtailed to a short visit of three days, as it was a new district, and the people were very rough and the crowds so great, that several times we were unable to speak on account of the noise. There are "tens" of villages comparatively near where the gospel had not been preached; my heart is often weary thinking of this, and yet we do all we can. When will the day come when every town, village, city, and hamlet, shall have its witness for Christ?

The Lord never lets me want anything that is for my good; when I am in need He always supplies that either, or something else which does as well. In looking over my accounts at the end of this year 1890, there was a small deficit in almost every branch of our work. I took the matter to the Lord, and the very last steamer of the year brought me gifts from two friends not only enough, but a balance to begin the new year with, and open an account for the boys we hope to train. "Bless the Lord, O my soul," I can say. "Goodness and mercy have followed me all the days of my life."

CHAPTER XVII

"Ye shall be sorrowful, but your sorrow shall be turned into joy."—
JOHN xvi. 20.

THIS year opened with dark clouds. Perhaps a letter written at the time will give the best idea of our position:—"The last few months have been filled up with joy and sorrow, loss and gain have held an almost even hand. The year opened with the death of one of our best and most efficient evangelists. He was brought to the Lord ten years ago, and for eight years has preached far and wide the gospel of God's grace. Supported by the native church, he laboured first in Dong-ling and latterly in Tung-t'sö district. In the former place he was much used of the Lord, and often adopted a rather novel way of gaining a hearing. He would choose his position, and then with a voice enough to frighten any civilised mortal would begin to sing a hymn. The tune attempted was generally 'Old Hundred,' but it ought to have been called 'Martyrdom,' for no one who ever knew that grand old tune would have recognised it. The people would flock out to hear the strange sound, and when the crowd was large enough to suit his purpose he would begin to preach. Well do I remember him telling us he had adopted this plan, and with a beaming face, he added, 'I caught four that day'; he was a veritable fisher of men. One thing was noticeable, those whom he instructed were wonderfully clear in the plan of salvation, and were able to answer any questions about the death and resurrection of Christ. Quite a number have been brought to the Lord through his instrumentality, especially in the district of Tung-t'sö, where not only a few men and women were converted, but five or six bright young lads of ages varying from fourteen to nineteen. Although they could not read a character, they learned from him a wonderful number of texts and hymns; indeed, their ability to learn was so marked that I have been induced to bring them into the city for two years' education and Bible training in the hope that by and by they will become useful preachers.

"Two weeks before his death Mr. Pöe came into the city to spend communion Sunday with us; and at the end of the service, with much earnestness, he told the church members they must come to his help. On every hand were open doors, and as it was impossible for him to enter them all, would not some one volunteer to come? On the 15th of January, 1891, he came from his station suffering from bronchitis, but did not seem dangerously ill. He called his son, and told him he must go and take his place, as the work could not be left. The son asked that he might wait a few days, and nurse his father. He answered, 'No; souls are important; I am all right, my younger sons are here who will look after me; you go at once and do the Lord's work.' The next day the son started at his bidding, and only a few hours afterwards the younger son, seeing a change in his face, said, 'Father, is the Lord calling you?' He answered, 'Yes, the Lord is calling me. I shall soon be at home. You have not been earnest enough; you must cleave closer to the Lord.' Then, after a pause, he said, 'Sing a hymn,' and at the close of the hymn our brother entered into the presence of his Saviour.

"Two weeks later our only other paid evangelist had to be put away for sin. These were heavy blows, and at first we did not know how their places were to be supplied. I had during the last year formed a band of unpaid preachers. They were seven in number, and went out every Saturday afternoon and held services in as many districts, and 550 cash (about 1s. 3d.) per month was given them as travelling expenses. To this band we naturally looked to supply the two vacant places. The native church had to select the one paid by them, and the choice of another fell upon me. Two of the most earnest were chosen, and on the same day two more joined our unpaid band; thus in the midst of trial we were greatly cheered.

"The work amongst the women has been most encouraging. During the year the numbers have increased so much that we have had to enlarge the meeting-room, and they have began a little evangelistic work on their own account. A few of our Christian women who live outside the South Gate and are surrounded by quite a number of little hamlets, meet for prayer every Wednesday afternoon, and the outcome of the prayer-meeting has been that they have appointed one of their number, in turn, to go out one day a week to preach the gospel to the women of these hamlets, the others joining in paying her boat expenses; this is besides contributing to the support of their Bible-woman, and was quite a little plan of their own, which I did not even know of until all the arrangements were made. At the beginning of the Chinese New Year I asked for a few who would undertake to visit sick and absent members, and the response was so cordial that I was able to appoint two for each month of the year, whose duty it was to visit all the sick and absentees. We have had quite a remarkable case just lately, which I think worth mentioning.

"During the autumn a good deal of my time was spent in visiting the Christians in their village homes, and on one of these visits I was much distressed by the extent and spiritual destitution of Yung-ko-dgiae. We have about ten members in that district. I was told that of the 108 villages, perhaps not more than a dozen had had an offer of salvation. On my return I asked my native sisters to pray about this place, and after a few weeks sent two evangelists to spend ten days and preach in as many villages as they could in that time. In one of those places they were told to go to the house of a woman who seemed to know something about their gospel. They went, and on talking with her found she answered like one who had known the truth for years. The preacher asked her how she knew these things, seeing she had never met with Christians? She told them that a Bu-sa (spirit) came and told her many things during the night. This Bu-sa, she said, was clad in white garments, and told her she must give up worshipping the idols, break her vegetarian vow (as there was no merit in that), cut off her opium-smoking, and put on white garments; and that he would send her a teacher who would tell her how she was to be saved.

"She told the preacher to come again, and if this doctrine was indeed the true one, the Bu-sa would tell her that night. He left a small book and a Gospel of John. She had already given up vegetarianism, had put on white underclothing, and given up opium for a fortnight; but her son, fearing his mother was going mad, had brought the pipe again, and pleaded with her to resume the drug. The son, who seems very fond of his mother, fearing the effect of a foreign religion, took away her book, and, going to the house of one of the Christians, gave it to him, telling him not to let any one from Wenchow visit his mother, as he did not wish her to have anything to do with the religion of Jesus. On the preacher's second visit she seemed much distressed; she said the Bu-sa had again spoken to her, and said she had done wrong in giving up the book (she could read fairly well, and was in easy circumstances), and that she must go to Wenchow and see the foreign lady teacher, who would pray for her. When she announced her determination to come and see me, her son was greatly distressed, but feared to oppose her. She arrived on a Saturday afternoon, and I had a long talk with her, and was much struck with her intelligent understanding of the Scriptures, which she had been reading. She said God had given her a new name.

"After Sunday, I told her that if she was willing to cut off her opium, and stay with me for two weeks or so, I would help her. She asked for time to think it over, and after dinner, very tremblingly, brought me her opium-tray. Poor thing, I knew she had entered on a hard struggle, for she had been smoking for ten years, but the native Christians, as well as ourselves, were much in prayer for her, and we expected victory. I had told her to come to our rooms whenever she felt bad, and we would play and sing and pray with her. She bore up until almost two in the morning, when they called me: she was then so ill that I allowed her to have a little of the drug. The next day, about three in the afternoon, being again very ill, I sat by her a long time, rubbing the twitching limbs, soothing and helping her all I could. In the evening I gave her a morphine powder, which quieted her for the rest of the night. Thus she continued for three more days, until the suffering had almost gone, and we looked for a happy issue, when there came a letter from her brother and son, urging her to come home, and not to give up the opium. I tried to encourage her to remain with us another week, but the next morning she decided she must go home. She could stand the terrible craving no longer, and she feared the disease, for which she took the opium in the first instance, was returning. With a heavy heart we had to let her go : it seemed grievous that just as she was escaping from the power of that terrible vice, she should slip back again, for we knew going home meant going back to it. She has been visited since, but while professing to trust the Lord for salvation, she keeps to her pipe. One could weep for the sorrow of those who are held fast in this dreadful bondage. Thank God, the prey is often snatched from the mighty, and we have not a few saved and delivered from the power of the devil.

"One dear woman, hearing of the gospel from her neighbours, and knowing that salvation and her opium-pipe could not go together, determined to give up the latter. She bought some opium medicine, and time after time as the craving came upon her, she prayed and continued the struggle until she got the victory. She has been a consistent Christian for nearly two years. Both her daughter and son-in-law were opium-smokers, and through her influence the latter gave up the pipe, but took to drinking instead. Do we not find in many cases, such as this woman's, that the old gospel has not lost any of its power; but oh! shall we not pray and never rest until this demon be swept from the land, as far as the traffic with England is concerned? Alas, for poor China! One's heart sinks when one thinks of her sorrow."

During this summer we had a rather amusing episode which frightened half the city, but, nevertheless, was used of God to the conversion of several of the school-girls. We were in our sitting-room, soon after prayers one evening, one reading aloud, the rest working, when suddenly we heard a cry of terror, "Sz-mo! Sz-mo!" We rushed out, wondering what could have happened, and running upstairs from whence the sounds came, our cook gasped out, "Look, look at the heavens!" Looking in the direction indicated, I saw a very bright reflection of an electric light, but where it proceeded from we did not know. The school-girls had fallen on their knees, and were praying in much fear. I explained the phenomena, and heard one of the servants say, with a sigh of relief, "I thought the day of the Lord had come." The next morning we heard that an English gunboat had come up the river, and so the mystery was solved. Several of the girls had become truly anxious, and the question was pressed home, "What if the Lord had come? we are not ready."

The Sunday following, just as we were retiring for the night, we heard the girls talking rather excitedly. Miss B. called to them to be quiet and go to bed, but they answered, "We can't be quiet, our hearts are so full, three souls have been saved to-night. Tell Sz-mo to thank God with us." After hearing who the three were, we knelt down and gave God thanks. The next morning before six o'clock we heard them all singing together, " Happy day when Jesus washed my sins away." After morning prayers I took them, one by one, into my study, and heard their simple story. One child was seen weeping, and when asked what was the matter she replied, "I am a great sinner." Two others were anxious, and they were led by the elder girls, who had been lately much revived in soul, to the Saviour, in whom they found peace and pardon. The following Thursday, at our usual meeting, I told the good news to our dear praying women, and asked them, while giving thanks for this, to remember the two elder girls, still unsaved. It was not often I took evening prayers in the school then, but on this occasion I did, and one of the two prayed for that afternoon was saved; and two days later another, and as far as we could see they were real cases. Two of the five were the most naughty-tempered girls we had, so the change in them was most marked.

September 5th.—Saturday was a busy day. All the afternoon and evening we were examining candidates for baptism. I spoke with each one in my study first, and in the evening they were again examined in the presence of one hundred or more members. Ten out of twelve were accepted and baptized next day. That Sunday was such a happy one. The morning service lasted three hours and twenty minutes, yet no one seemed tired. After the usual service and breaking of bread, the silversmith told how the Lord was blessing his work at Bah-zie (three of the new converts were the fruit of his labours), and of their need of a chapel. He told how much money he had received, and how much he still needed. The members responded nobly, and at once promised to contribute twenty-seven dollars (about £5), and this just after they had given the usual sum for one of their own evangelists. Later on other promises were added, so that altogether, including his own donation, he received fifty-five dollars from the native Christians alone.

But it was not long before our joy was turned to sorrow—sickness and death were to be again our portion. That very Sunday, Sept. 6th, I had a letter, written by Mrs. G., saying she was ill, and, if no better, would like to come into Wenchow to see the doctor. I wrote at once, telling her to come anyhow, little thinking she was so seriously ill. They were to arrive on Wednesday, early; and on Tuesday afternoon Miss W. with Miss T., who had only recently joined us, went for their usual walk on the hill. Soon after a man came running in to tell us that one of the young ladies had fallen from the city wall to the street below, a distance of twenty feet. In a few minutes she was carried in, and Dr. L. kindly came at once to attend to her. The elbow of the right arm was literally smashed, but the doctor dressed it as well as he could; and the next morning, at 6 a.m., the G.'s arrived. I now quote Miss B.'s letter, written at the time:—

"On Saturday, the 5th, the country Christians came in to be ready for the services, and amongst them were twelve candidates for baptism—four women and eight men. Mrs. Stott and the pastor saw them all in the afternoon, and had a talk with each one. I was present and much enjoyed the answers of some; they were so clear and bright. Two were asked to wait a few months longer, as they do not yet understand much; and the other ten were examined after the prayer-meeting in the evening, in the presence of about one hundred of the members. One of the unpaid preachers gave a nice testimony as to the reality of one woman's faith, saying that before she believed the doctrine she was in debt, but as soon as she became a Christian she set herself to pay her debts, and is now quite free. The next morning, at nine o'clock, the baptisms took place. Three of the people were from a new place, Bah'-zie, where a good work is going on, entirely through the efforts of one man, Ao-ming by name, a silversmith. About the beginning of last year he, with his wife, removed there from Wenchow, and at once opened a room for preaching. He has had services regularly ever since, paying all expenses connected with the work; and now there are quite a number of inquirers; and these three have been received into church fellowship. After the baptisms the collection was taken (the church supports the evangelist for the Tung-ts'ö district), then the service, at the end of which we remembered the Lord's death for us.

"Then Ao-ming asked to say a few words. He reminded the people of the time when Mr. Stott had come to their city, when the name of God had never been heard, and of how he toiled and preached the gospel all around, and of the result to-day. They had received all freely, the chapel in which they were sitting never costing them a dollar; and compared them to a vine which took root on Mr. Stott's arrival, the branches having spread into the districts around, the last branch being Bah-zie, where he is. He told now the Lord had blessed him, how the room he had rented could not hold the people who gathered, and that the few who had believed could not mortgage a larger one, so he looked to them as the parent to provide for the baby just born. The response was a noble one, twenty-seven dollars being given or promised on the spot. Altogether, from the Wenchow church, including his own donation, he has received fifty-four or fifty-five dollars. This from the native Christians alone.

"On reaching the house we found we had had a service of three hours and a quarter, not counting the prayer-meeting the Christians always have before we come in. There was only time to get dinner when the preachers met for their monthly meeting. They report any interesting cases, and sometimes their districts are changed, then they have prayer, immediately after that all gathered into their respective classes for the afternoon meetings, and those ended, many of the Christians returned home; thus ended a happy and full day of service for the Lord.

"*October* 14*th.*—I had written part of the above, hoping to post it at once, when we were suddenly plunged into sorrow by sickness and death, and I have been too much engaged in the sick-room to finish before this. On Tuesday, September 8th, Miss Tanner fell from the city wall a distance of twenty feet into the street below, breaking her elbow bone into pieces and receiving very severe bruising all down the right side. The next morning at six o'clock Mr. and Mrs. G. with their little girl came in from Bing-yie, Mrs. G. being very ill with dysentery. Dr. Lowry, who was exceedingly kind, said at once hers was a most serious case; he feared she would not pull through. We did all we could for her, but she gradually sank, and on Thursday at 5.5 p.m. she entered into the presence of the Lord Jesus—only thirty-six hours after being carried in. She was so sure she would recover, and several times thanked the Lord for the life spared, praying so earnestly that she might live more entirely to God's glory. Though unconscious on Thursday, she would always answer any question; she spent a good deal of the day in prayer. She prayed very earnestly about workers in Bing-yie. She thought she was in Shang-hai with Mr. Taylor, and again and again asked that the matter might be settled that afternoon. Once she said, 'Now, dear Mr. Taylor, will you pray?' About noon I repeated a text Miss Tanner sent her; she did not grasp the meaning, and I said, 'That means Jesus.' 'Oh, does it?' she replied; 'then that means everything, does it not?' She at once closed her eyes and prayed so beautifully; I will give what I remember of the prayer in her own words: 'O Lord, we come to Thee this afternoon in that precious, precious name of Jesus; we little know the meaning of that name, and of what we could do with it if we only used it. . . . Let us begin from to-day and start afresh in the power of that name . . . that we may live in it, act in it, move in it, and work in the power of that precious, precious name. . . .' Her one theme was Jesus, 'that precious, precious name,' as she said again and again. Once she turned to Mrs. Stott, saying, 'What do you think the Lord Jesus wants me to do for Him now?' and on Mrs. S. saying, 'I think perhaps He wants to call you home,' she said, 'Oh, do you think so; that would be lovely, if only I could think that.'

"I don't think she realised she was going, she had been so sure she would get better. Very soon after that she became quite unconscious and unable to speak. We buried her the next day in the little cemetery outside the city walls, near the little baby boy she lost last year, and near dear Miss Boyd who was taken from us last year, in sure and certain hope of a glorious resurrection. 'A little while and He that shall come, will come, and will not tarry.' A week later Mr. G. and his little three-year-old motherless child went to Shang-hai, and last mail we were terribly shocked and grieved to hear that little

Olive had died, after three days' illness, from cholera It does seem too terrible, and as yet we can hardly realise it. Truly 'God's ways are not as our ways, nor God's thoughts as our thoughts.' The 'love that spared not His own son' hath done this; we can only bow the head and say, 'It is the Lord; let Him do as seemeth Him good.' May the God of all comfort comfort and sustain His tried and sorrowing servant, for only He who has so bruised can heal.

"To return to Miss T., whom we left very much shaken and bruised: she has had a trying time, the arm could not have splints on as the wounds were very bad, and the whole arm much swollen; for a month she caused us anxiety, as we feared the spine was also injured; the fever was very high, but she has been getting up a little the last few days, and we trust she will now go steadily forward. She needed constant attention day and night for several weeks. All who have seen the place where she fell marvel she was not killed. We do sincerely praise God that so little injury was done, and for all the grace and patience He has given her.

"On October 4th we had eleven more baptisms; five were school-girls, four of whom were converted four months ago, and who have shown decidedly by their changed lives that they are 'new creatures in Christ Jesus.' One, an old man of seventy-seven years from O-dzing, gave a very clear testimony—I was much struck with the way in which he spoke of the 'precious blood.' One of the questions was, 'Have you any part in hell?' He replied 'No; I once had, but now I have part in heaven.' 'How has that come about?' was the next question. His face lighted up, and in his energy he threw out both hands and almost shouted 'By the precious blood!' There was another man from Bah-zie, Ao-ming's place, making four now in that village, not counting Ao-ming and his wife; the rest were from Wenchow and its outskirts. Thus twenty-one have been received during the last two months.

"The following Tuesday the preachers' meeting took place; we had a good day, and the Lord was present in the power of the Holy Ghost. The pastor, Mr. Tsiu, took the morning meeting, speaking with power, and the prayers after were very earnest. For six weeks we nursed Miss T. night and day, at the end of which the doctor advised her to go to Shanghai for further medical advice, and after lingering there for nearly two months, she fell asleep in Jesus."

CHAPTER XVIII

"All Thy works shall praise Thee, O Lord; and Thy saints shall bless Thee."—PSA. cxlv. 10.

IN November of this year I paid my first visit to O-dzing and give the following account written at the time:—

"Our visit to this place is never to be forgotten, the journey being one of unsurpassed beauty. In vain may I attempt to give you some idea of its grandeur. You must imagine yourself in a district surrounded by high mountains. The journey, occupying the greater part of two days, lay entirely amongst the mountains, the path winding along and often through a stream of clear, limpid waters, rushing in ceaseless music under and over great boulders which had fallen from the cliffs above in years gone by. In passing through these streams one has to hold one's breath; the chair-bearers are nearly knee deep, and a false step would give one an unseasonable bath with, perhaps, more serious results. The mountains are not rugged and bare, like those you are accustomed to in your more northern clime, but ridge after ridge high up the sides is cultivated, and only a few weeks ago the rich, ripe harvest was safely gathered in. On the higher and more precipitous mountains there is a perfect glory of dark fir, lighted up here and there by clusters of the light-green graceful bamboo. Along the foot of the hills and hedges the wild tea and bi-bo trees are in full bloom, the latter scenting the air with its delicious fragrance; the bright yellow flowers, some resembling the broom, others the daisy in form, give quite a glory to the scene; while here and there a scarlet azalea seems to have forgotten we are in the middle of November. Ferns of great variety are in abundance, while every now and again we come upon a splendid waterfall, whose white, foaming waters rush headlong down, regardless of all below.

"Altogether, it was a scene to inspire the commonest mind and send the poet and the painter into raptures. Yet in the midst of all this beauty, poverty and filth, sin and misery abound. Our hearts were drawn out in deep gratitude to God that in this remote mountainous region with its widely scattered villages the gospel of His grace was known and loved by not a few.

" The little church here has been baptized by fire ; some of the members have suffered much for Christ's sake, yet they have come out of the fire stronger and better for the testing. God grant that the little seed may grow into a strong tree, with branches spreading to all around.

"*Tuesday*, 17*th*.—We—*i.e.* Miss Bardsley, the evangelist, our cook and myself—left Wenchow about ten o'clock on Wednesday evening (11th), and ought to have reached the end of our water journey by dawn next morning, but strong head-winds and opium-smoking boatmen defeated our purpose, so at dawn we were only seven miles from the city. We managed to get chair-bearers, however, and started at 9 a.m., intending to make one-half of the journey that day. At two o'clock we reached the house of an inquirer, who gave us a hearty invitation to spend the night there and to preach to the villagers. This we consented to do, though we were more than an hour's ride from the place we had intended to stay at. We were hardly seated before a curious crowd gathered around us, for foreign women had never been in that district before. I tried once or twice to speak to them, but their excitement was too great, they would not hear; so I told them to go home, get their suppers, put their babies to bed, and return later. We gave the invitation, but were hardly prepared for the response; for scarcely had we finished our tea, when a large crowd assembled of men, women, and children. The room was dangerously full, the people standing so closely that they swayed to and fro in the most alarming manner; the lights were dim and those on the outer rim were struggling to get a sight of us; the noise was deafening; three times I essayed to get a hearing, but at last determined to retire, hoping that the preacher would get a quiet opportunity of telling them of a Saviour's love. On reaching our room we found it necessary to put out the light at once, as the women were following; we listened with beating hearts to the noise below, as the preacher in vain tried to get a hearing. In an hour or two all was quiet, but not before they had brought lighted torches and, inserting them through the partition, at last persuaded themselves we were really in bed and asleep. The next morning before starting we had a very quiet and orderly service.

"Six and a half hours' further riding brought us to our journey's end, and then what a welcome awaited us! The Christians had somehow heard of our coming, and came out part of the way to meet us, their faces beaming with delight. We were at once taken upstairs to the room they had set apart as a chapel, and indeed we were delighted with what we saw: a table at one end, three rows of stools to accommodate forty-five persons, while on the walls hung scrolls of scripture, the whole of the first chapter of John, the Sermon on the Mount, and other scriptures. It was indeed a refreshing sight, in the place where last year the devil seemed to have it all his own way.

"We have had quite a splendid time here; quiet

Bible readings, morning and evening, attended by thirty or more people. The three services on Sunday were as quiet and orderly as any I have seen in China. One blind man was proposed for fellowship; the Christians all gave testimony as to his changed life, and as his faith in Christ seemed clear and bright, he was unanimously received, and to-day he has been baptized in the clear mountain stream near by.

"Yesterday we went to visit a place seven miles off, where an interest in the gospel has lately sprung up. The youngest son of the family we are living with and an earnest Christian woman go there every Sunday to preach to them. We were rejoiced to find seven or eight persons interested in the truth. On arriving there, however, a bitter disappointment awaited these Christian workers. One old woman, eighty-one years of age, in whose house the services were held, had suddenly gone back to her idols, and refused to let them have her house for services any longer. The reason was that her eldest son, who had been away from her for two years, had just returned home, and being angry with his mother for receiving what he called a foreign religion, she gave all up to please him. Poor old thing! it seemed so sad to see her bordering on the grave, yet careless of her soul's salvation. Another family, almost next door, offered their house, so the meetings were not to be given up. I have no doubt but that the gospel will spread in the district, and many shall yet bow down to own our Lord and Saviour.

"This afternoon we have had rather a novel experience. We were invited to visit the wife of the chief persecutor of last year, the man who seemed possessed by the evil one, and who determined to keep Christianity out of the place. Of course we were delighted to have the opportunity, and were received most graciously, old grievances were spoken of but without bitterness. The old lady seemed so pleased to see us; she stroked our hands, and gave us tea and nuts, and led us to the hills to see the beauties of the place. We have no doubt that our visit will result in good, in bringing about a kindlier feeling towards the poor and despised Christians. We have been freely welcomed in every home.

"*Wenchow, Nov. 21st.*—The evening before we left we had the first Christian wedding that has ever been in that place, and a very rough, noisy time we had; all the village turned out, and there must have been one hundred persons to see us eat the wedding feast.

"Next day, 18th, we started for home about 1 p.m., halting for the night at a village half-way. In the evening we had a large audience of folk anxious to see and hear the foreigner. We managed to get quiet enough to deliver our message. Next morning before seven o'clock we were on the road again, reaching home about 5 p.m. Oh, it was good to get into our comfortable home and to find that all had gone on well during our absence. Will you pray that the work at O-dzing may prosper more and more?

"Next month we expect all our preachers (two paid and eleven unpaid) in for a month's Bible study. I have promised to give them a daily Bible lesson in Old Testament history. We feel the great need of having all our Christians, especially the preachers, well taught in the Word that is able to make them wise teachers of others."

Through the kindness of friends in Malvern and Dartmouth, we were able to give a Christmas-tree not only to the boys and girls, but also extended our invitation to a number of our men and women. This was not the first time we had dressed a tree, but it had been rather sorry work before, spending what little money we could spare on useful and pretty gifts, there was no little ingenuity required to make the thing a success. This year all was changed, and never had we seen such lovely dolls or pretty toys, all fitted to instruct as well as amuse our young folk, and the opening of the box was nearly as great an excitement to us as to the natives. The kind friends had put in personal gifts for each of us; these we kept until Christmas morning, which added greatly to the interchange of presents which we have always kept up on that day. Our riches made us bold, and we invited all the foreign community (which has never numbered more than twenty, including missionaries) to join in our fun. Some willingly responded, and much enjoyed witnessing the happy scene. After the children were supplied we had gifts enough to put into a good-sized bag, into which the women were allowed to dip and become the happy possessor of whatever they drew out.

The last day of the year was spent partly in prayer, ending in a watch-night service, a delighful home custom which we have always kept up.

CHAPTER XIX

1892.

"The kingdom of God is come nigh unto you."—LUKE x. 9.

IN February I was much impressed with the favourable opportunity which the first month of the Chinese year (February) presented for gospel work, and when our preachers assembled for their month's study I communicated my thought to them. They all gladly responded to the suggestion, that they should go two and two into as many towns and villages as possible in the time, and preach. Plans were made, districts divided up, and twelve men started on their mission. I gave each man three dollars (above seven shillings and sixpence) for this month's expenses, and they all had without exception interested audiences in the different districts they visited, and in one place permanent work has been maintained since. One of the preachers felt unable to give up his work for that month, explaining that, though his food was provided, there was nothing to leave for his wife, so our men contributed amongst themselves enough rice to send to his family rather than that he should be deprived of this opportunity. Of course, they all returned to their employments at the end of the month.

At the same time, we held evangelistic services in the city chapel, using the little organ as a special attraction, and we had large numbers at all the meetings. A few of the Christian women also went out evangelising. Some months afterwards Mrs. Liu visited one place where they had been, and found four families deeply interested. She returned with a splendid report, and brought with her a young wife, nineteen years of age, whose husband wished her to learn the truths he had himself accepted. She spent a fortnight with us, made good progress, and seemed really in earnest. I quote from a letter written in June regarding this young woman :—

"Two weeks ago we had the joy of receiving her husband, twenty-five years of age, and his brother, a young man of twenty-two. They were both baptized together, the firstfruits of these women's efforts. Now they ask that a preacher be sent to them every Sunday, and just as the request came to me, another of our men offered himself as an unpaid preacher ; so the open door was entered. Do praise God with me for all this mercy."

We had also encouragement in the more distant places. In one village the preacher was detained three weeks, six families wishing to be taught, and one of the inquirers came to the city to purchase Bibles and hymn-books. The young wife was baptized a few months later. Thus the seed then sown brought forth lasting fruit.

In the spring we had the pleasure of welcoming Miss Chalmers. She was engaged to Mr. Menzies, who the month previously had reinforced Mr. G. at Bing-yie. She remained with us for two years, learning the language, at the end of which time she was married, and joined her husband in his work there. We much missed her loving sympathy and hearty interest, though unable to take part in the work.

In the summer Miss Bardsley and I took a much-needed change to Japan, leaving the work in the hands of the native pastor, and the schools under the care of Misses Whitford and Chalmers. I append Miss B.'s letter, giving an account of our doings and places visited, also one of my own, written on our return to Wenchow :—

"ARIMA, *near* KOBE.

"We left Wenchow on Aug. 21st, reached Ning-po on Monday, spent there some hours visiting friends. In the afternoon sailed for Shang-hai, arriving there the following morning. Found all our friends at the mission-house well. Only the residents were there.

Spent a very busy three days shopping and visiting. It is a real treat being able to shop once more, for in Wenchow all is done by the servants. On Friday went on board the s.s. *Yokohama Maru* for Japan, a fine big steamer, beautifully fitted up. We had a delightful passage—the sea as calm as a mill-pond all the way, and the weather so warm that we wore muslin dresses even in the open sea. Our fellow-passengers were nice, pleasant people, several being missionaries. Dr. S., of Shang-hai, has been our companion all the way. She is an American, and we are greatly enjoying her society. We have been in the midst of Americans since we left China.

"We reached Nagasaki Sunday morning. The entrance to the bay is charming, and the bay itself is one of the six finest in the world. Surrounded by hills, you wonder how or where you came in—there seems no entrance. The English houses nestling among the trees on the sides of the hills, make it very pretty and gay with the various flags of the Consulates. There were numbers of steamers, men-of-war belonging to England, Germany, America, and Japan. We were very pleased to see our old friend, H.M.S. *Redpole* come in soon after us and anchor close by. The following morning two of the men came to see us. They told us six of them had been converted in Chin-Kiang through one of our missionaries soon after they left Wenchow (you may remember we had the men to tea twice and at that time there were no Christians on board). They were so bright and full of praise; it was sweet to hear them speak of the keeping power of Christ, and its reality. They have much to endure on board. In the afternoon the captain, doctor, and second lieutenant came to see us. They were going to England in a few months, so we may not meet again.

"We had intended calling on some of the missionaries in Nagasaki; but the weather was so hot we contented ourselves with going to church in the morning and a visit to the bazaars on Monday morning to get some tortoise-shell hairpins, for which Nagasaki is famed. On our return we hope to see a little of the work, &c.

"We left Nagasaki on Monday, and again went into the open sea for some hours, but the next day the scenery was lovely. We passed between islands all the way. Sometimes we seemed completely landlocked.

"Wednesday morning early we reached Kobe, and at once proceeded to Mrs. Ballard's, whose house is in a lovely situation on the hill overlooking the town and bay. She had kindly reserved her best room for us, and we were quite sorry to leave again so soon, but the weather was so hot we thought it best to come on here. We started for this place at 5.30 next morning, and had the pleasure of travelling a few miles by train; then we got kangos for the rest of the way. A kango is a short chair, with a cover of bamboo; the proper way is to sit with your legs under you, but if you cannot manage that, you must manage to stow them away somewhere, for the chair is so short. We were four hours and a half on the way. The country was very pretty, and we ascended the mountains for three hours and a half, then descended for one hour. Arima lies in a very narrow valley and is completely surrounded by hills; it is a lovely place, and abounds in flowers and ferns of every description.

"We are staying in a Japanese hotel, which is so quaint and clean, so different from a Chinese inn. Dr. S. is with us. We have two good large rooms, for which with baths (real mountain water), good food, and attendance, we pay one dollar a day, or two shillings and eightpence in English money. The food is very good, and they give us more courses than we care for. One girl speaks a few words of English, and we have great fun making ourselves understood. She is very anxious to tell us the Japanese of all we say, and we cause great delight when we remember to ask for what we want in Japanese. The people are so very clean and polite; they are lively, and laugh heartily with us over things. There have been and are still a good many missionaries here.

"*Monday.*—We had such a happy and refreshing day yesterday. Mr. P., from China, took morning service and gave a beautiful address on Psa. li. 10-13. 1. The necessity of regeneration. 2. Upholding of the Spirit. 3. Maintaining the joy of salvation for purposes of service, not for selfish enjoyment. At 4.30 we all met together to remember the Lord's death, and had a very precious season, the Lord's presence being very manifest. At 7.30 there was an open meeting and much prayer. There has been a good deal of blessing this year at Arima.

"We enjoyed our visit to Arima; the longer we stayed the more sorry we were to leave. The mineral baths were most enjoyable. We came to Kobe on the 15th, and on the 19th went to Kioto, the ancient capital. It was a great treat to travel by rail again. The carriages are very like our English ones, and the train goes as slowly as the Manx trains.

"We had a letter of introduction to Dr. and Mrs. Barry, of Kioto. They very kindly took us over the Doshishi, the largest and first college in Japan. It was opened by a Mr. Nissima, a Japanese. There are four or five buildings, one alone being as large as Manchester High School, and there are now over six hundred pupils. All the sciences are taught—in fact, as good an education given as in the colleges in America. There is also a large girls' school, and hospital and dispensary in connection with it. We spent all Monday afternoon in going over the buildings, and the evening with Dr. and Mrs. Barry. The next morning they kindly arranged with Jinriksha men, to take us to all that could be seen in a day. They took us to five beautiful temples. In one was a Buddha quite sixty feet high; in another were 33,000 idols, all so beautifully clean, and the bronze and lovely embroidering made them so much more beautiful than the ordinary Chinese temples. In one there were many hundred worshippers, sitting as quietly as a European audience, listening to a Buddhistic sermon.... It is so sad to see Japan, with all her civilisation, still so closely bound to her idols. Next we went to a porcelain warehouse, and saw the most exquisite ware being made, all hand-painted. Next to a silk warehouse; but the silk is neither so good nor so cheap as in China, though it looks very pretty. Kioto is a very fine city, the streets very wide and level, and surrounded by high hills. The hotel we stayed in was as large and as well fitted as the large town hotels and lighted with electric light.

"We next visited Osaka, the commercial capital of Japan; there is not much natural beauty there, a great deal of business going on, some fine large bridges, the city also lighted with electric light near the station and in the Concession. We stayed with

Dr. and Mrs. D., American missionaries whom we met in Arima, but as we had so short a time in Osaka we could not see much of their work. All the missionaries in Japan are engaged more or less on educational lines; they are not free to work where and as they like. The Japanese are most anxious to do without the foreigners, and even the Christians say, 'Give us the money and you can go home, we can manage our own affairs.' There is not a foreigner in any Government position now; they despise them more than the Chinese do I think. They don't like a Japanese to marry a foreign lady. They say 'Our men are too good for your women, but our women will do for your men.'

"We are very thankful that our work lies in China, for though we have trials and difficulties they have not, they have difficulties we know nothing of. The Japanese are lively, polite, clever people, beautifully clean, and in many respects lovable, but they have no depth. Quickly converted to Christianity, many as quickly go back; they often take offence and leave one church and join another. The Chinese, on the other hand, are quiet, sober people, filthy in all their habits, slow to take in an idea, and as slow to adopt it, but when once they do, nothing will move them If a Chinaman is truly converted to God he remains firm, in spite of persecutions."

On our return home I wrote the following:—

"WENCHOW, *Oct.* 28, 1892.

"We returned home last Thursday, and were so delighted to get back again; one would have thought we had been away a year to see the excitement. All our dear natives were crowded round the door to bid us welcome; all, including the babies, had to be spoken to, so that it was quite a few minutes before we could notice Miss Whitford and Miss Chalmers The latter has been very ill; for two or three days the doctor feared she might not live. We were so thankful to see her almost strong again, only looking thinner.

"The day after our return, the country Christians and candidates arrived; five were examined, but only two men were baptized. On Sunday we had a splendid day; the pastor spoke with much power on Christ cleansing the Temple. He also turned to Corinthians: 'Ye are the temple of the Holy Ghost.' He asked some searching questions, such as, 'What has our heart been during the last month, the temple of God, or a den of thieves?' I am sure all felt the power of his words, and we thank God for his faithful testimony."

As soon as possible we recommenced our autumn country work, our first journey being to O-dzing. Miss Whitford has written a journal giving details of our experiences during that and the Tong-t'sö visit, which will be more interesting than any words of mine. She writes :—

"*November* 10th, *Thursday*.—On the second of this month Mrs. Stott and Miss Bardsley left us for a trip to O-dzing, one of the out-stations. They left in the afternoon, and came to the end of their boat journey up the river too late to proceed any further that night, so composed themselves to rest where they were. Early in the morning they were ready to start, but owing to the difficulty of arranging with chairbearers, &c., it was quite eight o'clock before they could get off. The men were not well up to their work, and before long they began to grumble and say they could not carry them, and as it was a twelve hours' journey that was rather a bad look-out; it ended in their walking altogether about half the way, until they could do no more; and even then Miss B.'s men set her down within a short distance of her destination, declaring they could take her no further; but Mrs. S. pushed forward, and sent men back to fetch her. They went out with torches and brought her in in true festive style, and the hearty welcome they here received made up for all the hardships of the way. The journey is a very pretty and picturesque one; but the beauties were not so well appreciated this time, owing to the discomfort; one cannot enjoy beautiful scenery when too weary to put one foot before the other.

After supper, they left the preacher to conduct evening prayers, and retired at once, hoping to get a good night's sleep after the fatigues of the day. But alas for their hopes! They had just got to sleep when they were aroused by a regiment of rats, scrambling and squeaking in very close proximity. They got up and arranged the mosquito curtains so as to keep them at least off the bed, and once more composed themselves; but not for long. Again they were aroused by the same noises, and this time they lit the candle and left it burning all night, which seemed to scare away the intruders. Meantime the rats had visited the next room, where the wearied chairbearers and the preacher had forgotten their trials in rather noisy slumber, and in the morning the preacher was minus a stocking, which they had carried away bodily to their nest.

"Miss B. had taken with her a small medicine-chest, and the morning of the next day (Friday) was employed in seeing patients, doctoring bad eyes, bandaging sore legs, &c.; the rest of the day being spent in visiting the Christians and inquirers near at hand, and a visit was also paid to the wife of the arch-persecutor of two years ago, and she seemed pleased to renew the acquaintance made last year.

"On Saturday a visit was paid to two villages about seven or eight miles distant, where the gospel was preached and some inquirers visited. In one of these villages there were seven, four of whom seemed very earnest, and gave evidence of true conversion; in the other village there were only two.

"Sunday was wet, but notwithstanding the elements about thirty-four, mostly Christians and inquirers, turned out, and three hearty services were held, all of which Mrs. Stott took herself, as well as morning and evening prayers every day. She feels the importance of giving the Christians as much Bible-reading as possible during these visits, as it is almost the only opportunity they have. She was especially pleased with their interest during this visit, and the evident pleasure and intelligence with which they listened at all the services.

"Monday was wet, so the morning was spent in seeing patients, and the afternoon in letter-writing. In the evening there was a very good audience, and quite a number of strangers sat still and listened attentively all through, part of the address being for them and part for the Christians.

"On Tuesday morning Miss B. was to start about four o'clock for Wenchow. The cook, who is ever on the alert when there is anything extra to be done, first roused the people at one o'clock; on being told the time, he subsided again for a little while, but at 2.30 insisted on all getting up; before that the hostess had been preparing breakfast, which was ready. Soon after a start was effected, Miss B. and the cook leaving for Wenchow, the two sons of the house accompanying them with torches as far as necessary. After they were gone, Mrs. Stott finished the packing, &c.,

and after assembling the family for prayers, she also left just as dawn broke (about 6 a.m.) for a long journey across country to Tung-t'sö, another outstation. A halt was made at mid-day at a hall which is rented as a chapel by Mr. S. of the Methodist Free Church, and the night was spent at the house of some inquirers of his. It was dark when Mrs. S. reached their house, and they had shut up for the night; but they gave the travellers a kind and hospitable welcome, and soon hands were preparing the food which they had brought with them for supper.

"The next day they again set off, and Tung-t'sö (where I had already arrived) was reached about 3 p.m., after a wet and trying journey.

"But I must go back a little. The Monday after Mrs. S. left Wenchow an old woman, one of the members who had been ill some time, passed peacefully away. A few days before the Bible-woman had visited her and asked her if the Lord was going to call her. 'In a few days,' she said. 'Are you ready to go?' 'Quite ready; I see a crown and a white robe prepared for me.' 'Is Jesus with you?' 'Yes, He is with me.' 'Does anything trouble you?' 'No, I am quite happy.' This woman's daughter was one of Mrs. Stott's first and most earnest Christian women; she died about four years ago; but before that she literally prayed her husband and her mother saved, never resting until they were both within the fold.

"On the Tuesday I left Wenchow about 5.30 p.m. for Tung-t'sö. The first part of the journey was performed in a boat, my companions being one of the Bible-women and my servant. When I wanted to retire for the night I put up a shawl for a curtain to screen me from the boatmen, but they had to pass through, to take turns in rowing, during the night. Of course I did not undress, but I washed my hands and face in the morning, which was more than any of my companions did.

"We breakfasted in the boat, and soon after nine o'clock started to walk to our destination about seven miles distant, half of which was over a high and steep hill. As the day was very wet we had some difficulty in getting a man to carry our bedding, &c., and you may imagine in such weather our progress was not very rapid, the stone path over the hill being exceedingly slippery with the rain, so that we did not reach Tung-t'sö till about 1 p.m., just about two hours before Mrs. Stott arrived from the other direction. We both needed a rest that afternoon, and in the evening there were quite a number of strangers who listened to the preaching of the gospel.

"The next morning was wet, so we could not go out, but in the afternoon we went to a village a short distance off, where a service is held on alternate Sundays, and where there are several Christians and inquirers. It is a very poor place, and the people are very dirty; we spoke a little, but they did not seem to care much to listen, except those who were already interested. One old man whom we visited had been ill for two months with a trying disease: his wife is very much against his being a Christian, and does not treat him well; she needs our prayers that her heart may be changed and softened by God's Spirit.

"Friday (11th) was fair, so we started soon after breakfast to visit two or three places where there are Christians and inquirers; we took our dinner with us as the people around this district are so poor they have scarcely enough for themselves. After greeting our friends and doing some preaching, we were shown to a room to eat our dinner. I wish I could describe that room—the poorest barn would be a palace to it. We sat on the side of a bed, which was simply boards covered with a straw mat; the floor was stone, and all around was dirt and lumber of every description. One side was simply open basket-work, through which numerous pairs of prying eyes watched us eating our sandwiches; opposite was a large hole in the partition, also used as a peephole, and through which two basins of tea were presently handed to us to save opening the door, and while we were drinking our tea an arm and shoulder was again thrust in, to search for a key on the top of an old cupboard which stood conveniently near.

"After dinner we again spoke a little, and then

went on to the next place, to reach which it was necessary to cross a ferry. The boat was found to be two or three inches deep in water, and there was no one in charge, so after baling some of the water out, we disposed ourselves round the edges as best we could, Mrs. Stott's chair being set in the middle, the chairbearers pulled us to the other side, where we visited two villages, and met with a rather noisy reception. Some, however, listened to our message, though many were more intent on looking at us.

"On Saturday we only went a short distance, as we wanted to be back early in the afternoon, there being several candidates to be examined for baptism; so we went to a village just the other side of the hill I had crossed coming here, where there were three inquirers. We had dinner at the house of one of them, an old man and his wife, who were anxious to have some one come every Sunday to hold a service, or to stay there, because they say there are several people who would be willing to listen if there were some one to teach them. This can easily be arranged next year, when our boys, who are in for training, come home to live here, as they will go out on Sundays. When we returned in the afternoon there were candidates to be examined, seven in all, but one did not arrive till Sunday morning, so will have to wait. There were one man and four women from the place we visited on Thursday, and the old woman at whose house we dined that day; the latter was advised to wait, as she did not seem quite clear. All the others answered well, and seemed quite decided about conversion, and that they had experienced it. Two women were the wives of men who were baptized in the early part of the year; the husbands of the other two are not yet believers, and one of these especially needs our prayers. She was up for examination a few months ago, but was put off because she had not quite broken off the habit of coarse language; her husband is quarrelsome and scolds her, and is altogether very difficult to get on with, and she seems still afraid lest she should give way and answer him back in a wrong way; but we told her to go on praying for him, and the Lord would hear and help her.

"The baptismal service was held at daybreak at a stream just below the chapel; we had it thus early because the people seemed very much excited on the Saturday night, and we feared they might make a disturbance, so about a dozen of us went down quietly, and it was just over when the villagers began to stir; in another few minutes they would all have been round us. We had two good services morning and afternoon, about forty Christians and inquirers being present; in the morning we had communion, of which about twenty partook. We have had morning and evening prayers with the Christians each day, and every evening except one which was wet. We have had large audiences who, although rather rowdy at first, have listened attentively and quietly to the preaching of the gospel; and we cannot but believe that God will bless the seed thus sown to the saving of many more souls in this district.

"On Monday the 14th we started directly after breakfast for Si-kae, a place about twenty miles north-west of Tung-t'sö, where the gospel was first taken by the old firewood-seller, now a colporteur, who has been the means of opening up several places. He went there selling books, and, finding the people willing to listen, spent a few weeks with them, and one of the men came into Wenchow with him to buy a Testament and hymn-book. Now there are about ten inquirers, and the Tung-t'sö preacher goes there once a month to hold service and teach them. It was a day's journey through most lovely country hills and mountains; the river, now reduced to a mere mountain stream, rippling over the stones and winding in and out amongst the hills, requiring to be crossed and recrossed again and again as we proceeded. As it was entirely new ground we were not at all sure what sort of a reception we should meet with, and were agreeably surprised to find the people much quieter and better behaved than those of the Tung-t'sö district. The men were not in when we arrived, and the women did not seem particularly glad to see us, as none of them were Christians; but they soon sent for the others, and prepared to sweep out the best room for our accommodation.

"In the evening we had a good audience, who listened quietly and attentively to the gospel message, the inquirers who were present drinking in every word. Mrs. Stott asked one of them if he believed in Jesus the Saviour. He said, 'I can't find Him.' She said, 'Are you willing to worship Him?' 'I am willing.' 'Are you willing to trust Him?' 'Yes.' 'Then He will teach you what you don't understand.'

"When the people dispersed we retired, as we hoped, to rest, for we were very tired; but there was not much sleep to be got that night. We had been previously cheered by the information that there were a good many rats; but we were not prepared for the attacks of the fleas with which the bed evidently swarmed, and which proceeded to business with vigour as soon as we lay down; between them and the noise of rats gamboling about the room, together with the yelping of a dog just outside during the greater part of the night, we did not get much sleep during the two nights we spent there; indeed Mrs. Stott got none at all, and was consequently pretty well worn-out by the time she left.

"On Tuesday morning we went out to the house of one of the inquirers and spoke to some of his neighbours; then, being tired, I returned to the house, and Mrs. S. went on to another place, where she met with some Hunan braves, who are stationed there for the protection of the hills, and who listened very attentively, asking questions and buying books and tracts. One of them asked Mrs. S. how long she had been in Wenchow. She said, 'Twenty years.' He said, 'You have been there so long, and why have you never come here before to tell us the gospel message?' She told him she never heard of Si-kae till this year.

"In the evening we again had a good audience, who listened attentively to an explanation of the prodigal son. It is becoming more and more difficult to provide for these places, as they open up at greater and greater distances from Wenchow. We were told of another place, yet six miles further on, where one woman believed. Roughly speaking, between fifty and sixty miles from Wenchow as a centre, how are these places to get regular teaching and superintendence? The only way seems to be to take one or two into the city for teaching, then send them back to impart what they know to their brethren; but few have time for this, as they all live from hand to mouth, so to speak. However, three of the inquirers from Si-kae are hoping to come into the city in the 11th Chinese month, when the preachers come for a month's reading, and if these are satisfactory, and can spare time, two of them may stay for a year or two's training, as our other boys will be going home in the 12th month.

"*Thursday, 17th.*—After an early breakfast and prayers with the Christians we left Si-kae yesterday morning on our homeward journey. The first part of the road was got over very quickly, but shortly before twelve o'clock it came on to rain heavily, and continued the rest of the afternoon. About two o'clock we reached the riverside wet and tired, and found a boat just waiting to be hired; so, after a little bargaining as to price, we got in and established ourselves, heartily glad to be on our way home. We went to bed directly after supper, and before daybreak were anchored outside the east gate of Wenchow. We walked up in the morning twilight, and on reaching home the first step was to get a good bath and clean clothes, after which we felt respectable once more."

CHAPTER XX

1893

"In the fear of the Lord is strong confidence."—PROV. xiv. 26.

"YE shall see greater things than these." Such was the message I received from a dear friend in December, 1892. It came to my heart as a promise from my Father for the new year we were soon to enter; and, just as I determined to take it as my New Year's motto, another friend's message, "Greater things than these shall ye do," confirmed my faith, and I was enabled to claim them as promises. Mrs. Liu, our faithful and spiritual helper for years, was very ill, and twice we gave up all hope of her recovery. Her son was at Tai-chow helping in the medical work there, so I wrote asking Mr. Rudland to let him return at once, as I feared his mother might soon pass away. He came, and was thankful to find her out of danger. All through her illness her testimony to the Lord's nearness was very precious. One morning when I went to see her she smiled, and said, "The Lord has been with me all night; He showed me His face so

Group of Male Church Members.

lovely I wanted to see more of Him, and was sorry when morning came. I want to go to heaven to see Mr. Stott and Mrs. Oae, but best of all to see Jesus." She had been helping Miss Whitford in the school for three years and could ill be spared. Through the Lord's mercy she was restored.

There had been quite a revival in several of the T'ai-chow out-stations. We had heard of 170 persons baptized in a few months, and longed that we should see like blessing. I asked Mr. Liu if he would give us on Sunday afternoon a little account of the work there; so, instead of separating into our several classes, we all came together to hear what God had been doing in other places. Our hearts warmed as we heard of 147 baptisms in 1892. In the course of his remarks Mr. Liu said that Wenchow was considered the first station, both in numbers and spiritual power, while T'ai-chow was second. When he had finished I felt constrained to add a few words. I remarked that Wenchow had stood first, but could do so no longer. I contrasted our poor thirty with their 147, and asked who would join me in a week's daily prayer for deeper spiritual power in our own souls, and new life for others. Up went many hands. I asked what we should pray for, and one brother called out, "Seven hundred souls!" I was taken aback; my poor faith had not risen above one hundred. I said, " Let us think well before we speak.

God is able to give us all we have faith for." Then one dear man called out, "Up with your hands for three hundred next year." I pointed out that if each member would win one soul to Christ our numbers would just be doubled, and that seemed very little. So it was settled that as many as possible should meet for prayer every day during the first week of the Chinese year 1893; that after prayer we should make up several bands, and go in different directions, preaching the glorious gospel, and we expected much blessing.

We had a watch-night's service, and the next morning met at 10 a.m. for prayer. The room was quite full. I spoke from Titus ii., showing what sort of Christians we must be if we would receive the blessings we ask for. It was a heart-searching time. Our prayers were first for ourselves, that we might have more spiritual power, and be made more fit for our Master's use, and second for a large ingathering of souls. I cannot doubt but that these prayers were heard and answered, though not in the way we expected; for at first the answers seemed to come in disappointments—loss, not gain, was our experience during that week.

Mrs. Liu's serious illness was succeeded by the death of five of our members. One family was plunged into sore and continuous persecution. Worst of all, one man fell into open sin, while the pastor forgot his holy calling and gave way to wrath. We felt, like Jacob, "all these things are against us"; but, like Job, we could also say, " Though He slay me yet will I trust in Him." The pastor's case was particularly sad. On the Sunday afternoon following our week of prayer, during our women's missionary meeting, our coolie's wife had laid down the money she was about to give on the seat beside her. Next to her sat the pastor's wife, who, though unconverted, had been for some time attending our meetings. While I was speaking the coolie's wife was called away for a moment, and on her return the money was gone. No one had risen from their seat, and suspicion naturally fell upon the pastor's wife ; all the more so because she had done a similar thing before. After the service the coolie went to ask her if she had seen the money, when she flew into a rage and stormed ; he then returned, and told me what had happened. The next morning the pastor came, in almost as great a rage as his wife, said the coolie had accused her of stealing, and unless I made him apologise he would give up his position. He was too angry to reason with, so I told him to go away, and return when he could talk calmly. In the meantime I made inquiries, found that the coolie had neither said or done wrong, but that the woman had told a string of lies to her husband, who was not there when the thing happened. When Mr. T'siu came back he could speak more calmly, but was still angry. I pointed out that he, not the coolie, had done wrong, and that there were three Christian witnesses against the word of his wife; and as he had done the brother a wrong he was the one who ought to apologise. This he refused to do, and gave up his position as a preacher. Poor man, my heart ached for him. His worthless wife wasted his money so that even when receiving a good salary he was always in the depths of poverty. What he could do now I knew not.

A few weeks later the coolie came and asked that Mr. T'siu might be restored to employment again. He said, " I don't want him to confess to me that he has done wrong. I fully and freely forgive him, and have asked God to forgive him too. He is very poor and I am sorry for him." I was so glad to see such a Christlike spirit, and thought it might be God's way of breaking Mr. T'siu's proud heart. I sent for him and offered him employment as teacher to Miss B. and myself, telling him it was at Yung-ts'iah's request, mentioning what he had said, and that he owed his position to the man he had wronged. He was very glad to get back, and thanked me; but not one word of thanks to the coolie. How true it is that the one who does the wrong is the hardest to win!

This loss, which seemed so irreparable at the time, has only made room for one of the most able as well as Spirit-taught men I have ever known in China

Mr. T'sie was school teacher at the time, having come from Bing-yie, where he had for some years been helping Mr. G., and naturally stepped into the position of pastor in the stead of Mr. T'siu. He has been my greatest comfort, and the seconder of every active and good work ever since,

That was a sad, sad week. We had asked for more of the Holy Spirit's work in our hearts, and we got sorrow, and for increase there was scattering; yet we knew the Lord was answering our prayers, and could only ask Him to cleanse still further, until all that hindered His blessing should be taken out of the way. Over-strain of work, sorrow, and sleeplessness undermined my health, and while taking Chinese prayers one morning in April I grew faint, and had to be carried out of the room. The doctor was sent for, and ordered perfect quiet and rest for some days. After lying on the couch for a whole week doing nothing, he ordered me away for a change. I was unwilling to go far, or for long at such a time, so Miss B. and I went up the river by boat to a pretty waterfall for a week. I returned better, but still weak, and as I made very slow progress towards recovery the doctor advised me to take a sea voyage, and in June we went to Che-foo, where we had to remain four months under doctor's orders, Dr. D. refusing to allow me to return sooner. While I was ill we had the joy of baptizing five out of nine candidates; they came to my room one by one, as I wanted to hear their testimony, but of course I did not see them baptized.

In the month of April we were reinforced by Miss Stayner, from Canada; she at once set herself to acquiring the language, which she did both quickly and well, and has been a most efficient helper.

An extract from a letter written in that month states: "By God's grace the clouds have cleared; we have since had cause to praise Him for much blessing; many of the Christians have been stirred up to more earnest effort after the unsaved. Our large chapel, which seats 350, has several times been crowded with Christians and inquirers to its utmost capacity, and we are brought face to face with the question of enlarging our borders; either the chapel must be made bigger, or a new one opened outside the South Gate. Last month five were received by baptism, and yesterday we had the joy of adding ten more, while seven others who were not so clear in their testimonies were kept back. Some of the cases were particularly interesting; two were mother and son. The old woman told me when her son was very ill, and she feared he might die, she remembered some of the words told her that the living God could heal and help. In the darkness of the night she prayed to the unknown God. She saw no one, but heard a voice saying, 'If you will trust Me I will not only heal your son, but save your soul.' This was nearly two years ago, when her son also became a believer, and now they have been baptized together. Other two were uncle and nephew. We are beginning now to see families brought to the Lord more frequently than formerly, and it is a great joy specially to see the young men brought out on the Lord's side."

While I was in Che-foo I received a letter from Miss Chalmers, which proved that the prayers and promises of the early part of the year had not been forgotten. She spoke of one Sunday when Mr. T'sie preached from Rev. iii. 15–21. All seemed to realise that one-half of the year had gone and not as many souls been gathered as they had hoped, for the prayers were for more earnestness in that direction, and after the sermon Mr. T'sie asked one or two to pray, when Aoming prayed, and completely broke down. He stopped, went on again two or three times, and confessed he had been cold-hearted of late, and in the afternoon meeting the same spirit of confession prevailed.

I now insert a letter written after my return :—

"*Sept.*, 1893.—With very grateful thanks to our Heavenly Father I write again from Wenchow, the home of tender memories, of joy and sorrow, sowing and reaping; oh, it is good to be back amongst my dear people again; you would have supposed we had been away four years instead of four months. Misses W., C., and S. went down to the lower anchorage to meet us; we saw them on the shore, but the captain, who is a stranger, would not wait for them, and so they arrived home an hour after us. As soon as the anchor was down our two servants, with beaming faces, appeared; as we stepped on the jetty we were greeted by three of our women, who had taken a long walk to meet us, and when we entered our gates we were surrounded by men, women, and children, all eager for a word; they were delighted to see me looking so well, and said it was in answer to their prayers, for they had prayed every day that I might come back well and strong. Everything was in perfect order, even to flowers nicely arranged in all the rooms; my servants never spare themselves if thereby they can spare me.

"We arrived on our women's prayer-meeting day, and of course more than usual were present; all the prayers were full of thankfulness for our return. On Sunday we had a splendid day. I only took one service myself, for I mean to do less than formerly; indeed I have already arranged the work so that I shall only have three classes a week besides morning prayers, and I intend to confine myself to five hours' brain-work per day, except when the preachers are in. In another week or so we expect a number of candidates for baptism; I do not yet know how many.

We are still praying for greater things, but we want each member to be truly converted. Somehow I have a fear of large numbers. Perhaps it is want of faith, but in China it usually leads to trouble, and yet He is able to convert many as well as few. Do pray that no unsaved one may be received into the Church.

"I hope, if the Lord will, to start for O-dzing on the first journey of the season on the 18th of next month. Miss Stayner will accompany me; this will be her first visit to the country, and she is looking forward to it with much pleasure. Did I tell you that I had a very comfortable sedan-chair presented to me by a former captain of the s.s. *Haichang*. It will be a real comfort on our country trips, for the hill chairs take more out of me than the talking does, yet I did not like to buy one lest the natives might think I spent too much upon myself. The captain had left the Wenchow route more than two years ago, and we had neither seen or heard of him for a long while; surely the Lord put the thought of the chair into his mind. The other day in our women's meeting my subject was Phil. iv. 19, 'My God shall supply all your needs.' After I had finished one of the members prayed. She told the Lord one of their needs was a new chapel outside the South Gate, that they had been praying all the year about it, and now she asked for the fulfilment. When she finished I told them they must work as well as pray, and asked how many dollars they had contributed towards it; they replied not any yet, but they intended calling a meeting and ask what each one was able to give. I mean to leave them to carry out this project themselves, helping them a little when the time comes. I love to see them take more and more responsibility in church work, and shall be delighted when I can leave the acceptance of candidates entirely in their hands. Candidates are accepted by the church, but I see them all privately first, and while they sometimes keep back one whom I have passed, they would often pass one I would keep back.

"A little later I was all Saturday afternoon examining candidates; eight (four men and four women) were baptized yesterday morning. The prayer-meeting on Saturday night lasted from 7.15 till 10 o'clock; all gave bright testimonies, and some are very interesting cases. Yesterday was a grand day, the chapel packed in every corner; some of us had to sit on the platform. We began the baptismal service at 9 a.m.; there was no break, and the communion service closed at 12.10. We snatched a hurried meal, and at one o'clock I had the preachers' meeting for an hour; at 2 p.m. we had the afternoon service, which lasted until 3.30. Quite a number stayed all night, and at eight o'clock next morning I had a service with them; 75 were present. The

Lord is truly working in our midst. The preacher spoke with great power on the words, 'He will thoroughly purge His floor,' and it was a most searching address. Praise God for all these tokens of mercy. My soul is rejoicing in God my Saviour. Two of the schoolgirls have professed conversion, both having been led through the efforts of the elder Christian girls."

CHAPTER XXI

"Thy expectation shall not be cut off."—PROV. xxiv. 14.

EARLY in October Miss Stayner and I started for O-dzing, but I must leave Miss S. to give the account of that journey, for it takes all my time and strength to do the work at such times, so that writing about it has to be left to another pen, if not, the journey remains unwritten, as an accumulation of work forbids my giving details after my return home. If these journeys should prove interesting to the reader they are wholly indebted to the kindness of my young helpers, who often recount our experiences while I am resting. Miss Stayner writes:—

"The O-dzing pastor waited over in Wenchow for a few days so as to come on with us. We left the city on Thursday evening; at least, we got into our boat and settled down for the night, though the tide did not permit our leaving till about 1 a.m. This river-boat is covered by a thick mat called a 'bong,' arch-fashion, an uncovered place only being left at bow and stern for the boatmen. One end of our primitive cabin was boarded up, and a number of boards at a little height from the floor at that end formed a good bedstead. Our mat, and thin mattress, were laid on top of that, and, shutting ourselves off from our Chinese co-travellers by tying up a little curtain, we made ourselves quite cosy for the night. By daylight we were up so as to be dressed and have our breakfast before arriving at the place from which we were to take chairs. The boats only go about three miles an hour, so we had come up the river about twelve miles during the night. We then had to go nearly thirty miles across the country to O-dzing. How different travelling is in China from at home! Here we take a day and night to do what would take about an hour for our own slow trains to do. Our chair-bearers and those carrying our luggage were all Christians, or inquirers who had come down for us from this village.

"Mrs. Stott had brought her own sedan-chair, a light, open basket one, but I must really try to describe mine to you. It was a mountain-chair, and as such was of the simplest and lightest construction, as you may well imagine when I say that when one of the men brought it down to the jetty over one shoulder it seemed to consist of little else than the two long bamboo poles, with the shorter pieces at each end joining these together for the men to rest on their shoulders. But in a minute, with two short boards, he arranged a back and a seat, which swung from the side poles by ropes, and longer pieces of rope supported a stick upon which the feet were to rest. You will be saying that must be most uncomfortable to sit in for nearly a whole day; but wait, Mrs. Stott has not been over twenty years in China without knowing how to make the best of things. Our wadded bed coverlet was fastened round the back and seat, thus making a broad, comfortable seat, and softer back. Wrapping rugs round our knees, having warm jackets on, the morning air being delightfully cool, our caravan started in 'Chinese file.' It consisted of us, our two chairs, our cook, who trudged behind, a man with our bedding, and our servants, another with our big provision basket, &c., the preacher, and two other men who had come with us from Wenchow. We made quite a respectable and picturesque little procession as we wound along the path, through the plain, or up and down the mountain roads. Each man had his own loads over his shoulder, yet they walked that twenty-eight or thirty miles without faltering, only stopping two or three times for rest, and in the evening they were all at prayers, and the pastor gave quite a long, animated address. They are splendid walkers, these country fellows who live amongst the mountains, and their well-built, muscular frames are a pleasant contrast to the thin, skinny specimens which are so common in and around the city.

"The scenery is just lovely, and one can take it all in so nicely sitting quietly back in one's chair, no one to distract, and plenty of time to notice in detail, instead of dashing through in an express train. The plain through which we went for the first three hours or so is not very broad, high hills, and even mountains, I imagine, rising on every side. We followed the course of a picturesque little river for some way, now on this side of it, now on that, crossing it either by stepping-stones or else the men wading through where it was shallow. Often we felt inclined to take a good long walk, but we had to save up for a very high 'ling' (mountain pass) where the chairs could not carry us. This was near the end of our journey, so the bearers were pretty well tired out when we started to descend into the valley where O-dzing is situated, about two hundred chimneys (they thus reckon the size of their villages) nestling in the midst of the mountains, and with a clear mountain stream flowing by. We crossed the stream by stepping-stones, and went through the straggling lanes, some so closely built up our chairs could hardly turn the corners, and turned into this house, where we met with a very warm reception.

"As soon as we got into our room they brought us delicious hot tea, made out of pressed and dried oranges, sweetened, and ever since they have been heaping us with all their best eatables. We brought enough provisions with us to serve for a few meals, but Mrs. Stott knew there was no need to bring much, as they always insisted on giving us Chinese food. Fortunately they know our tastes somewhat, so we manage to get on very well, though they are greatly distresed at the small quantity we eat, they thinking nothing of a couple of basins of rice. Their food is so much less nourishing than ours, they are obliged to eat a greater quantity to support them. One boy brought us a quantity of fruit which he had been out on the hills gathering, a woman brought us cake, while a man who invited us to his house to-day, because Mrs. S. felt too tired to go, brought our dinner over to us instead. Our host, who is well off, allows an old blind man to live in one corner of his house, and half supports him; the other day our hostess came up with quite a fine fowl, which she said this old man had been feeding up for the last few weeks for Mrs. Stott.

"On Saturday three men came in from some villages to be examined for baptism, and two were accepted, the other being told he had better wait a little, as on some points he was not very clear yet, though all think he is a Christian. The baptisms took place down at the river, about six o'clock on Sunday morning, before many people were about, as these country people of course would not understand baptism, and we might gather quite a noisy crowd. As we stood there on the rocks beside the sparkling, running water, on that bright, clear morning, how our prayers did rise for these two thus definitely professing to follow Christ in the sacred ordinance so significant and so new to them; and how they needed our prayers! one just a boy of twenty-two, and both simple and ignorant, and so few opportunities in their distant mountain home of learning more about spiritual things.

"After breakfast Mrs. Stott and I went to sit for a while on the side of the hill, and had a little quiet reading, prayer, and singing, no one coming near to disturb us. At about nine we had service, Mrs. S. speaking from Ephesians ii., our position before we were converted, ending with a few earnest words to some strangers who were there, and then about twenty or so natives, with ourselves, partook of the Lord's Supper. We were greatly struck with the earnestness and reverence of all through the whole service. Early in the afternoon, for the convenience of those who lived at a distance, we had a second service, at which Mrs. S. spoke on the same chapter in Ephesians—what we are now in Christ.

"We were taken by our hostess to see several people living on the other side of the river, and, as Mrs. S. was too tired out to take part in the evening service, it was conducted by the preacher, Tsie-ming. Though he is the pastor of O-dzing, and his headquarters are here still, he is only regularly here once a month on Sunday, when they have communion; the other three Sundays he holds services in other villages, and the rest of the time goes round evangelising.

"The people of this house keep a spare room for his use, and ours when we are here, and they also give up the good-sized room next door for a chapel. It is fitted up with a table and benches, and Scripture scrolls are hung round the wall, making it quite a neat little room. Besides regular Sunday services, they have morning and evening prayers, and Thursday afternoon the women have a prayer-meeting, as in Wenchow. In the morning the people of the house meet at about six, the men having their rice immediately afterwards, just before going to the fields, but in the evening most of the Christians come to prayers.

"On Monday we went to Za-bie, where one of the inquirers live, a small village about twenty miles away. We left about nine in the morning, a bright beautiful day, cloudy in the afternoon, so that we did not suffer from the heat—altogether I can say I think I had one of the most enjoyable trips in my life. We went right through the very heart of the mountains, wandering up and down, in and out on the narrow paths, sometimes in really dangerous places, where a slip of one of the bearers would have dashed us down the steep mountain sides; but, strange to say, even in the worst places I did not really feel afraid, though naturally I have a strong aversion to precipices and high places in general. One seemed to realise that the Lord was keeping the feet of those who carried us. Two or three times one of Mrs. S.'s men stumbled and fell, but never in a bad place.

"I was greatly tickled once. In a very narrow, precipitous place her man slipped, and she said, 'Do be very careful'; for if he fell down here we would all be killed. In a most reassuring voice he replied, 'Oh, if we are all killed we shall go to heaven'; at which Mrs. S. said, 'No doubt, but she didn't particularly care to go in that way'; at which there was a great laugh.

"Za-bie is quite a small village, and must be situated several thousand feet above the sea, for coming home we noticed it took two hours and a quarter from there to the foot of the high 'ling,' during which time we were nearly constantly on the descent. We had a great affair of it going up the 'ling,' for before we had got to the steepest part Mrs. S.'s strength gave out, and though it was almost impossible to take her up in the chair, the men determined they would do it. So two got in front and two behind, and with the preacher and her devoted servant occasionally lending a hand at the difficult sharp corners, they did manage it. But I thought she was really brave to let them, for sometimes the path was almost straight up. For a time, after reaching the top of the 'ling,' our path led right along a narrow ridge of the mountain, so on either side we looked down into the deep valleys, and far away to height above height. It was a scene that would have rejoiced the heart of a painter, as we saw the sun set behind those mountains, and the next morning it was even more beautiful on our return trip. There was a heavy mist, and for fear of rain we started early. The mountains were invisible, but as we proceeded the sun began to struggle down and the mists to rise. It was just grand. I only wish I could picture it to you. Suffice to say Mrs. S., a true Scotchwoman, said she thought the scenery quite equalled if it did not excel the Highlands, and I agreed with her.

"We had a funny experience at Za-bie. When we arrived our host came out and welcomed us, and then retired to prepare our bedstead (two boards on two benches) while the wife was busy lighting the fire to get us something to eat, 'like Martha,' as the preacher remarked, so we were left sitting in the courtyard to admire a pig, some cocks having a regular fight, a cow, and various other domestic animals, while some of the village people came in to admire (?) us, being the first foreigners most of them had ever seen probably. While waiting we drank some tea, I being so thirsty as to indulge in two basins ; something for a person who never drinks ordinary tea at home. However, please do not let any one mistake the word basin ; it is only the size of an ordinary large breakfast-cup. After great preparations, and when we were nearly famished, the good wife brought us up our tea to our room, and really at first sight it appeared as though there was nothing we could eat but rice. Our servant was greatly distressed, so privately told our hostess, we liked eggs and potatoes, the latter sweet are considered so common they often don't like to offer us them, so at breakfast our inner man felt more satisfied.

"That evening sixty or more men and women gathered in the courtyard, so we went down, had a hymn and a gospel address from Mrs. Stott, after which the preacher spoke to them. Even after we had retired to rest we heard him preaching to those who remained, while a couple of others, our chair-bearers I suppose, were speaking to others in the kitchen and back premises—this after a hard day's tramp over the mountains at least twenty miles. Does not the earnestness of these young men put many of us to shame?—we who have known the gospel from the time we knew anything, who have many of us, been Christians for years, while those from O-dzing first heard the way of salvation but little over four years ago.

"It was very amusing; at night we had quite a reception, many of the women came up to our room to examine us and our possessions. Finding our native light insufficient, they lit long pieces of wood, with which they went poking round so close to us and to our bedclothes that it made one quite nervous. It is a source of astonishment to me that they aren't constantly burning down their houses, for this is the way they always light themselves round. Much to their disgust, Mrs. S. said we were now going to retire, and walking calmly to the door, as it were, took it for granted they were going out, so for shame's sake they felt obliged to, though one woman insinuatingly asked Mrs. S. just to lay her head down and let them see her rest before they left; however, she said she wasn't ready. The next day, when half-way home, I got hungry, an unusual thing; so as we had nothing with us, we stopped at a village in hopes we could get a 'basin' of sweet potatoes; however, they had none cooked, and all we could get were two heaping basins of 'mie-n,' that is vermicelli. You would have laughed if you had seen us sitting in the road, Mrs. S. in her chair, I on a small stool beside her, the centre of an admiring crowd, digging diligently with our chopsticks into this most inconvenient long stringy stuff, which, however, we pretty nearly managed to finish.

"We had intended going another trip the next day to the village where the two newly baptized men lived, but at the end of our six hours in chairs from Za-bie Mrs. S. was so exhausted she felt it wiser not to attempt anything further, but just rest another day, quietly visiting and teaching the Christians and inquirers, and then return home.

"We called at the house of the old persecutor, and were quite kindly received by his witchlike old wife, who gave us some 'z s' (fresh persimmmon) to take away with us. We had such a weird sort of visit, and all the time I could think of nothing else but the tale of the Witch of Endor. The men had some visitors to dinner, so we waited a few minutes for her in the usual dark, dirty Chinese kitchen and living-room, while she served them. In a small room just off we got a glimpse of the big old man and his four fine-looking stalwart sons and their guests, while the skinny old wife was leaning over the big round rice-pot and ladling out steaming bowls of rice and vegetables, &c. Some one else was feeding the big Chinese stove with brushwood, so that the whole scene was lit up by its blaze. Every now and then one of the young men would come out with a couple of bowls to be heaped up again with rice.

"One thing that strikes one most forcibly is the

utter lack of home comfort amongst even the well-off Chinese ; they seem to have no idea of it ; everything so bare and dark, the living-room as a rule with earthen floor, a good portion taken up with the stationary brick stove, and just furnished with the bare necessities of table and stools ; perhaps a couple of uncomfortable little bamboo chairs, a few farming implements it may be, and a pile of brushwood thrown down complete the picture. Oh, I forgot a pig and a few little ones snorting around, and a lot of fowls should be added.

"On the Thursday morning, after final prayers with our kind O-dzing friends, we once more mounted our chairs and started for home. About a dozen followed us right out of the village to the stepping-stones across the river, and remained waving their hands till we disappeared round the hills. We took a different and, I think, a prettier road down to the river, where we get the boat, reaching there as it was getting dark, though it was not much after six. As soon as we had our supper in the house of one of Mr. H.'s church members in the village, we got Nga-Koe to arrange our bedding in the boat, and retired. My principal reason for going thus early was so as to go to sleep before I had time to get hungry again, as I didn't want the bother of reopening up our provision basket. This time our mattress was just laid on the bottom of the boat crossways, but with curtains fastened up at either side, and nice warm rugs. We were quite comfortable, and slept the sleep of the fatigued pilgrim, though, in true Chinese style, our boatman made the most dreadful noise in starting about midnight, and putting up the sail (apparently just over our heads), and generally managing the boat. If we had been nervous people, sleep would have been utterly out of the question. It was a lovely bright moonlight night, and when we reached the city about 5.30, and walked home, the moon and stars were shining brightly at one side, while just over the eastern wall the rising sun was beginning to tint the sky, so that we thoroughly enjoyed our walk through the quiet city streets.

"And so my first real experience of Chinese travelling, of living in Chinese homes, and eating Chinese food has come to an end, and, looking back, I may say I have enjoyed my week most thoroughly, and it makes me long for the time when I shall be able to go out and teach these dear native Christians, and tell the gospel to those who as yet do not know it or its wonderful transforming power in their dark lives."

CHAPTER XXII

"Thou therefore endure hardness, as a good soldier of Jesus Christ."—2 TIM. ii. 3.

ABOUT this time Miss Bardsley began an Anti-foot-binding Society. She had been encouraged to this by Mr. M'Gowan, of Amoy, of whose work we heard a delightful account when in Che-foo, and the success of his Anti-foot-binding Society was so remarkable, that we felt quite ashamed that we had done so little in that direction. Mr. M'G. kindly sent us one of his pledge-books, which contained a threefold pledge. First, the woman was to unbind her own feet; secondly, not to bind her daughter's; thirdly, to unbind her daughter-in-law's; this last I thought too hard upon the daughter-in-law, so ours took the form of a twofold pledge only. Miss B. has been greatly encouraged in her efforts, and, I think, has something like seventy members; it has created a truly wholesome sentiment in the church on this question.

The year closed more happily than it began, for, although we had not seen the large numbers we had hoped and prayed for, and sorrow had marked a large portion of the year, yet many of the Christians had been truly revived in soul, and two new stations had been opened. We had a sweet and blessed watch-night service, the closing words being Psa. xviii. 2. My motto for the coming year was, " My soul, wait thou only upon God, for my expectation is from Him"; the words "Wait upon the Lord" I felt was to be the lesson for the opening year.

Our usual preachers' meetings this year were opened by a three days' conference upon methods of work, when Pastor T'sie gave three most searching, helpful, and spiritual addresses; indeed, I have seldom heard more so even from a foreigner. The first day his subject was, "How to explain the Scriptures." We give the merest skeleton of these addresses. (1) Knowledge of the Chinese character essential. (2) In speaking on the parables, first explain the story before giving figurative meaning. (3) Show clearly the plan of salvation, repentance, and faith—Mark i. 15. (4) Give first principles of the doctrine; then its use and application. (5) It is important not only to understand the Scriptures, but to have experienced oneself the truth one is seeking to impart. (6) Be careful to give the doctrines of Scripture, not one's own ideas. (7) Christ's words and His works and example the foundations of all your teaching. (8) Not only enunciate the truth, but seek to send home and apply them to the heart of both preacher and hearers. See Romans iv. 23, 24.

Second day: " How to preach so as to lead men to Christ." (1) United prayer necessary—Acts i. 14, 15. For the answer, see Acts ii. 41. (2) Not only prayer but preaching necessary—John i. 35–40. (3) Preach trusting in the power of the Holy Spirit to convict, following Christ's method in John iv. 16–19. (4) Have patience to teach and explain, as Christ in John iii. 3–21. (5) Sacrifice one's own time, comfort, &c., in order to lead others to the Lord—Luke v. 27–29. (6) Seek to be at peace with all, even outsiders—Rom. xii. 18. (7) Examine oneself as to reality of faith, and with what object one is preaching, whether for money, for glory, &c., or for the salvation of precious souls — Acts xix. 13–16. Third day: Acts xix. 23–41. Two lessons are here learned from Paul when in difficulties and persecutions. While contending for the truth, and never yielding there, yet he so conducted himself that the chief of Asia were his friends. We should show due respect to those in authority, and be considerate and yielding in all matters not affecting our religion—verses 35–37. (2) We must be careful not to revile the idols or idol-worship, but to preach the truth; when truth and light enter the soul, falsehood and darkness must fly. We should have fewer cases of persecution if we followed Paul's example in these things.

The subjects dealt with by the preachers were mostly parables, miracles, the life of Christ, &c., and we were greatly cheered by the able way many of these subjects were handled. A good portion of each day was spent in prayer, and the future seemed hopeful, earnestness and humble confession characterising most of the prayers. It was a month of deep soul-searching and blessing, and was doubtless an inspiration throughout the year.

During the Christmas week, when our missionary brethren from Bing-yie and Chu-chow were with us, the idea was started of building a cottage by the sea, or rather bay, within easy reach of Wenchow, as a sanatorium for the C.I.M. stations of Wenchow, Bing-yie, and Chu-chow. We began as early in the year as possible, hoping it might be ready by the summer; but, alas! for our hopes, it was not finished till September, owing to the difficulty and the expenses of transport. Much of my time, too, was spent in superintending details. The pastor was the only man able to help me, and he could not often be spared; but I had a double object in spending a week or ten days at a time among men, bricks, and mortar. There were seven Christians among them, and, though they rested on Lord's days, they were too far off to attend any services, so I once or twice included Sunday. We had a short service every evening and three on Lord's day, a few of the village people attending, and I doubt if the same number of Testaments and hymn-books could be found among workmen in England as were piled in a convenient corner ready for use when the day's work was over.

Our cottage will be a great boon as a quiet, cool place of rest for weary workers who cannot afford the time and expense of going to Che-foo; indeed, it has already proved a great comfort, and I believe its use will be more and more apparent as the years roll by. It is built Chinese fashion, three rooms long and two deep, two bedrooms on either side, while in the centre is a good-sized sitting-room, behind it being a large pantry which could easily be converted into another room if needed; there is a good verandah round three sides of the house, and a bath-room at either end; at the rear is kitchen and servants' room; in front there is a small garden, and a wall enclosing the whole; behind are the everlasting hills, where we can walk for miles without meeting a soul, while stretching before us is the large expanse of waters, with large and small islands dotted about, and is about four hours' journey from Wenchow by native boat.

It is furnished in simple cottage fashion, bamboo chairs and sofa, while packing-cases do duty for dressing-tables in each bedroom, covered by pretty art-muslin sent by kind friends from England; short curtains on the windows to protect us from prying eyes, for during the first months we had many visitors. The sitting-room is covered with Canton matting. When we go we take with us our photographs and other knick-knacks to make it home-like, while the hills provide us with wild flowers and grasses.

In the meantime Miss Whitford had become engaged to be married, and with the prospect of her going to another station came the necessity of some one to take her place. The request for one was responded to by sending two, and in the spring Miss Spink and Miss Williams arrived, the latter to take up the school, and the former more especially for country work; but of course both had to commence studying the language, and Miss W. kindly decided to defer her marriage a few months until her successor should be more able to fill her place.

1894. In the early months of the year Ba-zie and other stations were visited. In the former, six full and very encouraging days were spent. We visited fourteen villages (five of those were newly opened up to the gospel), in all of which there were Christians or inquirers. They told me of over ten persons who had themselves sought out the Christians and asked that a preacher might be sent to teach them. The silversmith accompanied me to all those places, but it grieved me to see that, although full of zeal, his addresses had too much of self to please God; this characteristic clung to him to the end, and I have lately heard that he was called home suddenly, in the very midst of his rejoicing over a degree he had just bought. There was no doubt of his salvation, but the suddenness of his death and the circumstances made a profound impression on the church. He was seeking the honour that cometh from man rather than that which cometh from God. "Hold fast, that no man take thy crown."

At the end of May I was called to O-dzing. One of the Christians was and had been suffering persecution, another had sinned and was now ill and penitent, and it seemed as if my going would be a help all round. It was late in the season for such a long journey, but I trusted the Lord to give cloudy weather, and He gave it. Through the Lord's grace I was able to do what we hoped, except that the penitence of the poor woman was short-lived; she had got under the power of the Roman Catholics, and soon after went over entirely to them, and has not yet been restored; thus the promise of a most useful worker has been blighted.

Two days before returning to the city I took a bad cold, which, with the extra fatigue, knocked me up altogether, and for more than a week I was unfit for any kind of work. I was conscious that steadily, though slowly, my health was giving way; I was no longer able for the same amount of work as formerly, and I felt that, unless a more vigorous hand took up the reins, loss to the church must be the result, for, unless the leader is able to keep well in the front of every good work, the natives soon relax their energies. I therefore asked the Director to send a suitable married man who would in time relieve me of the greater part of the responsibility. Such a request was not so easy to grant as might appear at first sight; married men who have been a few years in China had their own stations and work which could not be left, while a new and inexperienced man was hardly suitable for the post, and so we had to wait.

Again, in the beginning of August, while at the cottage, I was suddenly taken ill with an attack of cholera (not Asiatic), which led me aside for a few weeks; and, just as I was getting convalescent, Miss B. and Miss S. took ill, also several of our natives, so we had almost a hospital. Cholera was raging in the city, and hundreds died daily in deep darkness. "Oh! God, when will light arise in their midst?" In all our sickness we were most kindly attended without charge by Dr. L. of I.M. Customs, who never spared himself while others needed his care.

Hostilities between Japan and China had broken out, and the people were more or less excited, but, as the seat of war lay in the north, there seemed no cause for apprehension in our neighbourhood. In November Miss Stayner and Miss Spink had gone to the Tong-t'sö district, where they expected to be three weeks visiting the different villages; they returned, however, in less than one week in a sad plight, dressed in borrowed native clothes, partly men's, and partly women's; they looked such guys in their curious rig-out that we were forced to laugh in spite of our surprise and alarm. All had gone well with them until the Thursday before, when they reached a hamlet where there were a few Christians; they were well received, and after evening prayers retired to rest. But I will leave Miss Stayner to tell her own story:—

"We started on Monday morning, the 3rd inst., for a journey across the river, and on Tuesday and Wednesday visited several villages, where we were received very well by the people, and nothing but quiet was experienced till Thursday night. On that evening, about six o'clock, we reached Du-Kang, a small lonely village right away on the hills, inhabited by only seven or eight families, all of the name of Chi. We were to stop that night at the house of a Christian family living about five minutes distant. We were accompanied from the previous village by our private servant, a Bible-woman, preacher, and two Christian men, who were all to stay in the same house. We were received well, and quite a number gathered for the service which was held about eight o'clock; and soon after we retired to rest in a room in a loft, our Bible-woman and the woman of the house sleeping in an adjoining room, an open doorway leading from one to the other, the men of the party sleeping downstairs.

"About midnight we were aroused by great shouting and lights in the next room. A moment later our room was filled with a crowd of men (perhaps about a dozen) carrying flaming torches, who at once started pulling our clothes off the bed and emptying our provision basket. I attempted to speak to them, asking what they meant by this, but could not make myself heard; and when I tried to hold on to our bed quilt, one man struck me on the hand with his bamboo stick, and held on a minute or so, but at last I got free.

"The Bible-woman, who had been the first with the woman of the house to be attacked, had had some bracelets torn off her arms, and was also beaten with bamboo poles; but somehow she managed to get through them to us, and while the robbers were busy going off with our things (for by this time we saw that resistance was useless) she led us by a door into another loft, and we escaped down the ladder and out by the next house on to the hill behind the village. We were barefooted, and with only our night-dresses on, the robbers having stolen all our other clothing, bedding, books, &c. We climbed up through the wet grass and brambles, over rocks and stones, and at last, when we thought ourselves on a tolerably safe place, sat down in the bushes to see how things would shape themselves. We must have remained there over an hour listening to the shouting and yelling, and watching the flaring lights as the men went from house to house beating down doors and walls, and expecting each moment they might come out to search for us. Some of the villagers had escaped to the opposite side of the ravine where we were sitting, and soon we heard them say the robbers had left. In a few minutes more they let off several volleys from their guns, signs of triumph, or perhaps to intimidate any from following them. A little later two of the Christian men came out with lanterns to search for us, and were rejoiced to find we had not been carried off by the banditti. Fortunately they were able to find shoes for us to put on, as our feet were so hurt we could not have got down barefooted.

"We went back into the house, and remained up in the loft the rest of the night. The alarm had been given at the nearest village, Lao-o (about ten li distant), and a number of men started after the robbers, but of course were unable to overtake them. The poor villagers had also suffered much. The robbers, they say, were armed with spears as well as guns, and the old man of the house where we were staying had his arms and side badly cut. The people's clothing, grain, some of the cows, and other animals were taken off, the women's ornaments being torn out of their ears, hair, and hands.

"But what was most serious of all, our servant named Ui-yi-foh, the son of the house, and another neighbour were nowhere to be found; they were doubtless taken off by the banditti for the purpose of being held to ransom. Before dawn, the woman of the house and the Bible-woman having divested themselves of some of their clothing to give us, we started for the next village, Lao-o, one of the Christians having gone some time before to try to get chairs for us. We had only got a little distance when we met eight of the Christian women; from these we got a bundle of clothing they had brought for us. They had started off bravely with a lantern in the dark to walk all that distance, though their husbands had opposed their doing such a dangerous thing. We then took chairs down to the creek, which we reached about noon yesterday; here we took a boat to the city, and arrived before daylight this morning.

"To show that in this instance we have not done anything that might be considered dangerous or foolhardy, I may say that, though foreigners had not been in that particular hamlet before, the district round and just such lonely places have frequently been visited by Mrs. Stott and others, and no danger was apprehended by ourselves or any of the natives; the people of the place have suffered most, having had nearly everything they possessed carried away.

What the fate of our servant and the other two men may be we dare not think."

A few days later some of our people came in with the further information that the robbers, being unable to carry off all their booty, left some of it on the hillside, and two of their number, returning to take possession, were captured by the people of another village seven miles off, and were bound by them. Soon after another messenger arrived from Si-k'ai, saying that the chief of the robbers, with some of the booty, had been caught there and bound. But the officials delayed so long that the villagers were compelled to set the captives free. We were very anxious as to the safety of our Christian servant; we had received a message that he would be released upon our paying one hundred dollars; later on the demands became less and less, until it was believed that he would be released on the payment of ten dollars, and I was urged to settle the matter thus by the native Christians. I pointed out, however, to them that even the smallest sum must not be given for such a purpose; if we ransomed him we would never be safe, and not only our servants, but we ourselves liable to capture at any time; we must therefore wait and pray. It seemed hard to keep our brother in bondage when a few dollars might set him free, but the principle involved was too great, and I was firm, although gladly would I have given much more to see him once more amongst us.

We frequently met together to pray that our brother might soon be released, that he should not suffer hunger or ill treatment while in bonds, and that he might have good opportunities of preaching to the robbers. All these requests were granted by our loving Father: one day, just as we had risen from prayer, and I had asked that while we were praying the answer might come, the captive walked in. A stranger to us in the city, with whom our servant had business dealings, heard of his capture, and having a brother living in the village where he was bound, interceded with his brother, and without our knowledge they redeemed him for two dollars, he having been nearly three weeks in captivity. Oh, how our hearts did rejoice when we heard how they had listened to the gospel and treated him kindly, providing sufficient straw to keep him warm; the loss of the goods seemed as nothing. A little later the two other men were also released, but I do not know upon what terms.

At the end of this year we had ten candidates for baptism; a number were from a village across the river. They had been led and in some measure taught by a man who had been an inquirer for nearly six years; he never seemed to make much progress, and was, I feared, more bent on proving his fitness for employment as a preacher, than soul winning. He was a man of some character, and it looked as if the candidates of the district would stand or fall by his decision; some, therefore, were anxious for him to be baptized. There was no doubt that several of the others were truly converted, and it seemed hard to hinder them by not accepting him, and they were not prepared to stand independently; when, therefore, he appeared with six others, including his own son, it was with the confident hope he would be received. But as I had reason to believe he expected to be employed as a preacher, I put him through a rather stiff examination, and pointed out that there was no hope of employment. He said he did not want that; all he asked was to be sent out as a preacher, and get a dollar a month for expenses. I replied such a thing was impossible for two reasons. First, we never sent out newly baptized members as preachers. Second, our old and tried men only got fifty cents per month for their journeys; and indeed I made it plain that though I should be glad for him to tell the gospel to as many as he could, I had no intention of sending him out as a preacher. At this he said, "In that case I would rather wait." His son, about twelve years of age, was very clear in his testimony, and so were the others, but they also withdrew, as they considered it not good form to be baptized before the one who had taught them,

It was soon apparent that the Lord had delivered us out of a snare, for there is now no doubt that had we received this man he would have caused much trouble; and indeed he has tried in several ways to injure the work. Since then, several of those who withdrew have been baptized, though at that time only four out of the ten were received.

CHAPTER XXII

1895

" Both he that soweth and he that reapeth may rejoice together."—
JOHN iv. 36.

IN February, Mr. and Mrs. Woodman arrived in Shang-hai, from England. Mr. Taylor, who was on the look-out for a suitable couple to send to Wen-chow, recognised in them the ones most likely to fill the position, and without delay designated them for our city. They were most gladly welcomed, and ere long were fully installed not only in our home, but in our hearts also. They differed as to gifts, but both had that warm loving sympathy which won all hearts. They came at a busy time, for on the 12th of March I was to celebrate my jubilee, and at the same time complete my twenty-five years in China—for it will be remembered I arrived on my twenty-fifth birthday. What a change had taken place in that time, the little one had literally become a thousand, and it seemed a most fitting opportunity for a day of thanksgiving.

It was my intention that invitations should be

issued to all the church members, including those also in Dong-ling and Bing-yie, who had been received into church fellowship by my husband ; but our accommodation proving insufficient we were obliged to restrict ourselves to two in each family, where more than that number were in fellowship; even then the invitations extended to over three hundred, sixty or seventy of whom would have to remain our guests for three days, because of the distance they must travel. Part of the programme was a Chinese feast, which is a necessary adjunct to all celebrations. Preparations on such a gigantic scale had to be begun betimes, so that the event was known and talked about months before. For some days every one wore an air of delighted mystery, which I attributed to the anticipation of the coming event; on the 11th the chapel was in the hands of many willing workers, who had taken upon themselves to decorate the building in true festive style. In the afternoon I went to see how they were progressing, when I was turned back and told I must not try to look in until I was invited to do so. I knew then some surprise must be in store for me, but never could have dreamed of anything so costly and beautiful as what they had devised. I had invited all the missionaries to supper on the Monday evening, knowing that Tuesday would be given up to the natives. About nine o'clock we were all invited into the chapel, to see, as I thought, how nicely the natives had decorated it: the sight nearly took away my breath; there hung behind the platform a large satin banner, and scrolls to match, besides thirteen others, two in satin and silk, but all inscribed in gold letters. Many pairs of large red candles, and some other things, including a handsome pair of candlesticks of stags, the horns and hoofs gold plated. As soon as the pastor had hinted that it would be nice to present me with a banner, the Christians took it in such a hearty way, that he saw they meant to have it done in the best possible style; hence such a costly present. A few days after, when asking him why he had allowed them to spend so much money upon me, he remarked, " If you had only seen the joy with which they brought their presents you would not be grieved;" he had not intended anything so grand, but after everything was paid for, and even boxes added in which by and by to convey them to England, there were still ten dollars over. It was just wonderful the amounts those poor people gave, many of them hardly able to buy rice. That same evening I had another surprise, quite as great; my dear fellow missionaries in Wenchow and Bing-yie, including those of the Methodist Free Church, united in presenting me with a lovely gold watch. It was just overwhelming that day, and even now I can hardly write about it without emotion. During the meetings every speaker referred to my beloved husband in the most tender and loving way, showing how blessed his memory was.

In the midst of the festivities one of the mandarin ladies, dressed in her official robes, with a four-bearers chair, came to offer her congratulations as a representative of the Yamen ladies, few of whom had ever seen me. The devotion of my cook, who had served me for fifteen years, touched me much; he took all the work of providing for my numerous guests upon himself, at far less cost than I could have done, and worked almost night and day that the burden might not fall upon me. After all was over, and the guests gone, I called him into my study and told him that while I knew that money could not pay for the services he had rendered, yet, being pleased, I wished him to accept a little present to express my appreciation. He only answered, "If you are pleased, that is all I want." He took the money, but a little while after his wife, who was our first school-girl, came with a message that as he could not express what he wanted, he had sent her back to say that "they did not look upon themselves as servants; I was both father and mother, and parents did not pay their children for doing their duty." Tears ran down her cheeks when she added, "When you are pleased we are pleased; when you are troubled we are troubled; when you are well we are well; and when you are ill we are ill too." She then asked me to take back the money; but I replied, "Mothers will sometimes give a gift to a child, and would feel hurt if it were returned." She then took it with a smile; such devotion is humbling. I have done what I could, but others have done far more, and have received less, "to Him alone be the glory!" Mr. Woodman, giving a touching and graphic description of that wonderful day, writes as follows:—

"Just now, when so many eyes are turned towards this far-off land in the East, you will be glad to hear a little of the Lord's doings among His own people, I should like to describe, if possible, to you the events of one day, March 12th, in this city of Wenchow, with its eighty thousand or more population; it is what we call in our own country a 'red-letter day,' the event being the fiftieth anniversary of Mrs. Grace Stott's birthday, and the completion of her twenty-fifth year of work here. Invitations had been issued to the Christians to gather for a day of thanksgiving and praise to God, and as many of them lived thirty and forty miles away, they arrived two days and even three days before, so as to be in time; the large church and native quarters were taxed to their utmost powers of accommodation. It was most touching, as you walked about the compound, to see the Christians gathered about in little groups, studying the Word, or praying for a mighty outpouring of the Holy Spirit upon them and all who should be gathered together. All through the previous day the church, with its bare white-washed walls, had been in the hands of the native Christians, and at night, when all was finished, Mrs. Stott was sent for, to find waiting her surprises of their love, for on entering the place there hung a most beautiful and costly scarlet satin banner, with ornaments of silk tassels and fine polished jade stones, the gift of the church, speaking by its very beauty the depth of their gratitude and love to her who had led them to Christ, out of darkness into His marvellous light. In the finest gold characters there was inscribed upon it a very suitable inscription referring to Mr. and Mrs. Stott having been the first to bring them the good news of the gospel, with the quotation from Dan. xii. 3 linked to their names. Besides this, on all sides other scrolls and banners to the number of fifteen, tokens of individual love, chief among them being one from her girls' school on which was written 1 Kings iii. 9-13, in Chinese characters. One of the most touching gifts received were some very large Chinese red candles from her old blind men's home, which to them meant much from their poverty; and last, but not least, there were four pairs of scrolls from the heathen tradesmen of the city, which perhaps spoke louder than any other thing of the value and result of a Christ-like life lived in the midst of heathen darkness and idolatry, especially when one remembers the terrible persecution and narrow escapes of life which Mr. and Mrs. Stott passed through in previous years.

"The morning of the 12th commenced with a service in the church at 10 a.m., and the sight that met one on entering was one that never could be forgotten by those who were privileged to see it; the place was crowded to its very utmost extent by nearly four hundred Chinese Christians, whose bright and happy faces shone with the love of God in their hearts. 'This is the Lord's doing, and it is marvellous in our eyes' were the words that rose to our lips, and one's thoughts went back to the time, a little more than twenty-five years ago, when, among all the teeming thousands of Wenchow, there was not a single soul who knew of the true God, until one solitary man, Mr. Stott, filled with love for souls, came and settled in their midst and was joined two years later by his wife. One thought of those terrible first years, when the very people they came to befriend sought their lives, and in every way tried to drive them out by bitter persecution and opposition; especially did one long that he who had spent and been spent for the salvation of these people might have been there to join in the thanksgiving. Truly heart and voice of all present united in the singing of the opening hymn, 'O bless the Lord, my soul.'

"The first word came from Mr. S., of the Methodist Free Church, who spoke all our thoughts by first referring to Mr. Stott; he said he wished he were present to share in the joy of that meeting, but it had seemed best to the all-wise God and Father to take him to Himself. 'But,' continued he, 'perhaps God may tell him; perhaps he knows all about us to-day. I would like to compare to-day with twenty-five years ago; think of the difficulties then, the people suspicious of the hated foreigners, and their opposition. Mr. Stott was the only foreigner here until Mrs. Stott joined him. Then they lived in a little three-roomed Chinese house.' He remembered hearing how ill Mrs. Stott was during one of those early years. 'Just think of her, the only foreign lady in the place; what would some of you native women have done in such a case? Would you not have grumbled to your husband, "Oh, why did you ever bring me to such a place as this, over twelve thousand miles, to dwell alone in a strange land?" But Mrs. Stott stood bravely at her post encouraging her husband. Think of those early days, and the two first converts, now there are in the whole Wenchow prefecture (including Methodist Free Connexion) 1,050 persons in church fellowship. In addition there are two thousand men who meet regularly every Sabbath to worship—say, in all, three thousand souls. I would ask you, first of all, to pray that Mr. and Mrs. Stott's example may be followed, and I am sure in twenty-five years more the three thousand will be thirty thousand. Just twenty-five years ago worship was held in the centre room of Mr. Stott's little three-roomed house; now there are sixty districts where regular Sunday services are conducted. I would ask you all to use your life, your possessions, your abilities in spreading the gospel; let every act of your life be a service to God for the spread of the gospel.'

"Then followed a deeply touching address from Mr. Tsie, the native pastor, one whom Mr. Stott had taught and trained, of which we can only give brief notes, but as we listened to words which spoke of a man filled with the Holy Ghost, taught by God, again we felt, 'What hath God wrought'! He said, 'What is the meaning of all this? It is not Sunday, as some outsiders might think; no, to-day Mrs. Stott is celebrating her fiftieth birthday, and we have come here to rejoice with her, and give her our presents and congratulations. But what is our great object in thus assembling to-day? When we look back over the last twenty-five years and think of all God has done for Wenchow, we are led to meet together to give glory to God. Look at 1 Thess. i. 2–3 and 1 Thess. ii. 1–4, 9; this, too, might be written of them, for at that time we, in our ignorance thinking ourselves superior to any country, persecuted and shamefully ill-treated them; but such things did not dishearten them, they were bold to speak unto us the words of life. To-day we see the results, but I know I shall only echo

Mrs. Stott's sentiments when I say 'Let all the glory be to God.'

"It was now the writer's privilege, as one who had so recently come to live and work among them, to say a few words. 'First a word as to the past; let it be Psa. cxxvi. 3, "The Lord hath done great things for us whereof we are glad"; then a word as to the future, Joel ii. 21, "Fear not, O land; be glad and rejoice: for the Lord will do great things"; whichever way we look, past or future, we have cause for great rejoicing.'

"Mr. G., from the Bing-yie Church, an outcome of the Wenchow work, then spoke. He referred to the past twenty-five years as a picture from Rom. xiii. 12. First the dark night of Mr. and Mrs. Stott's coming; then the bright starlight night, the stars coming out gradually one by one. 'Therefore sprang there even of one, and him as good as dead, so many as the stars of the sky in multitude' (Heb. xi. 12); and lastly there has come the clear full moonlight, the church now lighting up the darkness of the night around, waiting until the day dawns and the Sun of Righteousness arise with healing in His wings.' One thing only is to be dreaded, the clouds of sin hindering the light of the moon.

"The meeting was closed by a few remarks from Mrs. Stott herself, the rapt attention of the whole church proving how deep a hold she had on their hearts' affections. Mrs. Stott commenced by saying, 'Never had I a harder thing to do than to speak to you to-day. I am in a strait; my heart longs to speak, but my tongue almost refuses to utter the words. Last night when I saw your beautiful present, Mr. S. well expressed my sentiment when he said, "When I looked at your precious gift I saw not it, but your hearts." I knew before that you loved and honoured me, but did not know how deeply that love went, until I saw the expression of it in that gift. You have been as children with a mother, listening to my counsel and following my advice, and I thank you for all your loyal devotion, but when I hear all that has been said about my twenty-five years' labour among you, I feel unworthy, and others ought to be here to share the honour. My one thought is let us give all the glory to God, the work has been His and the power of service too; comparisons have been made between the past and the present, and we rejoice together over the hundreds that have been saved; but who have been the means of their salvation? You, my brethren, and my sisters—you have carried the message of salvation to your friends and neighbours, into towns and villages, and souls have been won. If only those whom I have personally led to Christ were here, how few there would be; it is true I have been your teacher instructing you in the Word of God. In thanking you all for the rich gifts you

"HE THAT SOWETH AND HE THAT REAPETH" 341

have presented to me last night, and in which you all have had a share, I must refer to two others that have especially touched my heart. Look at that scroll, the gift of the school girls; they have little money of their own, it must have taken months of saving; and these large candles the gifts of the blind men, out of their deep poverty they have offered them. May I say in closing, that the one desire of our hearts is that God may be glorified in our midst, and that souls may be saved, may we live and work together for this object alone!'

"We knelt in heartfelt praise and prayer, and then there burst out the grand praise note of the doxology with an earnestness and fervour that even in our own dear homeland is seldom heard. We broke up, to gather again in happy fellowship over a real Chinese feast, and the much to be remembered day was brought to a close by an evening meeting, when, among others, two of Mr. Stott's old schoolboys, both of them preachers of the gospel, spoke of the days gone by, lovingly referring to that life which, in its beauty and patience, and its intense love, had done so much for so many of them gathered there—one reference to 1 Cor. iv. 15 being especially touching, showing how dear he was to them still: indeed, the thought of him was as a gold thread running through every memory of the past, 'who being dead yet speaketh.' The whole was brought to a conclusion by Mr. Menzies (of Bing-yie) urging that as the day had been a feast of fat things, not to forget to send portions unto them for whom nothing is prepared. May we ask the prayers of all who read this simple testimony of the Lord's goodness, that in the days to come our God may do still more wonderful things for us."

" Along with the photograph of the banner I append the translation :—

(Inscription on Banner.)

"'ON MRS. STOTT'S FIFTIETH ANNIVERSARY.'

" Dan. xii. 3. We hear of light as of the gracious stars, but God's own light has shone into many of these far-distant lands. Those who have received this light are joyful, and sing everlasting songs of praise. Our Zöa Sz-mo (Mrs. Stott), with her husband, Pastor Ngo-dji-Zöa (Mr. Stott), were the first to come to Wenchow to preach the holy doctrine of Jesus. When they had newly come, and the gospel had not yet been preached abroad, they were very badly treated by some, who, without any reason whatever, maligned them in every way possible—all which they bore most patiently. Afterwards, trusting in God's help, they were at last able to reach the country districts with the gospel. Later on Mr. and Mrs. Stott together returned to England.

From there Mr. Stott was called home to heaven; but Mrs. Stott, understanding what the mind of the Lord was, and in accordance with her husband's desire, again returned, remembering all the Wenchow Christians, and not hesitating at the thought of the long sea-voyage, and perils, and discomforts she would have to endure if she came back to Wenchow, in accordance with the promise which had formerly been made to the Church. While in Wenchow she set herself to teach the Church members, and to feed them with spiritual food. It is now well nigh ten years since she began this work. And now in Wenchow-fu, 10 hsiens, and all the districts round about, there are many white-haired old men, besides young men and numbers of women, who have all heard the gospel and received her instruction. I, Tsang Ts'e (the Pastor), with many others, have for years been taught by her, and we have learned to love and respect her much. To-day we are celebrating her birthday, and have prepared a banner to present to her, which may be compared to that jewel in the old story which the grateful bird sought and picked up to present to the master who had found the poor little fledgling and had fed and nourished it ever since. All those who met together to consider the idea of presenting the banner were only too delighted to put it into execution. On the eventful day the chapel and compound were opened wide and beautifully decorated; the Christians all met from the city and different districts round about, and spent the time in singing joyful hymns, and praying God to bless Mrs. Stott and spare her to us till her hundredth year.

(Right-hand Scroll.)

"In her twenty-fifth year [Mrs. Stott] sailed to China: in, as it seems, a moment's time she has reached her fiftieth birthday.

(Left-hand Scroll.)

"During these couple of decades great grace has come to us from God. The gospel has spread. We congratulate her on her birthday, and pray that from to-day she may have long life."

Banner presented to Mrs. Stott by the Native Church of Wenchow on March 12th, 1895, the completion of her twenty-five years' work in their midst.

CHAPTER XXIV

"Be not afraid of them that kill the body, and after that have no more that they can do."—LUKE xii. 4.

FOLLOWING this happy day came sorrows thick and fast; indeed, in looking back upon the year (1895), it was the one bright gleam in the midst of a cloudy sky. Seldom has so much sorrow been crowded into one year as we experienced in this, and one can but adore the wonderful grace and sustaining power of our God, who doeth all things well. He is good and doeth good, is the language of our hearts.

During the summer a very serious persecution broke out in the district of Shiae-koa-diu, an outstation from Bing-yie, where there were a goodly number of inquirers. A man still heathen was ill, and as his family feared he might die, they called upon the preacher and a few of the inquirers to pray for his recovery. On entering the house the preacher saw an idol there, and remarked that he could not pray to the living God while it occupied the place of honour. The family were afraid themselves to take it away, but asked the evangelist to do so, which he did. Whether this incident gave rise to false reports we do not know, but on the 18th of June a band of men went to the house of an inquirer, an old man, and accused him of taking out the eyes of an idol near by, threatening to bind him hand and foot and carry him to the temple; instead, however, they went to the house of a scholar, who is the head of the clan, and obtained from him a flag as an insignia of authority. They then, with the accompaniment of gongs and drums, again proceeded to the old man's house; he, however, escaped and made his way to the chapel. The third son was ill, and so unable to escape, and him they kicked and ill-treated.

On the matter being reported to Mr. M., who was in charge, he sent the pastor to inquire into the matter, but, on nearing the place, found he dared not proceed further, owing to the serious turn affairs had taken; he learned that the people were banding themselves by hundreds, and were inciting to riot, determining to turn out all who professed Christianity, and burn down their houses. Mr. M. then communicated with the magistrate, who at once sent out runners, who, however, never reached the place of trouble, having, no doubt, been bribed by the rioters to say there was no disturbance of any importance. On the 20th, at N-so district, the local constable informed the preacher that some men were accusing him of taking out the eyes of the idols, and meant to lay hands on him; he therefore advised the preacher to leave the place at once; but he decided to remain, as to fly would seem to confess himself guilty of the charge brought against him. An hour or two later he was seized by a band of men, bound hand and foot, and carried to the seaside, with the view of throwing him into the water; the constable, however, appeared on the scene just in time to save him from the hands of the mob, but an inquirer who stood by was badly beaten.

On the 24th, at another village named Dzing-ko-to, the constable of the place, instead of exhorting the people to keep the peace, and using his authority to this end, led on and incited a band of men with the same cry of "idols defaced," and the mob were not appeased until they had entirely demolished two of the young Christians' houses. By this time the whole neighbourhood was in an uproar. The 27th was the annual dragon festival of the village O-chie, which included a boat race. The crew who were beaten in the contest charged the only Christian in the place with defacing the idols, hence their defeat. They beat him and partly destroyed his house. These cases were duly reported to the magistrate, who sent out his runners, but with no good result.

On Saturday the 29th, matters came to a crisis, when the rioters commenced a wholesale work of destruction. In the early morning a large band of men proceeded to the village of Shiae-Koa-du, and levelled our new chapel to the ground, also the house and property of the pastor, who had just time to entrust his wife and family to a kind neighbour, and fly to Bing-yie with the news. Immediately on hearing of this fresh outbreak, Mr. M. duly communicated with the local officials and asked for an interview, which was granted. The mandarin promised to do his best to put down the rioting, and an official, with a body of soldiers and runners, at once left for the scene of the outbreak. Meanwhile, the rioters busied themselves by pulling down and burning the houses of the Christians, so that by the same evening five houses had been destroyed, and by the following morning (Sunday) the number had increased to eleven, and by Wednesday twenty houses had been partly or utterly destroyed. The inmates made their way to Bing-yie, where no fewer than fifty-nine men, women, and children were thrown upon Mr. M.'s resources, the majority of them having nothing more than the clothes they were wearing. The officials and soldiers, who had gone to quell the disturbance, returned the following evening without doing anything to restore order, and on the 30th Mr. M. again visited the magistrate, when he dolefully confessed that he was powerless; the outbreak was too large for him to cope with, but he offered to issue official notices to the scholars of the district, and lay upon them the responsibility of putting a stop to the riot. He also promised to restore to the Christians all that had been destroyed by the rioters.

On Thursday, July 4th, another large and newly built house, in which a family of sixteen had only lived two months, was destroyed, and without a moment's warning the inmates were cast adrift, without a roof over their heads. Another Christian in the same place saved his house and goods through the efforts of a literary man; twice the mob assembled for the purpose of destruction, and twice were restrained by the scholar, who called upon them to go with him to the temple, and he would show them that the face of the idol was eaten by rats, and the defacement was not the work of man; but though the house was left, the occupant, with his wife and aged mother, had to make their escape at midnight and join the outcasts at Bing-yie.

A fresh outcry was then raised of more idols being deprived of their eyes. A crowd gathered to discuss the question, but as no one had been seen committing this outrage, it was determined to ask the idol himself. A man in the crowd was chosen to represent him; the priest wrote certain characters, or incantations, burned the paper over the man's head, thus transforming him into the idol, which was minus its eyes. He was asked who had stolen his eyes, and the man immediately replied, "Those who have believed the foreign doctrine." Of course this was to them conclusive, no other evidence being required.

The damage done during that terrible fortnight amounted to nearly five thousand dollars. This was a great trouble and anxiety to Mr. M., who had had but little experience of such ways. We shared the burden and helped him as best we could, and the English Consul took up the matter, and eventually brought about a settlement, and indemnity for their losses was given; but months elapsed before their houses could be rebuilt and the people return to their work.

Following these came troubles nearer home. One of the stations of the Methodist Free Church was the scene of a most determined attack against Christianity. One Sunday morning, while the people were assembled for worship, a band of rowdies made an attack, scattered the assembled people, broke lamps, seats, etc., and threatened to expel from the village any who should join this religion. It was long before any steps were taken to redress this wrong, and as the Bing-yie troubles were not at that time settled, a spirit of bold defiance was manifested in other places. In one village, just across the river, where we had conducted services for years, a most determined opposition was set up; the villagers refused to allow the Christians to have meetings even in their own houses, and each attempt was met with personal threats and stone throwing. They plainly intimated that any house thus used should be pulled down, and the occupant expelled, though no charge whatever was made against the Christians. It seemed monstrous that the laws which gave perfect freedom and toleration to all religions, should be thus defied under the very eyes of the officials. Their attention was called to the matter, when they politely asked me to defer our sending preachers for a few weeks, until the excitement of the Bing-yie troubles was over. I complied with this request, but at the same time pointed out that the settlement of the case would be more difficult later on, as the seeming victory of the opponents would embolden them and others, and I put the responsibility of future disturbances upon them.

A few weeks after we made another attempt with a like result, stones and mud were freely thrown, and the meeting broke up in noise and confusion. The mandarins either would not or could not maintain order, and the villagers, feeling their power, waxed bolder. So far as I know, services have not yet been resumed in that place.

Mrs. Menzies and baby, with Miss B., were in the meantime at the cottage for the summer months, and so she mercifully was spared much of the trouble and anxiety her husband was in, and part of the time she was so ill that it was not deemed advisable to tell her how serious matters were. At the end of September, I joined them, hoping to rest a fortnight, but had only been there one week when the terrible news of the massacre at Ku-chang reached us. That tragic story filled us with horror, and as Fu-chow is the next province, south of us, the Consul felt somewhat alarmed, and ordered us to return at once to the city, which order we reluctantly obeyed, as we felt really safer where we were. I had only returned about a week when my health thoroughly broke down. For months I had been steadily failing, and the hope of staying a few years longer in Wenchow vanished, but I expected that with cooler weather a measure of health would return, so that I might be enabled to visit the country stations, introducing Mr. and Mrs. W. to what we hoped would be their future work. Then I thought, if the Lord should will it so, I might leave in the spring. "My ways are not as your ways," saith the Lord.

The preachers had come in to their autumn week of study. Feeling unequal to the task, I had asked the pastor to conduct the first day's meetings, promising that I should be there. At the close of the afternoon meeting, although taking no part, I became so prostrate, that my fellow-workers became uneasy, and called in the doctor. Work was at once prohibited, and in less than a week after, I was ordered to England without delay, and was told that I must not attempt many good-byes. The news of my coming departure filled the dear natives with concern, as Mr. and Mrs. W. were not yet able to speak the language, and there was no one of experience to fill my place; but when they were told that it meant either going now or the probability of not being able to return, they said, like the sorrowing disciples of old, "The will of the Lord be done." When I heard the people were disappointed at the thought of not seeing me again, I sent a message that, if they could restrain their feelings, I would try and come to the chapel on Sunday morning and see them all once more. As might be expected, the place was full, and as I was carried on to the platform the sight of the red eyes of my dear women nearly took from me the little courage I had left; many prayers were going up that I might have power given to speak to them once more, and for nearly ten minutes I was strengthened to give the message which the Lord had given me the day before, after which I was again carried down, when the whole congregation stood and, without a sign of emotion, watched me out of sight.

The following day I received a message from them that they would do as I desired; they would not come to the steamer, or make any attempt to see me again, but would pray every day for my return, and then come *en masse* and carry me home in triumph. A few days before, the preachers came to my room, when I was able to speak a few farewell words and present each of them with a complete copy of the Bible in Chinese, which was received with many tears. Mr. and Mrs. Menzies, who could not bear the thought of Miss B., who accompanied me, and I leaving without their seeing us once more, were told they had better not come in, as I was too weak to bear the excitement, so instead of seeing us off, as they had hoped, they had to send their adieus by letter.

CHAPTER XXV

"I was dumb, I opened not my mouth, because Thou didst it."—
Psa. xxxix. 9.

"As for God, His way is perfect."—2 Sam. xxii. 31.

ON the evening of September 18th we went on board our Wenchow steamer, where most of our foreign friends assembled to say good-bye, and the following morning at daybreak we started for Shang-hai. Little did we then think of the cloud that was about to burst over our loved friends left behind. I was able to send a tiny farewell note to each, and Mrs. Woodman's reply, received before starting for Japan, and probably the last she ever penned, was so touching in its loving devotion to and trust in the Lord that I offer no apology for inserting it here:—

"WENCHOW, *September* 28, 1895.

"MY DEAREST MRS. STOTT,—Thank you very much for our bit of yourself; it told the story that you were a little better, and indeed you ought to be, and you would think so could you have heard the volume of prayer that went up for you both, as a sweet smelling savour unto God, on Saturday evening and Sunday morning. But I will try and do my chat decently and in order, though C. will bring all news; still, I want you to hear it from my lips as well, and in my way.

"We came back from the ship feeling we had taken a large slice of our life out and put it outside the city gates on board that vessel, and my husband has, among other fresh complaints against me, the one of starting up in bed with some tale of a man opening the shutters; he got out and went to the window, and succeeded in overturning the large lamp, waking up servants and household by the crash; we felt after that we had really done something to herald in our taking charge.

"The next day we became too busy to think, especially as the work-people arrived to commence proceedings. C. and K. helped splendidly, and by night we had put away even the odds and ends that reminded us of you; for another purpose we will have another such day when we make ready to receive you back again. Since that one day of clearing up we have steadily gone in an opposite direction, and tonight 'confusion worse confounded' reigns; the stairs, destroyed by white ants, are strewed in pieces about the passage; the sitting-room is not at home; instead, a carpenter's shop seems to have taken its place; and the study is a bare, blank place, having its walls done; still, as we understand the joy of meeting far better after parting, the love of home after the far country, so we shall revel in the comfort of our house after its discomfort and mess, and I want, if possible, to be able to welcome K. and C. back with us and our surroundings in our right mind. Am I writing trifles? Well, I want to write to you as I write to mother, who says, 'Tell me down to the smallest detail.'

"Now for the other side. The prayer-meeting had you all in spirit with us, I am sure. May God use that meeting time, week by week, to be the hand that shall open windows of blessing here; and wherever you are, somehow I felt that last Friday evening you were among us in the quiet communion service, that the Lord just took the links of love that united us and riveted them afresh, placing upon each one the seal of His love again. Then, and now, I thank Him for doing this; I thank Him with all my heart that He has let my husband's life and my own cross yours and A.'s, and that He has made them richer by your love.

"Saturday was another full, busy day. For one thing I was rather alarmed by having great requests for medicine. They evidently thought A.'s mantle must have fallen on some one, and my reputation went abroad as the one, when I gave a simple dose to a woman who pleaded for it for her daughter, and who arrived back full of glee at the cure. Many came in from the country, and it was what well-nigh every day is, a fresh finding out of weakness and helplessness. Seven applied for baptism, with a probable three more; later on in the afternoon, three from Koa-diu, among whom was the policeman's son, and the others from Yung-ko-djiae. My husband decided it was far better to wait for the pastor's return, and just had them in, and asked them if they would come next month, telling them it was your wish this should be done. They were quite willing, and we heard them say, as they left, 'Yes, that is right: God first, then Zoe-Sz-mo.'

"The prayer-meeting at night was an earnest, powerful time. The new shepherd summoned up courage for a couple of Chinese sentences; Zing-Lie prayed, that as freely as he drank Wenchow water, might he drink in the Wenchow words. Then, as we had no baptisms, my husband thought it would be very nice to start Sunday with a prayer-meeting, and asked them to gather together at nine, especially remembering you and A. The chapel was full, and eight or nine prayed quite rapidly, with very full hearts I am sure, for the absent ones. We had a crowded communion, but all passed off quietly and well. I fear the strange faces must keenly have reminded them of their loss: love begets love, though, so I pray steadily on for a great love towards each one, and then I know they will by and by learn to love us back.

"Monday brought us an unexpected bit in the arrival of Mr. and Mrs. M. and baby. The little fellow is very poorly, such a little white-faced boy, and they were anxious to put him under the doctor's care. He is evidently upset by his food, and thoroughly out of order. You know how easily Mrs. M. makes herself at home, so I have scarcely felt having them at all; only the house is in such a mess for them. Mr. M. left last night, leaving his wife and child behind until the latter is well. Things are not very peaceful in Bing-yie yet; they beat and ill-used twenty going to the Mo-z-ka.

"I went down to the South Gate, on Wednesday, with Liu-sy-mo, a nice meeting place, but I missed A very much; somehow it was not the same to me: I don't know how the natives felt. Everything in the church is quite quiet. We have had a request from the Yung-ko-djiae people, to allow them to have a house or place taken for meetings. They will give four dollars a year towards expenses: there are four wishing to join them, interested through Dr. Hogg and his ministrations. We told them the matter should be seen into when T'sie came back. Now I have, I think, told you all. 'Pray for the peace of Jerusalem.' 'God will do the best for those who leave the choice to Him.' He knows the under-currents of life, and this work is dearer to Him than it is to us. Don't you think He watches over Wenchow with a jealous love, and says, 'Here have I commanded my blessing.' We shall be able to plead with Him that strong prayer, 'For Thy name's sake.' And now, 'God be with you till we meet again.' I have such a nice word which I have been connecting with your name, 'Thou shalt have joy and gladness,' 'For ye shall go out with joy, and be led forth with peace.' May the dear home country mean to you rest, strength, and gladness. Thank you, again and again, for your lovingkindness to us. Our first months in China have been happy ones indeed, by your goodness and love. The old place in the hearts of these people, 'the Mother's corner' here is being 'kept for thee.' Our prayers will follow you step by step, wherever you go they shall form a three fold cord, with 'goodness and mercy.' Take this letter as from both of us: we are one in Christ. Our fond love. Oh the blessing of the Lord that maketh rich be yours richly.

"Ever yours lovingly,

"FANNY WOODMAN."

Eleven days later, she, with her husband and the others, entered into the full atmosphere of love, where she ever seemed, while here, to dwell. Before going to China, Mr. and Mrs. W. had been for some years engaged in Christian service in connection with a soldiers' home at Lichfield. Their work had been wonderfully owned of God; many souls were saved, and Christians helped and encouraged to more earnest devotion. Sincere were the heart regrets of the men at their leaving, as letters written by them afterwards proved. To some it seemed a mistake to leave a work they were so well fitted for, and in which God was blessing them; but they heard the call, "Go ye," and that to them meant going. Nor do I believe they ever regretted, for one moment, the step; and had they known the issues, they would still have gone in simple obedience. But the few months were not lived in vain, for our lives have been made the richer for knowing them, and our love, hope, and sympathy increased by their example. The friendship and intercourse, though so short, will ever be a sweet and hallowed memory. "They were lovely and beautiful in their lives, and in their death they were not divided."

At the time we left Wenchow, cholera was raging in many parts of the city, especially outside the East Gate, where several hundreds had died; but, as this was an almost yearly occurrence, no special uneasiness was felt, while medicines were freely given by our people to the sufferers. As mentioned in Mrs. W.'s letter, Mrs. M. had come in to Wenchow, on Monday, Sept. 23rd, with her baby boy poorly; but as it was thought to be nothing more than indigestion caused by change of food, there was no alarm felt, even by the parents; and on Friday Mr. M. returned to his station, although much weakened by the anxious strain of the past few months, leaving Mrs. M. and her baby to complete the convalescence. However, on the evening of Sunday, 29th, the dear little fellow was taken ill with undoubted symptoms of cholera, and after a night of extreme suffering, his little spirit was welcomed by the Saviour who said, "Suffer the little ones to come unto Me." Mr. M. was recalled, but only returned in time to commit the precious dust to the earth.

On Tuesday, symptoms of the dread disease developed in the girls' school, and on Oct. 2nd (next day) two died within two hours of each other. On the 3rd, one of our old women on the premises was attacked, and died soon after, leaving a bright testimony of her clear confidence and faith in Christ her Saviour.

The following day, 4th, another school-girl died, also an old man. These cases were lovingly nursed by Mrs. W. and Miss S. who did all in their power for the relief of the poor sufferers. By this time there was a panic in the school, all wanted to fly from the presence of death and danger; and by the evening of that day the last of the girls had been taken to their homes by their friends.

On Sunday, 6th, Mr. M. showed symptoms of the

disease, and after twenty-four hours' suffering, he too passed into the presence of the King.

And so our dear sister was doubly bereaved, and left alone after less than two years of a singularly happy married life. Bravely, and with most remarkable trust in the perfect will of God, she drank the bitter cup, never so much as questioning the love that had dealt such a heavy blow.

Mr. W., who had been suffering for a few days previously, now manifested the disease, though still hopes were entertained of his recovery, as he rallied two or three times and lingered longer than either of the others: but, by Tuesday, 8th, all hope was gone. The same day, fully realising her husband's danger, Mrs. W. met the doctor with a peculiar smile, saying, "I too have taken it." She was advised to lie down at once, but, with characteristic unselfishness, she waited to put things in order, as she did not expect to recover. Early on the morning of the 9th, she too passed away, and her husband a few hours later; so death and desolation reigned. Before she was taken ill she devoted herself with untiring energy to the care of others, and when Mr. M. was attacked, she put her arms round Mrs. M., and said, "Gladly would I give up my laddie to save yours, because you have lost your baby."

Mrs. M. and Miss S., together with Drs. Hogg and Lowry, nursed the dear invalids night and day, and all that skill and love could devise was done. Our Father had need of them, and we are silent. They rest in His glory, and wait until that day when Christ shall bring them with Him, for they without us shall not be made perfect. We, too, rest and wait; rest in the perfect will of God, and wait until we shall be caught up to meet them in the air, so shall we ever be with the Lord: "Even so, come Lord Jesus."

While all this scene of sorrow and death was being enacted at Wenchow, Pastor T'sie and the cook, when returning from Shang-hai, suffered shipwreck, the steamer they were in, from some cause or other, having gone on the rocks, and for a time they were in imminent danger, but ultimately a Chinese gunboat, seeing their distress, rendered what help they could, and brought the passengers to Wenchow. Thus they were mercifully preserved.

After a fortnight spent in Shang-hai, during which time sleep and strength were slowly returning, we sailed for England, *via* C.P.R., which route the doctor had advised for me. Misses S. and W., seeing us off, all in utter ignorance of what was going on then at the dear home we had left behind.

We had not been many days at sea when I was able to walk the length of the deck, and ere we reached Vancouver there had been more progress made than even the most sanguine had expected. After a few happy days spent at Toronto and

Montreal, we went to New York, and there suddenly and without any warning were told that a telegram had reached London that Mr. M. and the W.'s had been called home through cholera.

The news was astounding, and yet even then we did not know the full extent of the blow. That was a dreary week across the Atlantic. We clung to the hope that a mistake had been made in the reading of the telegram and that at least only one of the W.'s had been taken. But on arrival we found that not the half had been told, for instead of three, which we thought the extent of our loss, we found that nine foreigners and natives had in ten days been carried off by the hand of death from our compound; and yet how much of mercy and of lovingkindness has been revealed to us in this. My illness, which seemed so inopportune, occurring when I could least be spared, was the very cause of myself, Misses B., S., and W. being absent, beside the pastor, who is a delicate man, and might readily have fallen a victim, thus fewer lives were sacrificed than might otherwise have been the case. It has been said, "God buries His workers, but carries on His work." God can do without us, but He does not, and it is still true that "through the foolishness of preaching" He saves men. Who will be His ambassadors, and carry His message even to the uttermost parts of the earth? The dark places of the earth are still full of the habitations of cruelty; and yet the missionary's life is one of surpassing joy, for who has ever tasted a delight more intense than that of seeing souls born into the kingdom, and perhaps no country has given larger results for the amount of labour bestowed than China. It is true that as a nation the people are dirty, treacherous, and in many instances cruel; but while they have these and other unlovely national characteristics, I can bear testimony to a warmth of devotion, fidelity, and patient endurance, not exceeded by any country, not even by our own beloved England; and I still hope to spend my remaining years in their midst, though much of the burden and responsibility must henceforth rest upon younger shoulders.

And now my story is ended, many incidents have been forgotten, others too sacred for the public eye necessarily omitted; but if what has been written of the joys and sorrows, encouragements and disappointments, of a missionary's life, will serve to cheer some lonely heart and strengthen some feeble knees that are apt to be weary through the difficulties of the way, by reminding them afresh of the Lord's own promise, "In due season ye shall reap if ye faint not," my effort will not have been in vain.

www.ingramcontent.com/pod-product-compliance
Lightning Source LLC
Chambersburg PA
CBHW032029220426
43664CB00006B/414